THE BEST OF
BIRDS&BLOOMS
2008

THE BEST OF BIRDS&BLOOMS 2008

Editor: Stacy Tornio
Art Director: Monica Bergwall
Editor, *Birds & Blooms*: Heather Lamb
Art Director, *Birds & Blooms*: Sue Myers
Copy Editor: Susan Uphill
Contributing Editors: Melinda Myers, George Harrison, Tom Allen
Photo Coordinator: Trudi Bellin
Assistant Photo Coordinator: Mary Ann Koebernik
Editorial Assistant: Kirsten Sweet
Senior Editor, Retail Books: Mark Hagen
Creative Director: Ardyth Cope
Vice President, Executive Editor/Books: Heidi Reuter Lloyd
Editor in Chief, Home & Garden: Jeff Nowak
President, Home & Garden and Health & Wellness: Alyce C. Alston
President, North American Consumer Marketing: Dawn M. Zier
President and Chief Executive Officer: Mary G. Berner

Birds & Blooms Books ©2007 Reiman Media Group, Inc.
5400 S. 60th St. Greendale WI 53129
International Standard Book Number: 0-89821-531-5
Serial Number: 1553-8400 Printed in U.S.A.

To order additional copies of this book,visit
www.countrystorecatalog.com or call 1-800-344-6913.
Learn more about *Birds & Blooms* at *www.birdsandblooms.com*.

Magazine covers this page, clockwise from top left: Maslowski Productions, Donna and Tom Krischan, Maslowski Productions, Marie Read, Bill Leanman/The Image Finders, Nancy Rotenberg
Magazine covers opposite page, clockwise from top left: Maslowksi Productions, Jo Williams/The image Finders, Maslowski Productions, Rolf Nussbaumer, Marie Read, Maslowski Productions
Front cover photos, from top left: Nancy Rotenberg; Richard Day/Daybreak Imagery; Richard Shiell; bottom photo: Francis and Janice Bergquist
Back cover photos, from left: Anthony Mercieca; Robert L. Potts; Roland Jordahl

WELCOME

With the *Birds & Blooms* annual, we're bringing together two very important components—quality and convenience.

You'll find the quality stories you expect from both *Birds & Blooms* and *Birds & Blooms EXTRA*. And, at the same time, you'll get the convenience of having them all in one spot.

Among these pages, you'll find the best photos and stories of the year along with great tips and ideas for attracting more birds to your backyard and growing a better garden.

Don't forget to keep your eye out for our popular "Editor's Picks" throughout the book. We added these to honor some of our favorite stories.

Be sure to check out our Bonus chapter, starting on page 226. We've added 13 features, including a birdhouse plan, easy gardening projects and a plant guide for attracting more hummingbirds.

You've shared your best stories, advice and photos. Now it's time to sit back and enjoy the results!

Heather

Heather Lamb
Editor, *Birds & Blooms*

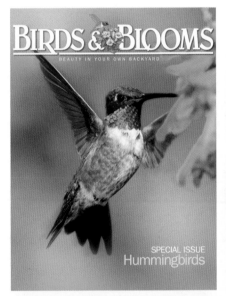

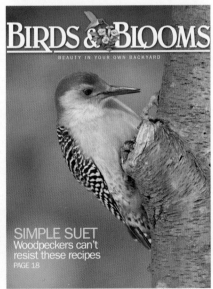
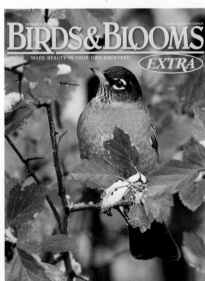

CONTENTS

6

64

128

PHOTOS OF THE YEAR 6

CHAPTER 1

TOP BILLING 14

Screech-owl	16	House Wren	35
Yellow-rumped Warbler	19	Northern Cardinal	38
Steller's Jay	22	White-breasted Nuthatch	42
Tree Swallow	25	Downy woodpecker	46
Great Egret	28	Evening Grosbeak	49
Tufted Titmouse	32		

CHAPTER 2

NO. 1 GREEN THUMB 52

How Her Garden Grew	54	Neighborly Gardening	73
Painting a Garden	58	Backyard Metamorphosis	76
Flower Man	61	Life on the Beach	79
From Sea to Shining Sea	64	Living a Garden Dream	82
Teamwork Equals Treasure	67	Lifetime of Gardening	85
Arkansas Rain Forest	70		

CHAPTER 3

BACKYARD BIRD HAVEN 88

Birds & Blooms:		Home Tweet Home	100
A Perfect Pair	90	More Birds, Less Work	104
Setting the Table	92	Fantastic Feeders	107
Little Trees, Big Benefits	96	Berries for the Birds	108

CHAPTER 4

FLYING FLOWERS 110

Pearl Crescent	112	Question Mark	124
Meadow Fritillary	114	Hummingbird Clearwing	126
Monarch	116	Aphrodite Fritillary	128
Anise Swallowtail	118	Orange Sulphur	130
Milbert's Tortoiseshell	120	Spicebush Swallowtail	132
Spring Azure	122	Hackberry Emperor	134

CHAPTER 5

BLOOMING BEAUTY 136

Lavender	138	Gladiolus	155
Coral Bells	140	Pentas	158
Pansies	144	Zinnias	160
Crocus	147	Yucca	163
Asters	150	Snapdragon	166
Oriental Poppies	152	Amaryllis	168

CHAPTER 6

ALL ABOUT HUMMINGBIRDS 170

Hummingbirds Quiz	172	Did You Know?	179
Feed Hummingbirds		A Hobby That Took Over	180
by Hand	174	Hummer Happenings	182
Rufous Hummingbird	176		

CHAPTER 7

PLAN A GREAT GARDEN 188

Life of a Plant Hunter	190	Country Retreat	199
Secrets to Grow on	194	Best Garden Ideas	202
Santa's Garden	196		

CHAPTER 8

GLAD YOU ASKED! 206

Critter Combat	208	Beauty and the Bugs	218
Moths vs. Butterflies	210	That's an Imposter	214
Problem Soils	212	Glad You Asked! Best	
America's Most Wanted	214	Butterfly Questions	220
Butterfly Gardening on		Gardening Questions	222
a Budget	216	Birding Questions	224

CHAPTER 9

THE BEST OF BIRDS & BLOOMS BONUS 226

Easy Oriole Feeder	228	Dive Right In	240
Pint-sized Pond	230	Winter Wonderland	242
Cozy Abode	232	Spice Up Your Windowsill	244
A Bright Idea for Birds	234	Gardeners on the Go	246
Make a Splash with a Birdbath	235	Plant a Hummingbird Haven	248
No Deadheading Zone	236	Birdhouse Guidelines	250
Do-It-Yourself Containers	239	What's Your Zone?	251

INDEX 252

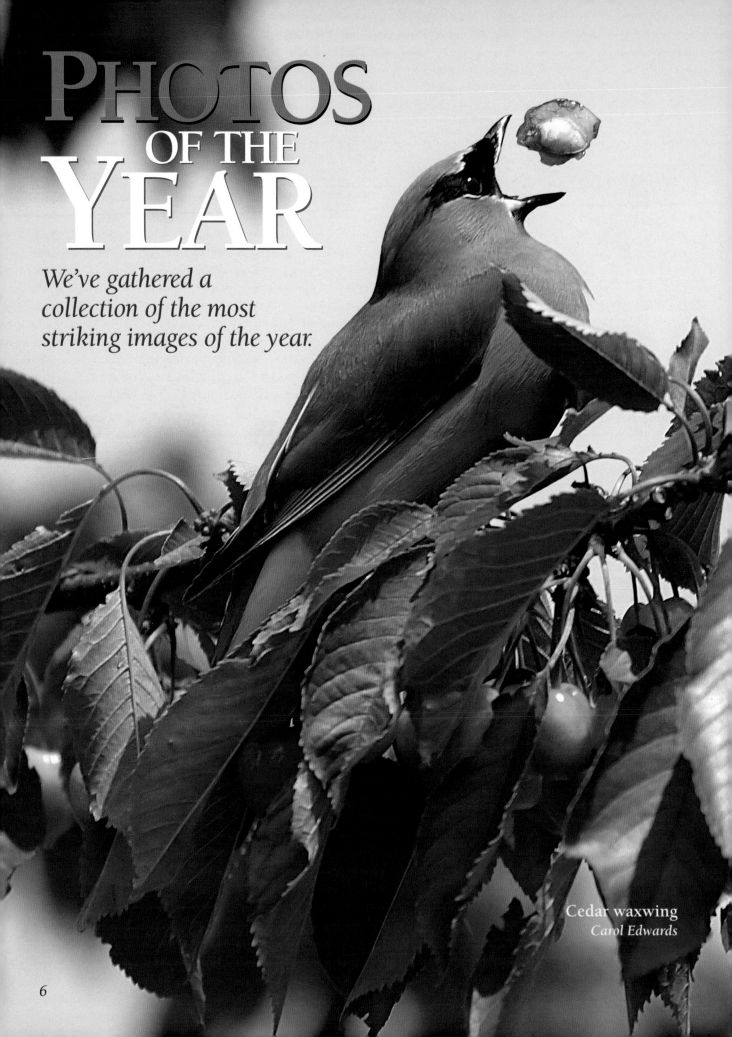

PHOTOS
OF THE
YEAR

*We've gathered a
collection of the most
striking images of the year.*

Cedar waxwing
Carol Edwards

Northern cardinal
Carol Edwards

Eastern bluebirds
Barbara Dunn

Fawn lily
Robert L. Potts

The Best of Birds & Blooms Bonus

Canada goose
Marvin Cattoor, The Image Finders

American goldfinch
Richard Day/Daybreak Imagery

Spring tulips
David Hammond

Christmas tree for the birds
Marie Read

9

Cecropia moth
Nancy Rotenberg

Baltimore oriole
Ken Thommes

Snowy egret
Jason Stuck

Lupines and California poppies
Nancy Rotenberg

American pride
Dianne Dietrich Leis

Squirrel
Randy Quinn

Northern
mockingbird
Maslowski Productions

12

Tufted titmouse
Jim Simek/Nature's images

Spiderweb and bloom
Nancy Rotenberg

Buff-bellied hummingbird
Rolf Nussbaumer

16

49

22

25

19

TOP BILLING

46

Photos: Screech-owl, Jack Milchanowski/Unicorn Stock Photos; Steller's jay, Francis and Janice Bergquist; Evening grosbeaks, Sid and Shirley Rucker; Tree swallow, Larry Ditto/KAC Productions; Yellow-rumped warbler, Rolf Nussbaumer; Downy woodpecker, Bill Leaman/The Image Finders; Great egret, Roland Jordahl

Screech-Owl	16
Yellow-rumped Warbler	19
Steller's Jay	22
Tree Swallow	25
Great Egret	28
Tufted Titmouse	32
House Wren	35
Northern Cardinal	38
White-breasted Nuthatch	42
Downy Woodpecker	46
Evening Grosbeak	49

28

*These creatures of the night
will light up your yard.*

By George Harrison, Contributing Editor

Chapter 1

SCREECH-OWL

On many a winter evening, in the afterglow of sunset, the loud pronouncement of, " 'Screechie's' out!" resounds through our house. It means the eastern screech-owl roosting in our wood duck house has made an appearance.

Sleepy-eyed, but ever alert to passing songbirds and mice, Screechie lingers at the entrance until dark, and then the hunt begins.

These owls, like others in their family, are largely nocturnal and use their keen senses of eyesight and hearing to search out food at night. Their ears are hidden beneath feathers on the sides of their heads, nowhere near the decorative ear tufts on top.

East Meets West

The screech-owls we see in our Wisconsin yard are of the eastern variety. They are virtually identical to the western screech-owl, which is found west of the Rocky Mountains. The two species are very similar in appearance, so their calls and location are the two best ways to distinguish them.

Screech-owls of both species can be either reddish-brown or gray, though the purpose of these color "phases" is a bit of a mystery. Color apparently has nothing to do with sex, age or geographic location.

However, the red phase does appear to be less tolerant of cold temperatures—many more reds die during severely cold weather than do grays. Perhaps for this reason, there tend to be more red eastern screech-owls in the South and more grays in the North.

Among the western species, most are gray. Yet, those western screech-owls living on the Pacific Northwest coast are either gray or chocolate-red. Together, they are the most common owl species in North America, and the only one that regularly nests in yards.

A few years ago, our screech-owl extended its stay and settled in to raise a family. Although we were pleased, the songbirds in our area weren't too happy about the new neighbors.

The handsome, gray-colored male spent its daylight hours quietly trying to sleep on a limb outside the nesting house, which was 30 feet up in a sugar maple tree.

As it slumbered, black-capped chickadees, American goldfinches, blue jays and others scolded—and even attacked—the little owl.

At 8-1/2 inches long, it's roughly the size of an American robin, and is the smallest owl with tufts in America. So why all the fuss?

I found the answer when I cleaned out the birdhouse in fall. The food the owls procured for their young at night was some of the same songbirds that scolded them during day.

I found feathers of downy woodpeckers, northern cardinals and American robins inside, and rose-breasted grosbeak feathers on the ground below the house.

Family Comes First

During all the commotion outside, a red-colored female eastern screech-owl stayed tucked inside the duck house incubating four white eggs for 26 days.

Each night, the male carried food to her and sang his descending trill, a strange tremolo sound that makes some

"HOO" ARE YOU LOOKING AT? During the day, screech-owls lurk at nest entrances. Below is an adult eastern peeking out of a nest box. At right, the curious pair with glowing eyes are juveniles. At left is an eastern species in the red phase color.

Rolf Nussbaumer

Gary Meszaros/Dembinsky Photo Assoc.

HIDE-AND-SEEK. A screech-owl's color and markings help it disappear in a tree. Above, the western screech-owl is virtually identical to its eastern counterpart, though their calls differ.

people cringe. According to folklore, the sight or sound of an owl portends an imminent death in the family.

About 3 weeks after the eggs hatched, the owlets became curious about the world outside. Each evening for a week, I saw them take turns sitting at the entrance hole, sometimes two at a time. They reminded me of the pet fledgling screech-owl I had when I was a youngster myself, when keeping wild birds was still legal. Of course, I had named it Screechie, too, and it rode on my shoulder everywhere I went, even to school.

Once the owlets were about 4 weeks old, they all flew away, just as my childhood owl friend had done. In fact, the whole family disappeared overnight, and the woods around our home were quiet again for the first time in a couple of months.

The survival chances of a young screech-owl are not good the first year. Like virtually all birds, 70 to 80% don't live to their first birthday. If they do survive the first year, their chances improve greatly, with almost 70% surviving year to year, according to screech-owl longevity studies.

Though I must admit I wince a little when I find the remains of a lovely songbird under our duck house, I also realize that it is all part of the natural world, and a fair trade-off for being able to watch screech-owls year-round.

As far as I'm concerned, our duck house is always open for Screechie.

BIRD-WATCHER'S SECRET

It's a myth that owls can swivel their heads all the way around. Instead, an owl typically can rotate its head 270 degrees.

Backyard Birding Bio

Common Names: Eastern screech-owl and western screech-owl.

Scientific Names: *Otus asio* and *Otus kennicottii*.

Length: 8-1/2 inches.

Wingspan: 20 inches.

Distinctive Markings: Gray, red or brown with heavy streaks below and darker bars on back; has small tufts that look like ears.

Voice: Not a screech, but a tremulous cry or whinny.

Nesting: In a natural cavity or large birdhouse, the female lays four to five white eggs, which she incubates for 26 days before they hatch. Both parents feed the young for the 4 weeks they're in the nest and for some time thereafter.

Diet: Insects, small mammals, birds, fish, spiders and reptiles. Owls swallow their prey whole and later regurgitate indigestible parts as so-called owl pellets.

Backyard Favorites: A large birdhouse in which to roost and nest. Wood duck houses work well (10 inches square and 24 inches tall with an elliptical 4- by 3-inch entrance near the top.) May also use birdbaths at night.

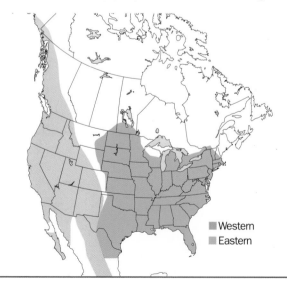

■ Western
■ Eastern

YELLOW-RUMPED WARBLER

Rolf Nussbaumer

Summer or winter, these gorgeous birds are always a bright spot in backyards all across the country.

By George Harrison, Contributing Editor

There aren't many warblers that can be described as "backyard birds," but the yellow-rumped warbler fits that label, especially if you live along the coasts or in the Southeast.

While visiting friends Ed and Betty Komarek in Thomasville, Georgia one winter, I watched as northern bobwhites, hermit thrushes, red-bellied woodpeckers and many others traversed their yard in search of food.

But the most thrilling attraction was the small flock of yellow-rumped warblers that flitted around bird cakes

Francis and Janice Bergquist

Common Name: Yellow-rumped warbler.

Scientific Name: *Dendrocia coronata.*

Length: 5-1/2 inches.

Wingspan: 9-1/4 inches.

Description: The distinguishing markings of both males and females are the bright-yellow patches on their rump and flanks, best seen in flight. Males also have a yellow crown, but are otherwise grayish. Females are brownish.

Voice: The male's song is a high-pitched, quiet series of rapid notes that sound like "swee swee swee swee swee."

Nesting: A neat, deep cup of small twigs and plant down, lined with hair, fine grasses and many feathers of other birds, about 20 feet above the ground on a horizontal branch of a spruce, cedar or hemlock. The female incubates the four to five white eggs, which are peppered with brown specks, for 12 to 13 days. Young fly a short distance from the nest after 10 to 12 days.

Diet: Primarily insects in summer, and berries such as bayberry, wax myrtle and poison ivy in winter.

Backyard Favorites: In the North, during nesting season, they will use birdbaths. In the South, during winter, they will eat bird cakes made of cornmeal, peanut butter and suet, as well as fruit.

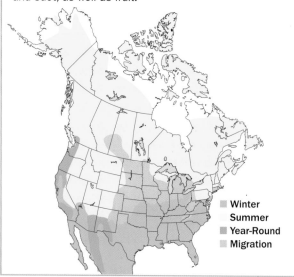

- Winter
- Summer
- Year-Round
- Migration

Betty had hung in netted bags. They were also gathered on a cypress stump, where a grapefruit half was filled with a variety of chopped fruit.

Most North American wood-warblers are summer birds that never eat from bird feeders, but not the yellow-rumped warbler. They are summer birds in the North and winter birds in the South, where they flock to feeders that offer fruit or bird cakes. No other wood-warbler consistently winters so far north.

My father, Hal, used to attract yellow-rumped warblers to his home in Ft. Lauderdale, Florida by putting out orange halves. He also described watching one of these birds skimming across his swimming pool in a swallow-like fashion, picking insects from the surface.

Eye-Catching Migrants

To travel between their winter and summer ranges, yellow-rumps pass through backyards across the country in spring and fall. That's when many people get a quick peek at this little bird with a yellow rump.

If you see one, you'll notice they are constantly on the move, sometimes hanging upside down on a branch in search of a caterpillar or beetle. But they never linger. In fact, it is always a challenge for me to get binoculars up to my eyes before the birds have moved from where I spotted them.

A fourth-grade class in Palm Coast, Florida got a treat when a small flock of yellow-rumped warblers descended outside their school last October.

"The children had a difficult time seeing them as the birds are so tiny and blend into the dry grass," writes their

BIT OF SUNSHINE. Yellow-rumped warblers are unique among warblers because they will visit feeders for suet (below) or fruit. One of the best ways to attract warblers is to offer a birdbath.

Roland Jordahl

Roland Jordahl

MALE OR FEMALE? Though male and female yellow-rumped warbles resemble one another, there are subtle differences. Males are grayish overall while females (above) are brownish.

teacher, Lisa Tilton. "They finally noticed them, and I explained that they are called yellow-rumped warblers. One student said that he couldn't see any yellow on them. I told him to wait."

As the birds flew away, the little bit of yellow on their rumps showed through. The children were amazed.

"That's when I told them the nickname for this warbler was 'butter butt,' " Lisa says. "They giggled about that and thought it was a fitting nickname."

During migration periods, these warblers will often visit birdbaths. Last fall, I watched a wave of warblers pass through my yard. Several yellow-rumps fluttered over the moving water in my birdbath, and one stopped long enough for a sip. Most of the yellow-rumps were juveniles, but they still carried the distinctive bright yellow on their rumps and flanks, making them easy to identity.

Their feeding behavior is much like that of a flycatcher. They'll often dart out from a tree branch to snag an insect in midair and then return to the tree branch to eat.

What's in a Name?

The yellow-rumps used to be divided into two different species, the Audubon's in the West, and the myrtle in the East. The only noticeable difference between the two is the yellow throat of the Audubon's and the white throat of the myrtle—named for the wax myrtle berries it eats. Today, both are called yellow-rumped warblers, and their combined summer and winter ranges reach from coast to coast and into Canada.

Yellow-rumped warblers typically place their nests in conifers. One of the remarkable traits of a yellow-rumped

nest is that the female uses many feathers from other birds to line the nest. She weaves the feather shafts into the cup, forming a screen for the eggs when the female is off the nest. The feathers make the eggs invisible to predators.

Room for More

If all goes well, the couple raise two broods, with the male feeding the fledglings while the female builds a second nest.

When the nesting season is over, the yellow-rumps head south. They are among the first waves of migrating warblers through my backyard in Wisconsin. For me, they are a seasonal indicator. When I see them in the fall, it means that summer is over. When I see them in the spring, winter is over.

Bring on the spring migrants!

Maslowski Productions

The yellow-rumped warbler is just one of 53 species of these birds that nest in North America. Because they primarily dine on insects, warblers migrate to tropical climates for winter.

The black-and-white warbler (pictured at right and featured on the cover of the F/M 2007 issue of *Birds & Blooms*) nests in the forests of the eastern U.S. and much of southern Canada. You're most likely to see it visiting yards during migration. This strikingly marked warbler is known for its habit of creeping around tree trunks like a nuthatch as it searches for insects in the bark.

Some of the most widespread species include yellow warblers, yellow-rumped warblers and common yellowthroats. Other common species include Kentucky warblers in the South, the black-throated green warbler in the Northeast, Virginia's warblers in the Southwest and the Townsend's warbler in the Northwest.

BIRD-WATCHER'S SECRET

Do you know how to tell the difference between a western and eastern yellow-rumped warbler? It's all in the throat. Look at the throat of a yellow-rumped. If it's white, it's an eastern species. If it's yellow, it's a western species.

STELLER'S JAY

These clever birds will win you over with their charm.

By Brianna Randall
Missoula, Montana

It's tough to be a member of the crow family. The Steller's jay, a common visitor in my western backyard, belongs to this group.

I'm an avid birder, and the Steller's jay has never been on my "most wanted" list. Instead, I'd rather look for rare species found in the nearby Rocky Mountains.

I'm not alone in my dismissal of these aggressive and numerous birds. Countless times, I've been hiking with friends who excitedly point out a bird gliding through the Ponderosa pines and Douglas firs. Upon closer inspection, they mutter, "Oh. It's just another Steller's jay."

What is it about ravens, crows, jays and magpies that causes folks to sigh and turn away? Perhaps it's just the sheer number of them found in our backyards.

After all, the calls of these non-singing birds is hardly impressive and even somewhat rowdy. Though they are the most intelligent birds in the entire feathered kingdom, it seems many people have reduced them to "ordinary" at best and "pest" at worst.

Change of Heart

I used to think the same way of this family of birds, thanks to the backyard squawks of Steller's jays. However, I've since changed my tune.

It happened a few years ago as I was sitting on my patio soaking up some sunshine. Soon, a loud "shek shek shek shek" shook me out of my reverie.

Grabbing my binoculars, I located three Steller's jays perched amid the branches of a western red cedar. I let out a sigh of disappointment upon recognizing the iridescent-blue bodies set off by a black head and neck.

Darn! It's not a berry-picking bohemian waxwing or giant pileated woodpecker, I thought to myself.

I was about to put down my binoculars when one of the Steller's jays turned its head in my direction. Its crest was boldly puffed-up atop its head, and its beauty surprised me. I later discovered that these jays have the honorable

Larry Dech

IT'S ALL RELATIVE. The Steller's is just one of several "blue" jays found in North America. Relatives include blue jays, pinyon jays and scrub-jays (like the western scrub-jay above). The male and female Steller's look alike, but the birds do differ slightly by region. On the Pacific Coast, they have all-black heads; those farther inland have a white "eyebrow" (below left and opposite).

distinction of sporting the largest crest of any North American bird.

Their jaunty crests certainly captured my attention that afternoon. It inspired me to look more carefully at these gregarious birds, rather than dismissing them as "just some jays."

Steller's jays are part of the elite group of birds that thrive during winter months without migrating to warmer surroundings. By using their strong, all-purpose bills to eat just about anything, Steller's jays are able to survive even the coldest climates of a northern Rocky Mountain winter.

A Matter of Survival

These adaptable birds inhabit forests from Alaska to Nicaragua and to coastal regions east to the Rocky Mountains. They eat everything from berries and seeds to eggs, meat and even other young birds.

The Steller's jay wisely prepares for long winter months by hoarding food. They hide nuts and seeds under the soil or in trees all year. Up to 95% of a jay's winter diet comes from its stored cache of food.

From late spring through summer, Steller's jays choose the crotch of evergreens 8 to 15 feet above the ground for their bulky nests of sticks held together with mud. Females lay four pale-blue or blue-green eggs.

Francis and Janice Bergquist

With my binoculars still glued to the boisterous jays, I thought about the fact that these small, warm-blooded creatures are much better at surviving Montana winters than I am.

The ingenuity exhibited by members of the crow family in finding new niches and exploiting resources reminded me of humans' adaptability. Shouldn't this bird's resourcefulness, careful social structure and clever use of tools endear it to humans instead of eliciting a bored sigh and a jaded glance?

One of the jays interrupted my thoughts as it flew away from my backyard with its characteristic flap-flap-glide flight pattern. Its remaining two cohorts sent up a loud warning call of raucous cackles.

I smiled. Steller's jays are like watchdogs of the forest. They sound alarms to keep other critters aware of danger.

I looked around for any present threats to my new friends—the neighbor's cat, perhaps—when one of the jays let loose a screech uncannily similar to the call of a red-tailed hawk. I nearly dropped my binoculars at the sudden, high-pitched call.

All members of the jay family are excellent at mimicry. This jay was copying the sound of a large bird of prey to scare off any lurking predators. It certainly startled me!

After a chorus of squawked warnings, the last two jays burst from the cedar tree. They maneuvered effortlessly through the crisp, sunny air with their short, rounded wings and long, rudder-like tails. The light bounced across pigments in the birds' feathers, reflecting flashes of bluish-green black down to my awestruck eyes.

In the Eye of the Beholder

Those three jays inspired a newfound respect for the tenacity and intelligence of the crow family. Just because a bird is common doesn't mean it deserves cynical dismissal. After all, "peskiness," like beauty, is in the eye of the beholder.

Now when I'm hiking with a friend, I look at birds differently. Sure, I still hope for a glimpse of a rare songbird or an illustrious bird of prey. But I also make sure to stop and acknowledge the clever Steller's jay, rather than simply grumbling in disappointment and walking away.

Backyard Birding Bio

Maslowski Productions

Common Name: Steller's jay.

Scientific Name: *Cyanocitta stelleri.*

Length: 11-1/2 inches.

Wingspan: 19 inches.

Description: Darkest of all North American jays; crest and front part of body is a sooty black. The rest of body is cobalt or purplish.

Voice: A harsh, descending "shaaaaar" is common. Another call is a rapid "shek shek shek shek."

■ Year-Round

Nesting: Bulky nest of large sticks held together with mud. Usually built in crotch of evergreen, 8 to 15 feet above the ground.

Diet: Forages for acorns, pine seeds, fruit, insects, frogs and young of other small birds.

Backyard Favorites: Sunflower seed, peanuts or chicken scratch.

BIRD-WATCHER'S SECRET

Keep your eye out for these clever birds. They cache their food in trees and other protected spots, relying on this stash for 95% of their winter diet.

ONE STELLAR NAME. The Steller's jay gets its name from Georg Wilhelm Steller, a German zoologist who was one of the first to describe the dark-blue jay during an Alaskan expedition in 1741.

Derrick Ditchburn/Unicorn Stock Photos

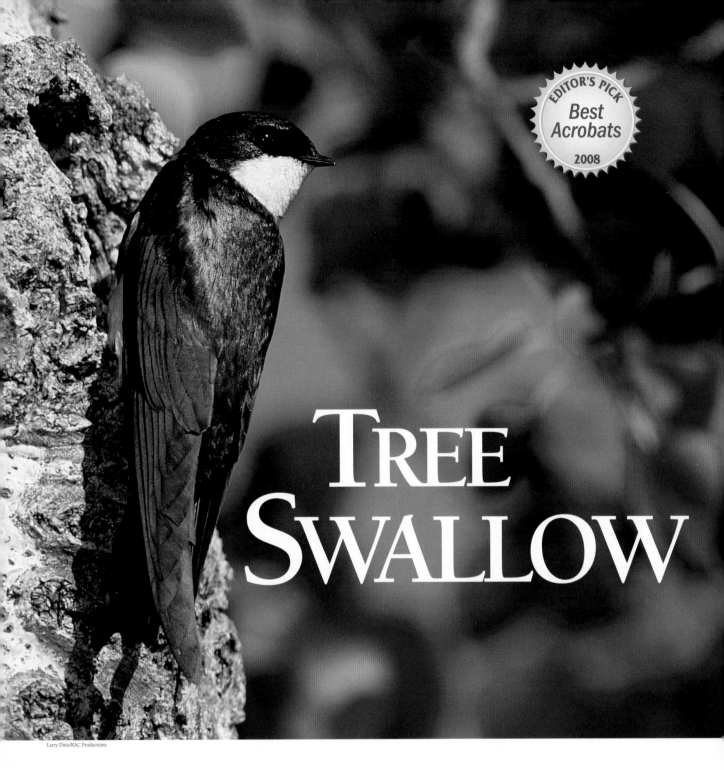

EDITOR'S PICK
Best
Acrobats
2008

TREE SWALLOW

Larry Ditto/KAC Productions

Aerial acrobats are a sure sign of spring's return.

By George Harrison, Contributing Editor

The "day of the swallows" is a big event at my house. On that day in mid-April, hundreds of swallows suddenly swarm over the little lake near my southeastern Wisconsin home. Mostly tree swallows, the chattering birds skim the water for insects and fly loop-the-loops, their metallic-green backs flashing in the sun. They seem to be celebrating spring.

As with all swallows, it's almost impossible to watch tree swallows through binoculars. They fly so fast, and zig and zag around so much in pursuit of insects, that getting a single bird in focus may drive you nuts. It often gives me a

Marie Read

Marie Read

Mark Werner/Unicorn Stock Photos

headache when I try to get a good look. I have much better luck just watching their antics from a distance.

Putting on a Show

I find them most enjoyable when I am fishing from my rowboat. Though I am concentrating on casting and retrieving the line, I am constantly aware of the tree swallows darting around me. Sometimes, when the lure hits the water, a tree swallow will be right there to check out what made the splash.

Tree swallows are the first of their clan to return north in spring, because they have a shorter distance to fly. They are the only swallows that remain in the United States year-round, spending winters in parts of the Southeast and Southwest, as well as in Mexico and Central America. For nesting season, they spread out across the northern two-thirds of the United States, into Canada and to Alaska.

Among the most sociable of birds, tree swallows gather in great flocks in late summer, migrate south in masses, and remain together in huge numbers through the winter and spring for their flight to northern breeding grounds.

I witnessed one of these mass migrations at Cape May, New Jersey one September. Not only did the thousands of tree swallows fly in swarms around the lighthouses there, they perched on utility wires in long rows near the beach. During the previous week, the tree swallows were so thick over Wildwood, New Jersey, that they darkened the skies and made tourists uneasy.

Stick Together

Tree swallows are so sociable that even when they break up in spring to nest, they often select different cavities in the same trees. I remember seeing several tree swallow pairs nesting in dead trees on a flooded marsh at Pymatuning, Pennsylvania.

They are not as colonial as cliff, bank or rough-winged swallows, but they like to have other members of related species as neighbors. For example, it is not unusual for several families to live in purple martin apartment houses.

There are nine species of swallows, including purple martins, in North America. All are graceful fliers, very sociable and eat insects while in flight. Tree swallows are a bit different from their relatives because they will dine on weed seeds and fruit if necessary, allowing them to survive cold

BIRD-WATCHER'S SECRET

In spring, keep your eye out for tree swallows migrating in from their winter homes. They travel in great masses and are amazing to watch.

Todd Fink/Daybreak Imagery

Chapter 1

Richard Day/Daybreak Imagery

FOOD DELIVERY. A male tree swallow swoops in with a meal (above). Opposite page, a female gathers material for a nest, feathers surround a partially completed clutch, a male and female vocalize during a courtship ritual, and (below) a group of swallows prepare to fly south during the migration season.

snaps that may kill their main food source—insects.

What really makes the tree swallow a common backyard bird is that they readily nest in bluebird houses, sometimes at the expense of the bluebirds. If this happens on your property, you can keep both families happy by putting up another bluebird house nearby.

One spring, a pair took up housekeeping in a bluebird house along the road near my property. I watched the pair gather grasses and feathers, sometimes while in flight, and carry the materials inside. The female laid one white egg a day for 6 days, and then began her 2-week incubation.

Several times during that phase, I peeked into the house while the female was away, but she had covered the eggs with feathers before leaving, and I could not easily see them. I was surprised when the swift-flying male grazed the top of my head while I peered into the house. He was fearless when it came to protecting the nest.

Feed Me!

A week or so after the eggs hatched, the fluffy nestlings, resembling little frogs with immaculate white throats, looked out the entrance, hoping to catch the next shipment of food. When an adult would zoom past and let out a "silip," they stretched their little necks and held their yellow mouths wide open to receive a meal of insects.

The youngsters got really noisy as the days passed. After about 2 weeks, they left the house, one at a time, making their solo flights much better than most fledglings. Within a day or two, the youngsters could fly and perch well enough to line up on the telephone wire above their house, where other tree swallow juveniles and parents joined them. The flocks had begun to form.

Although this meant that they'd soon be leaving, I knew I could look forward to their return in spring. And when the day of the swallows arrives, there will be a cheerful feeling in the air—that all is well with the world. ✒

Backyard Birding Bio

Common Name: Tree swallow.

Scientific Name: *Tachycineta bicolor.*

Length: 5-3/4 inches.

Wingspan: 14-1/2 inches.

Distinctive Markings: Adults are blue-green above and white below. While the sexes do look like, you can distinguish the two because males are brighter than females. Their wings on tree swallows are as long a their wedged-shaped tail.

Voice: Their song is a sweet, liquid twitter—a variation of "weet, trit, weet." The call note is "cheet" or "silip."

Nesting: In cavities, such as an old woodpecker hole, fence post, hole in a building, mailbox or birdhouse (even as large as wood duck house). Nest is a collection of dry grasses lined with feathers, often white chicken or gull feathers. Once the nest is ready, the female lays four to six pure-white eggs that hatch after 13 to 16 days. Gray and white fledglings leave the nest in about 3 weeks, or whenever weather conditions are favorable for their first flight.

Diet: Mostly insects, but unlike other swallows, they occasionally eat weed seeds and fruit.

Backyard Favorites:
Tree swallows prefer a small birdhouse, attached to a post or tree at eye level near water, with a 1-1/2-inch entrance hole 6 inches above the floor. In addition, look for these birds swooping through your yard in search of insects.

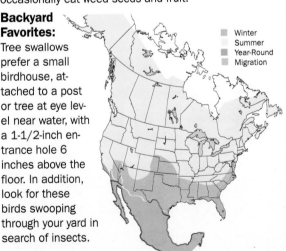

Winter
Summer
Year-Round
Migration

GREAT EGRET

*These majestic white wonders have
beauty, grace and personality.*

By George Harrison, Contributing Editor

Chapter 1

"Just wait 'til you meet 'Joe.'"

That's how my friends Don and Jean Hyde greeted me when I arrived for a visit at their winter home in Marathon Key, Florida.

I would soon learn that Joe is the great egret that settles into the Marathon community every winter, and visits Don and Jean every morning and night.

Sure enough, at cocktail time that evening, a tall and slender, pure-white great egret walked up to the Hydes' waterfront home.

"Good evening, Joe," Don yelled, as the huge bird came to the porch.

Don threw Joe several pieces of fish he got from the local bait shop, and Joe gobbled them down its long, white neck.

Everyone Knows His Name

"Along the water, we all know Joe," Don said. "Many people can't believe how close he comes to us, and how friendly he is."

Egrets have a way of making a lasting impression. These big and beautiful birds will often visit backyards in search of handouts, mostly in winter in coastal areas.

Diane Motsch of Louisville, Kentucky remembers a great egret that visited their winter community in DeLand, Florida for more than a decade. The residents nicknamed him "Stumpy" because the bird's foot had to be removed after it got entangled in fishing line.

"This unique bird encountered many challenges," Diane says. "Other egrets tried to run him off, perching could be a problem and even flying was difficult. Despite these setbacks, however, Stumpy thrived."

Joe and Stumpy are modern representatives of a species that was near extinction a century ago.

During the late 1800s, people hunted great egrets and smaller snowy egrets for the hat-making trade. Milliners throughout the world used egrets' graceful, flowing courtship feathers to decorate women's hats.

Worse yet, hunters killed most birds during breeding season when their feathers were most beautiful and valued at as much as $32 an ounce, twice the price of gold at the time. And when parent birds were killed, they left nests of eggs and young to die as well.

Protection of the plumed birds, forced by the newly formed Audubon Society and other conservationists at the turn of the 20th century, came just in time. Those organization had a large hand in saving the egrets from extinction. To this day, the symbol of the National Audubon Society is a great egret in flight.

It isn't difficult to understand why the great egret's feathers have attracted so much attention. Ornithologist Arthur Cleveland Bent probably said it best when he described the feathers in these glowing terms.

"Its long, graceful, flowing plumes, reaching far beyond its tail like a bridal train, and the exquisite purity of its snowy-white plumage make a picture of striking beauty when sharply outlined against a background of dark-green foliage, or when clearly mirrored on the surface of a

BEAUTY IN MOTION. Pure-white plumage makes great egrets majestic in any situation, whether they are snapping up a lizard for a quick meal (above), feeding young at a nest (below) or displaying their "bridal train" during courtship (left).

William Weber

Bernard Hehl/Unicorn Stock Photos

THERE'S ALWAYS STRENGTH IN NUMBERS. In winter, it's common to see great egrets feeding together in the water (below right). These birds often nest in groups, too. At right, an egret shows off its long black legs. Great egrets have black feet, while the similar, but smaller, snowy egret species has yellow feet.

quiet pool."

Today, great egrets are common on the East, West and Gulf Coasts and along many inland waterways throughout the country.

They remain close to water sources, which provide the mainstay of their diets in the form of fish, frogs, salamanders and the like.

In fact, many bird-watchers get a big kick from witnessing a great egret as it stealthily stalks its prey.

On the Prowl

"I got very excited the first time I saw a great egret feeding," says George Walker, who spends his winters at Sanibel Island, Florida, home of the Ding Darling National Wildlife Refuge.

"I watched this huge white bird creeping very slowly along the edge of the marsh," he says. "I was spellbound by the way it slowly placed one foot in front of the other, and then shifted its weight. Slowly, very slowly, it moved through the shallow water, head, neck and sharp yellow bill at the ready.

"Then it struck, as if fired from a gun. Its head and bill stabbed the water, and up it came with a small fish."

These birds' hunting habits aren't the only impressive thing about their behavior. After a spectacular courtship of displaying their famous plumes to help bond the pair, the male selects the site in a tree where both birds build a bulky nest of sticks and twigs.

Great egrets nest in small colonies, building their stick platforms in trees and close together, roughly 10 to 40 feet above the ground or wetland.

BIRD-WATCHER'S SECRET

If you want to see a great egret in person, you're best bet is to head for the water. Since these birds are big fish eaters, you can often find them wading through ponds, lakes and along the coasts.

Roland Jordahl

The Next Generation

For more than 2 months, the parent birds incubate eggs and then spend time to teach the young to fly. The juveniles typically climb out of the nest in about 3 weeks and fly in 6 to 7 weeks.

The egret nestlings are very aggressive toward each other, and they will often push a sibling out of the nest. Any youngster that falls from the nest before it is ready to fledge is doomed.

Today, great egret populations are again healthy. They migrate in the spring as far north as southern Canada, and fly south in the autumn to the southern U.S., Mexico and South America.

Watching great egrets fly, singly or in small flocks, is a beautiful sight. With its neck tucked back against its shoulders, and long black legs flowing behind white plumes, the elegant bird's slow wing beat gracefully carries it across the sky.

Larry Ditto/KAC Productions

Backyard Birding Bio

Common Name: Great egret.

Scientific Name: *Ardea alba.*

Length: 39 inches.

Wingspan: 51 inches.

Distinctive Markings: All-white, tall, wading bird with black legs and feet. Green between eyes and bill during nesting season.

Voice: Deep, gravelly "kroow" and other low croaks.

Nesting: Males choose a site, often in a small colony. Both parents gather the sticks and twigs for the large platform nest, and together incubate the three to four blue or greenish, oval eggs for 23 to 24 days until hatching.

Diet: Mostly fish, along with a few crustaceans, frogs, salamanders and snakes.

Backyard Favorite: A small pond surrounded by grasses or shrubs where they can fish.

- ■ Winter
- ■ Summer
- ■ Year-Round
- ■ Migration

Gerhard Schulz/Dembinsky Photo Assoc.

TUFTED TITMOUSE

Anything is fair game when this bird is looking for nesting material.

By George Harrison, Contributing Editor

Every year, Carolyn Langlinais watches as her dad helps the tufted titmice build their nests. She lives in Mandeville, Louisiana, and says titmice think her dad's silvery hair is the perfect nesting material.

"They hover right above his head, searching for the right spot to land," she says. "Dad says it doesn't hurt when they pull it out. Instead, he claims they cut it."

Though many birds line their nests with hair and fur, the tufted titmouse is probably the most aggressive about procuring the material. They've been known to pluck hair from wild animals, pets and humans.

When I was a kid, I remember watching a titmouse destroy the decorative raccoon tail tied to my bicycle handlebar. As much as I loved that tail, I loved birds even more. So, I just stood there on the front porch of my western Pennsylvania home in a kind of trance as the bird plucked away at the tail.

After hurriedly pulling fur from the raccoon tail, the titmouse would then flit off the porch, around the corner and across the fence where it disappeared into a woodpecker hole in our neighbor's apple tree.

While the female titmouse continued to make trips between my bicycle and its nest, her mate was busy searching for juicy insects from our garden. After gathering lunch, he called her out of the nesting cavity to eat.

Bonding Time

Among titmice and many other birds, a male feeding a female is a way to strengthen their bond. Until recently, scientists thought titmice mated for life. Now, DNA research shows this is not the case for titmice and virtually all other songbirds.

Nevertheless, pairs remain together all summer, busily raising youngsters. They also stay together through winter in groups with similar birds, foraging for insect eggs, seeds and berries.

We know spring is arriving when the male tufted titmouse begins to sing his courtship song, "peto, peto, peto."

This is a pleasant change from the harsh and scolding win-

SOUTHERN SPECIES. The tufted titmouse has a southern race, the black-crested (below), which lives in Texas and Mexico. It looks exactly like the tufted titmouse except for the black on its high crest. Below right, a titmouse gathers nesting material.

ter call of "day, day, day" that seems to match the bird's sharp crest, which rises with each pronouncement. The song is sometimes mistaken for the three-syllable notes of a Carolina wren or the spirited whistles of the northern cardinal.

Tufted titmice are among the most delightful of all backyard birds to watch. Like their close relatives, the chickadees, they are tame, bold, curious, acrobatic, noisy and never still. Also like chickadees, they can easily be lured to eat sunflower seeds from your hand.

The titmouse was the first bird to ever thrill me by eating from my hand. It quickly snatched a sunflower seed and darted to a nearby tree. Then it placed the seed between its tiny black feet and pounded the dickens out of the shell until the seed surrendered the meat inside.

Seconds later, the titmouse was back at my hand for another seed. It was so little that I could barely feel it on the tips of my fingers.

During nesting season that year, the titmouse pair in our neighbor's apple tree finished off their finely lined nest with a piece of snakeskin, perhaps to ward off predators. Then the female laid five spotted white eggs, which she incubated for 14 days.

The male fed her frequently while she sat securely on the eggs, rarely leaving the cavity. During that time, I mistakenly tried to scare her from the tree cavity to see if the eggs had hatched, but she sat tightly on them and would not come out.

Even after the eggs hatched, she remained inside, brooding the tiny, naked and blind babies while the male gathered and delivered food to the whole family. When the young finally exploded out of the cavity and fluttered in various directions, there was a great commotion as both parents tried to keep the fledglings fed and somewhat organized.

A few days later, the female was back to my raccoon tail,

BIRD-WATCHER'S SECRET

Don't let this bird's songs confuse you. While it sounds a lot like the chickadee's "dee, dee, dee" call, it is actually coarser in tone and more like "peto, peto, peto, peto."

Top Billing

gathering more soft fur for a new nest. This time she found the tail tacked to our porch railing because it was no longer fit to be a bicycle decoration.

Titmice Around the Country

Unfortunately for westerners, the tufted titmouse is mostly an eastern bird. Like the northern cardinal, it originated in the Southeast and then pioneered into the upper Midwest and Northeast.

Western bird-watchers have their own titmouse species, including the oak titmouse in California, and the juniper and bridled titmice in the Southwest.

A race of the tufted titmouse, the black-crested, lives in Texas and south into Mexico. It looks exactly like the tufted titmouse, except for the black on the front of its higher crest (see the photo on the previous page.)

Titmice are not migratory, but when autumn arrives, they join other families of their clan, which include chickadees and other woodland birds like nuthatches, brown creepers and small woodpeckers. Together, they roam the woodlands throughout winter in search of food and good places to roost at night.

Come spring, they will be hard at work again, gathering the finest materials around for their nests. So if you feel a tug at your head next year, take a close look. It just might be that a tufted titmouse wants to use some of your hair for its nest!

COME AND GET IT. The tufted titmouse is a common backyard visitor. Try offering sunflower seeds in a tube feeder or peanuts (below) to attract these friendly birds. They will also readily eat out of your hand. You just need some seed and patience.

Photos this page: Maslowski Productions

Backyard Birding Bio

Common Name: Tufted titmouse.
Scientific Name: *Baeolophus bicolor*.
Family: Titmouse.
Length: 6-1/2 inches.
Wingspread: 9-3/4 inches.
Distinctive Markings: Adults are larger and stockier than their close relatives the chickadees, with a plain gray head, short crest, short, broad gray tail and orange flanks.
Voice: Their song is a low, clear whistle of "peto, peto, peto, peto." The call "day, day, day, day" is somewhat like the chickadee's "dee, dee, dee" call, but wheezy and coarser in tone.
Habitat: Oak woodlands, moist bottomlands, swamps, orchards, shaded suburban parks and backyards.
Nesting: Never excavates its own nest cavity, preferring to find an abandoned woodpecker hole or a birdhouse, 2 to 80 feet above the ground. The nest is made of shredded tree bark, dead leaves, moss, grasses, hair, fur and sometimes a snakeskin. The female incubates the eggs for 13 to 14 days. The young remain in the cavity for another 15 to 16 days.
Diet: Mostly insects and seeds; eats nuts, berries, fruit and seeds in winter.
Backyard Favorites: A small birdhouse with an entrance hole that's 1-1/4 inches in diameter and 6 inches above the floor. Readily eats sunflower seeds and peanuts.

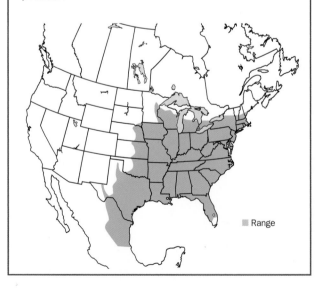

■ Range

Chapter 1

HOUSE WREN

Little brown bird wins admirers with its colorful personality.

By George Harrison
Contributing Editor

Top Billing

The little house wren surely must be the most tenacious bird in the world when it comes to nesting. Once it decides that your yard is its home, nothing will keep it from nesting there. Here's an example.

During the year we rebuilt our home in southeastern Wisconsin, a pair of house wrens laid claim to their usual summer residence—the birdhouse in the second apple tree from the garage—and got busy building their nest. On the day our basement was excavated, the wrens had completed their own construction project, and the female had laid her first egg.

I was certain the wrens would desert their nest because of all the commotion in the yard. But not only did they ignore all the construction work around them while raising a brood of five spunky youngsters, they persevered to bring up a second brood in the same house.

Another house wren bonded to a house in the backyard of Arlene Clouston, who remembers an incident from her youth. Arlene, who now lives in Lake Placid, Florida, recalls that her family was late putting up the birdhouse one spring, when her brother Glenn spotted the wren looking for it.

"Jenny Wren is here!" he hollered, "and we don't have the house up yet." Glenn raced out to the shed, grabbed the wren house and ran to the apple tree with it. As soon as he got there, the wren recognized the familiar abode and flew right into it…while Glenn was holding it!

Their mother fetched the step-ladder, and they quickly put the house up in the tree. Amazingly, the wren stayed put in the house the entire time.

A Welcome Visitor

That tenacity is part of the house wren's charm. It also makes them one of the easiest birds to entice to a birdhouse. That, plus the effervescent, joyous song of the male, explains why the house wren is a favorite among backyard birders.

"The wrens are not shy at all," says Teresa Zefo of St. Charles, Missouri. "We have several house wrens that nest in our birdhouses every year. When they are searching for food, they will often get quite close to us on our patio, and even hop right across my feet while searching for bugs.

"They have stolen our hearts," she says.

Though they are among the plainest of all backyard birds, they are also the busiest. Never still for more than a second or two, they're always flitting here and there, searching for insects, twigs for their nests, running off intruders, and all the while bursting with song.

RIGHT AT HOME. House wrens are among some of the easiest birds to attract to nest in backyard birdhouses. Basically, you just have to set out the right size birdhouse. These birds are tenacious busybodies, and the males have an effervescent song.

There is also a dark side to this robust bundle of brown feathers. House wrens have a violent temper and aggressively attack other birds—even those much larger than themselves—that invade their territory.

They will also attack other birds that nest in nearby birdhouses, including bluebirds, chickadees and tree swallows. They have been known to enter other birds' houses and pierce the eggs.

When a male house wren arrives in the spring from his wintering grounds in the South, he will establish a territory, usually in a backyard, and build dummy nests in every nook and cranny he can find.

Tour of Homes

When the female arrives a week or two later, she selects a mate and his territory. The male may take her on a tour of the dummy nests he has built. If she likes one of them, she may remove most of his sticks and replace them with sticks she gathers herself. You know who the boss is in the wren family.

Though they will readily take to a small birdhouse with a 1-1/8-inch entrance hole, house wrens are famous for other odd nesting sites, too. My father, Hal, photographed a pair of house wrens in Pennsylvania that built their nest in the leg of a pair of overalls hanging on a clothesline. The owner of the pants tied up the leg and relinquished the overalls to the birds. Eggs were laid, and young successfully raised inside.

Watering cans, fishing creels, sun hats, teapots, old boots, as well as a bathing suit on a clothesline are other places that have housed wren nests.

House wrens are as eccentric about the nesting materials they use as the sites they select. One house wren nest in Iowa reportedly contained hairpins, nails, tacks, staples, paper clips, wires and hooks.

The most common nesting materials used by house wrens are twigs. One of the more amusing sights in the bird world is watching a wren maneuver a 6- or 8-inch twig through a 1-1/8-inch entrance hole. It may take many attempts, but somehow the long stick finally gets placed inside, though the end often pokes out the door.

House wrens are not permanently bonded to their mates, and may change partners during the breeding season for a second brood. Some males have several female mates, who raise broods at the same time in different nests nearby. In these cases, the male seems to leave most of the domestic chores to the females while he is busy visiting his families, bubbling over with song, and keeping an eye open for intruders.

Backyard Birding Bio

Maslowski Productions

Common Name: House wren.
Scientific Name: *Troglodytes aedon*.
Length: 4-3/4 inches.
Wingspan: 6 inches.
Description: A small, plain brown bird that is dark above and lighter below. No streaks or eye lines. Males and females look alike.
Voice: The male's bubbling, chattering, repetitive song rises and then falls at the end. Its scolding notes are a series of "zzzzzzsssszzz" sounds.
Nesting: They're known for nesting in strange places—boots, car radiators, mailboxes—as well as in small birdhouses. They build their nest of sticks and line it with grass, plant fibers, feathers and rubbish. The female incubates the five to eight cinnamon-speckled white eggs for about 13 days. The young leave the nest 12 to 18 days after hatching.
Diet: Insects, including caterpillars, grasshoppers and spiders.
Backyard Favorite: A small birdhouse with a 1-1/8-inch entrance hole that's 6 inches above the floor, hung or attached to a small tree.

Winter
Summer
Year-Round
Migration

*This bird brings cheer
wherever it flies.*

By George Harrison
Contributing Editor

NORTHERN CARDINAL

Northern cardinals may be the perfect backyard bird. Though they are found only in the eastern two-thirds of the country, these red birds with the jaunty crests have everything going for them.

The male northern cardinal is gorgeous, devoted to its mate, aggressive toward competitors and a good father. The birds are also hardy in winter and sing beautiful melodies in summer. Their most alluring quality, though, is that they love to eat at backyard feeders.

Anyone who has watched cardinals would likely agree with John James Audubon's assessment. He wrote that the northern cardinal "in richness of plumage, elegance of motion, and strength of song, surpasses all its kindred in the United States."

Seven states have selected it as their state bird—Illinois, Indiana, Kentucky, North Carolina, Ohio, Virginia and West Virginia. This earns cardinals the most "state titles" than any other bird.

For me, the northern cardinal's cheerful song and bright-red feathers are like a breath of fresh air. I am continually amazed at how many months a year cardinals sing. The only time I don't hear them sing is during October, November and December.

In late winter, these lovely birds can light up a bleak and snowy woods with its lively "what-cheer, what-cheer, birdie, birdie, birdie" song.

A Bright Spot

Last winter, a male northern cardinal stopped in the Reston, Virginia backyard of Joyce Fleming. It made quite an impression, too. She was amazed at the way the single brightened her entire yard.

"When I first caught a glimpse of the bird, I threw some seed on top of the shed roof, and in no time, the bird showed up to eat," she says.

Joyce's other feathered friends usually fly away when they see her, but the cardinal was willing to put up with her prying eyes for a few minutes. It even turned its head and looked directly at her.

"It was great to have that up-close experience, even if it

was freezing outside!" Joyce says.

I've also had the opportunity to get eye-to-eye with "Big Red," and once, a little too close. Years ago, I was bitten by a male cardinal while trying to place a U.S. Fish and Wildlife Service band on its leg.

As I held it in my hand, the big finch took a chunk of meat out of my finger with its sharp bill. It hurt! I learned the hard way how they can effortlessly snap open a sunflower seed. That's a strong bill!

One other "too-close-for-comfort" situation was the spring a male cardinal awakened me every morning at 5:15 with "thud, thud, thud" sounds as it fought its reflection on my kitchen window.

As the males establish a territory for the nesting season, it's not unusual for them to battle perceived rivals in a house window, a car's rearview mirror or a shiny hubcap. One bird-watcher in Pennsylvania even reported a cardinal that attacked a piece of red cardboard.

Birds that fight their reflections don't really harm themselves. Most give up the "fight" shortly after it starts.

FLASHES OF BEAUTY. While male northern cardinals (like the one at left) steal the show with their brilliant red colors, the females are a beautiful addition to backyards, too. Below, this female perched on an evergreen has eye-catching red accents on her crest, wings, bill and tail, but she's tan overall.

BIRD-WATCHER'S SECRET

Want cardinals to become regulars in your backyard? It just takes two simple steps to make that happen. First, offer black-oil sunflower seed, and second, put out a birdbath.

Perfect Couple

Cardinal courtship, which begins in late winter, is often quite touching. To please his mate, the male will pick up a sunflower seed and pass it to her, even though they are both perched on a feeder full of seeds.

Following this courtship behavior, the female selects a nesting sight and builds a bulky cup of twigs and leaves in a thicket, at about eye level. Though the female does most of the work, the male does his share of feeding her and the young after they hatch.

Two weeks later, the young make their solo flights out of the nest. Although the fledglings don't return to the nest, the parents continue to feed them for another week or two, and at the same time, they may be making preparations for a second or third brood.

"I will always have a special place in my heart for cardinals," says Tracy Tillman of Belmond, Iowa. Tracy was pregnant with her son, Andrew, when she noticed a cardinal's nest in the shrub outside her kitchen window.

"I felt a special connection with that mother bird outside of my window. Every day as I did my dishes, I watched her sitting there on her nest as the male cardinal brought her food," Tracy says.

Five nights after the three eggs hatched, a storm blew the nest out of the shrub. Tracy was frantic. She ran outside and picked up the naked little nestlings and placed them in a butter dish, which she wired to the spot where the fallen nest had been. Ten days later, the fledglings left the nest.

For 3 years after that, a single cardinal frequented that

FEEDING "BIG RED." Sunflower seeds are a favorite of northern cardinals (like the female at right), but they will eat a large variety of foods. Below, this male plucks a piece of cactus fruit in Texas. They will also visit backyards with birdbaths.

Larry Ditto/KAC Productions

Maslowski Productions

Chapter 1

shrub outside Tracy's window. "I like to think it was one of the little birds from the nest," she says.

Centuries of Admiration

From the earliest times, people have been attracted to the cardinal, especially to the flamboyant male.

The first published illustration of the bird was in a 1599 work by Aldrovandus, the director of a botanical garden in Bologna, Italy. Apparently, the model for the drawing was a cardinal that had been captured in the New World and presented to Aldrovandus. (Today, they are protected species in the U.S.)

That's probably when the species acquired its religious moniker. The bird is named for the cardinals of the Roman Catholic Church, who wear scarlet-red robes.

The "northern" part of their name helps separate them from a couple of other cardinals farther south: the pyrrhuloxia, a lovely gray bird with a red breast, red crest and yellow bill that's found in the Southwest; and the red-crested cardinal, also called the Brazilian cardinal, that has been introduced into Florida, California and Hawaii.

Beyond the North

Over the years, northern cardinals have expanded their range—showing up farther north and west to the Rocky Mountains and into the Southwest.

Though adult northern cardinals are not truly migratory, young birds of that year do wander around a great deal in search of mates and territories. Most don't wander far, but there are exceptions.

One male was banded in Hartford, Connecticut and recaptured later in State College, Pennsylvania, a distance of 270 air miles. Cincinnati, Ohio is sometimes called the cardinal capital of the world, because it seems to have more than the usual number of red birds, especially in winter.

However, luckily for bird-watchers, northern cardinals often will stick around the same backyard all year long. No wonder they're a favorite.　　　🐦

UNDER ITS WING. Both male and female northern cardinals are attentive and devoted parents. The male (above right) feeds the young in the nest and after they fledge. Cardinal pairs typically raise two to three broods of three nestlings per season.

Backyard Birding Bio

Common Name: Northern cardinal.
Scientific Name: *Cardinalis cardinalis*.
Length: 8-3/4 inches.
Wingspan: 12 inches.
Description: The only red bird with a crest in North America. The male has a brilliant red body with a black face and throat, and a conical-shaped large, red bill. The female is fawn-covered with touches of red on her crest, bill, wings and tail. Juveniles look like females with dark bills.
Voice: Although both males and females sing, the male's loud "what-cheer, what-cheer, birdie, birdie, birdie" song is the one most people recognize. Hers is similar, but softer and quieter. A harsh "chip" is their alarm and communication call.
Nesting: The female constructs a loose nest of twigs, vines, leaves, bark strips and rootlets in dense shrubbery, generally no higher than 10 feet above the ground. The three to four pale-blue or greenish-white eggs blotched with brown are incubated by the female for the 12 to 13 days before hatching.

Fed by both parents, the nestlings sprout feathers and are ready to fly from the nest in another 12 days.
Diet: Seeds in winter; insects such as beetles and cicadas in summer; berries and other fruits when they're available.
Backyard Favorites: Sunflower seeds of any kind, served in a tray or hopper feeder. They will readily use birdbaths to drink and bathe throughout the year.

🔲 Year-Round

WHITE-BREASTED
NUTHATCH

This topsy-turvy bird has it all backward.

By George Harrison, Contributing Editor

When Europeans watched a nervous little bird wedge nuts into tree crevices and hack them open with its long bill, they called it a nuthack. Colonists on American shores saw the same kind of bird doing the same thing, and, as language evolved, the name changed to *nuthatch*.

The white-breasted nuthatch is the largest and best known of the four North American nuthatches. As I watch them daily in my southeastern Wisconsin backyard, they remind me of feathered circus performers presenting a variety of amusing acts.

While the other backyard birds behave more sedately, white-breasted nuthatches seem to always be on stage, like comedians, acting and entertaining wherever they go.

Two-Way Traffic

Especially noticeable is their seemingly ridiculous manner of walking down tree trunks headfirst. While all other birds walk up trees in search of food, the nuthatch does the exact opposite.

In this flip-flopped mode, aided by strong claws that keep it from falling, the nuthatch has access to insects, eggs and larvae tucked into the top sides of tree bark, hidden from the view of birds that shimmy up trees.

Their upside-down feeding behavior caught the eye of Karen Carlsen, a *Birds & Blooms* Field Editor in Elgin, Oregon.

"One winter, while taking pictures of my busy bird feeder, I noticed a white-breasted nuthatch high on the trunk of a pine tree," she says. "With an apparent disregard for the laws of gravity, this little scrap of a bird began descending the trunk headfirst."

As Karen continued to watch, she saw a tiny brown creeper at the bottom of the tree, inching up the trunk in a jerky, spiral manner.

"I watched as both birds mined the bark for insects," Karen says. "I was suddenly struck by the fact that these birds were both fashioned for the same purpose, but in a totally different way. The brown creeper finds insects from the bottom, looking up; the white-breasted nuthatch approaches the tree from the top, looking down. Between the two of them, I'd say they cover the insects pretty well...as long as they don't collide somewhere in the middle."

But their trademark upside-down feature is just a warmup to other, less understood behavior, such as their bill-

SEARCHING FOR SUET. When they aren't scavenging for bugs down the trunks of trees, nuthatches look for suet in backyard feeders. Even then, these quirky birds usually hang upside down (like the one above), enjoying treats from a different perspective.

sweeping performance. That's when a nuthatch sways from side to side, sweeping its bill in a motion so exaggerated that the bird's whole body moves to and fro.

I've seen this act staged at the entrance to the bird's nesting cavity, as though it is sweeping off the front steps. A male I observed sweeping had food in his bill, presumably meant for the female that was inside the cavity incubating eggs. Some people believe that it may have to do with the protection of the nest from predators such as squirrels.

Another unique nuthatch stunt is the white-breasted's courtship dance, which includes sound effects. Throughout the year, I hear the nasal "yank, yank, yank" call of both males and females that sounds like the toot of a little toy horn.

Starting in early January, I also hear a totally different "whi, whi, whi" call, which is the male's spring courtship song. That's when I see the pair engage in their courtship dance, initiated when the female responds to the male's song by swaying side-to-side until he floats down to her, like a parachute, with his wings and tail spread.

Landing next to her, he puffs up his colorful feathers, as if to say, "Take a look at me."

Feathered Busybodies

Despite their strange behavior, or maybe because of it, white-breasted nuthatches always seems to be in a hurry, as if they are late for their next performance. If that's true, they're always well dressed and groomed for any such eventuality. (Males and females look alike, though a close exam-

Francis and Janice Bergquist

Maslowski Productions

Richard Day/Daybreak Imagery

ination will reveal that the male's cap is deeper black than the female's).

The nuthatch's feeder behavior, much like the black-capped chickadee, with which it associates most of the year, is to take one sunflower seed at a time, and fly to a nearby tree to crack it open. But instead of holding it between its feet, like a chickadee does, it will wedge the seed into a piece of tree bark.

The bird quickly consumes the seed meat, and in a flash it's back to the feeder for another seed. And so it goes for half a dozen trips before the bird zips off to another backyard, presumably to its next performance.

Always in Motion

I watched a nuthatch pair raise a brood in a hollowed-out limb scar, about 10 feet up the trunk of a sugar maple tree along the lake road I walk every morning. My daily observations started with the female carrying bark shreds into the hole in May, and ended with the fledging of the gawky youngsters in late June.

Though I could not see inside, I assumed that the female

laid about eight eggs and then incubated them for 12 days while the male faithfully fed her, sometimes sweeping the front door en route. Both parents became very busy after the eggs hatched. They were carrying food into the cavity every few minutes, sometimes both arriving at the same time to feed all the hungry mouths.

And what a clamor there was when the young left the cavity. It was as if little toy horns were tooting from every corner of the neighborhood. Clearly, the whole family was now in the act.

BIRD-WATCHER'S SECRET

At first glance, you'd think that the males and females of this species look exactly alike. There is a subtle difference, though. The male has a deeper black cap on the top of its head compared to the female.

CLOSE RELATIVES. The red-breasted nuthatch (pictured below) is one of the other three nuthatches in North America. Below left, while many songbirds only lay three to four eggs, nuthatches lay up to eight. That is a lot of hungry mouths to feed! At left, a baby peeks out of the tree.

Greg Bergquist

Backyard Birding Bio

Roland Jordahl

Common Name: White-breasted nuthatch.
Scientific Name: *Sitta carolinensis*.
Family: Nuthatch.
Length: 5–3/4 inches.
Wingspan: 11 inches.
Distinctive Markings: A small, bluish bird with a white breast and black cap and nape, tawny flanks, white patches on each side of the tail and black beady eyes. Males and females are alike in coloration.
Voice: The song is a soft and slightly nasal "whi-whi-whi." The call is a sharp "yank, yank, yank."
Nesting: Usually a natural tree cavity 15 to 50 feet above the ground, but may use an old woodpecker hole or a birdhouse. Female lines nest with bark shreds, grasses and rootlets, fur and hair before laying seven to eight eggs. She incubates the eggs for 12 days before they hatch.
Diet: Primarily insects gleaned from tree trunks. Will also eat tree nuts, and the seeds and berries of various plants.
Backyard Favorite: Relishes sunflower seeds, in the shell or cracked, offered in virtually any kind of bird feeder.

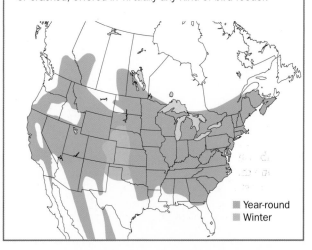

■ Year-round
■ Winter

Downy Woodpecker

These little woodpeckers are true "feathered friends."

By George Harrison, Contributing Editor

Chapter 1

There's a reason many people call downy woodpeckers the "friendly woodpecker." These birds are frequent backyard visitors and often remain at feeders or on trees even when people are around.

In my yard, downies are constant companions any time I'm outdoors—on the patio grilling dinner, reading in my favorite lounge chair or photographing other birds. I frequently watch them back down a tree trunk to the suet feeder while I am only a few feet away. When I fill feeders or clean birdbaths, a downy will often continue quietly feeding nearby. They are always around, summer and winter.

Downies can sometimes be confused with the similar-looking hairy woodpecker, but there are several ways to distinguish them.

Both species are named for the feathers at the upper base of their bills, but the downy woodpecker has a downy knob of nasal feathers, while the hairy's is more bristly. Downies also have a shorter bill and are smaller than the hairy woodpecker.

At two-thirds the size of the hairy, they are the smallest woodpeckers in North America. They're also more common, so if you're not sure whether you're seeing a hairy or a downy, odds are, it's a downy.

Although downies are around all year, I am especially grateful for their presence in winter. That's because the si-lence of the winter woods is often interrupted by the tap, tap, tap, tap of a solitary downy woodpecker. That sound is reassurance that spring will arrive…someday.

While most birds whistle their courtship songs, downy woodpeckers tap theirs against the bark of a tree. Occasionally, much to the irritation of some home owners, downies drum their mating calls against the wood or aluminum siding of a house.

Both male and female downy woodpeckers perform this staccato tapping, which may echo through the naked trees of winter as early as January. Downy woodpeckers may keep the same mate for life, and in midwinter, they start drumming to find their mates and rekindle bonds.

> *One of the great bonuses of feeding birds in summer is seeing adults introduce their youngsters to the feeders.*

It's Time for the Dance

Once they have found each other, the actual courtship begins with a curious dance by both the male and female. With their necks stretched out and bills pointed in line with their bodies, they pivot their head and body from side to side, effortlessly balancing with the tips of their tails. They also flit about and chase each other from branch to branch as part of the ritual, waving and weaving their bodies, and sometimes spreading their wings and tail feathers. It's an amazing display to watch!

This display is accompanied by considerable chattering. It's just another way downies bring the winter woods to life.

Sometime during this courtship period, the pair selects a place to nest. The female, who dominates her mate, is usually the one that picks the site. Both work to dig out the cavity, which is located 3 to 50 feet above the ground in the trunk of a tree.

The pair works 15- to 20-minute shifts over the course of a week to excavate the cavity so it's ready for their four or five pure-white eggs. When the clutch is complete, the pair takes turns incubating during the day, while the male usually sits on the eggs at night.

After 12 days, the eggs hatch into naked, red and homely chicks. For the first few days, the parents take turns staying with the babies, while the other gathers food. The male usually broods the youngsters at night.

The parents feed their ever-hungrier youngsters a diet of insects, as often as every 2 or 3 minutes. As the youngsters grow and sprout tail feathers to support them, at about 14 days old, they begin to take turns sitting in the entrance of the cavity. There, they stick out their heads and beg for food. At 21 to 24 days, they fly out of the cavity, never to return.

Carol McCormick of Arnold, Pennsylvania was lucky enough to witness some young downies and their parents in her backyard.

"The young chattered most of the time during the final

LONG AND SHORT OF IT. Up close, it's easier to see that the downy woodpecker (top left) has a shorter bill than the hairy woodpecker (left). From a distance, the best clue to differentiate the two is their body size. Downies are much smaller.

Top Billing

SITTIN' PRETTY. Downies and other woodpeckers use their tails and specially shaped feet to cling to vertical surfaces. Above, this downy clings to a suet feeder mounted on a post.

2 or 3 days, taking turns looking out the entrance hole at the strange world outside," Carol writes. "Then, one at a time, they made their maiden flight from the cavity.

"The first chick left immediately after being fed and watching the parent fly away. It flew from the nesting hole straight to the tree where its parent landed, 60 feet away. Then it followed the parent up the trunk of the tree in that hitching manner that downies use, as if it had been practicing this vertical locomotion all its life."

It is easy to distinguish juvenile downies from their parents. The youngsters have red caps that extend from their bills to the back of their heads. They keep their red crowns until they molt in fall. That's when they get their first adult plumage, including a red spot located at the back of the head of males. One of the great bonuses of feeding birds in summer is seeing adults introduce their youngsters to the feeders. I consider it entertainment all by itself.

A Lesson in Dining

Downy parents divide the brood and feed their individual charges for a couple more weeks after they have left the nesting cavity.

BIRD-WATCHER'S SECRET

If you want to attract downies to your backyard, you can't go wrong with suet. To make an extra-special treat, add seeds, berries and other high-protein bits to the suet. The birds will love it.

And if you happen to see what appears to be two adult male downies, and one is feeding the other, it likely is a father feeding his offspring. This is the behavior Shannon Beaudoin of Troy, New York observed in her yard.

"For several days, I watched two male downy woodpeckers at my suet feeder," she writes. "While they were both clinging to the cage, one repeatedly fed the other."

Insects make up the majority of a downy's diet. They gather beetles, wood-boring larvae, caterpillars, weevils, ants and the like from tree bark. The remainder of their diet, about 25%, is wild fruits, seeds and nuts. In winter, they eat the tiny grubs inside goldenrod galls.

To make downy woodpeckers feel at home in your yard, start by setting out suet or some cracked sunflower. Then wait to see who shows up. You just might make a "friend" that will stick around all year long.

Backyard Birding Bio

Common Name: Downy woodpecker.

Scientific Name: *Picoides pubescens*.

Length: 6-3/4 inches.

Wingspan: 12 inches.

Distinctive Markings: White on the belly and black-and-white markings elsewhere. The male has a small red spot on the back of its head.

Voice: Both male and female "sing" in early spring by drumming on trees. Their call note is a single, abrupt syllable, like "tchick."

Nesting: Pair creates a cavity in a live or dead tree, 3 to 50 feet above the ground. The female lays four or five pure-white eggs. After a 12-day incubation, the eggs hatch and the young fledge about 3 weeks later. One brood a summer is the norm in the North, while pairs may raise two broods in the South.

Diet: Mostly insects, but also fruit, seeds and nuts.

Backyard Favorites: Suet, bird cakes, cracked sunflower seeds and safflower seeds.

■ Year-Round

Anthony Mercieca

EVENING GROSBEAK

You'll take notice of these flashy birds that travel in packs.

By George Harrison, Contributing Editor

As the dentist came at me with his drill, I saw a flash of yellow and white out of the corner of my eye. I held up my hands and gurgled for him to stop.

When I sat up, I looked out the window and saw a bird feeder loaded with evening grosbeaks. It was the first time I had ever seen these lovely winter visitors from the North.

I watched in amazement as dozens of the big yellow, white and black birds fluttered around, vying for positions on the crowded feeder filled with sunflower seeds. It was the perfect diversion for a nervous dental patient like me.

Dr. Joseph Hummer owned that country dental practice in Pine Grove Mills, Pennsylvania, just a few miles from Penn

Top Billing

Sid and Shirley Rucker

BIRD CLIQUES. Evening grosbeaks tend to travel in groups, even during nesting season. So if you see one at your feeder, you're bound to get the whole pack, too. Watch out! In winter, a flock can empty a bird feeder in just a matter of minutes.

itime provinces of Canada. They are even so common in New Brunswick that, unfortunately, cars sometimes hit them on highways when the birds gather salt left from winter highway treatments.

Not Night Owls

In June, I was visiting New Brunswick when I saw a group of these birds along a coastal highway. I did a double take when I first saw them because they were in their breeding plumage and had light-green bills (like the bird at left) instead of the pale cream ones I'm accustomed to seeing in winter (like the birds above).

Even during nesting season, evening grosbeaks often travel together. They nest in a dense leaf clusters near the ends of branches. Females lay three or four bluish eggs, and the youngsters leave roughly 14 days after they hatch.

Don't let the name of these birds fool you. The first recording sighting of the species happened during the evening in August 1823 near the Thunder Bay district of Ontario. The recorder, Major Joseph Delafield, wrote, "At twilight, a singular bird that cries at this hour perches about the tent..."

Two years later, an ornithologist tasked with giving the bird an official name read the major's report. He had never seen the bird in the wild and assumed from the account that the bird was most active in the evening. Therefore, in his mind, "evening grosbeak" was perfect.

To the contrary, evening grosbeaks are morning birds and often roost for the night as early at 2 p.m. during winter. Perhaps "morning grosbeak" would have been a more accurate name!

Though these birds are charming, they are also gluttons. An average flock of a couple dozen birds can eat you out of sunflower seeds in a matter of minutes.

Francis and Janice Bergquist

State University, where I was a journalism student.

I was so excited about seeing the grosbeaks at the dental office that I phoned my father, a nature photographer and writer. The next weekend, he drove 150 miles to Dr. Hummer's office just to photograph the birds and see them in action for himself.

Eastward, Ho!

During that time in the 1950s, evening grosbeaks were a rare sight in Pennsylvania. Today, they are much more common as they have expanded their traditional range from the West and Northwest, eastward all the way to the mar-

MEET AND GREET. Courting season was in full force when this picture was taken. You can tell by looking at the male's bill. The male evening grosbeak (on the right), sporting a light-green mating-season bill, is feeding the female during a courtship ritual.

Big Eaters

"I've fed a couple of tons of sunflower seeds to grosbeaks in a single winter," says Konnie Hunter of Rhinelander, Wisconsin.

Konnie has been feeding evening grosbeaks every winter, and some summers, for 40 years.

"If you see one or two evening grosbeaks at your feeders and you don't have a good supply of sunflower seeds on hand, you'd better head to the feed mill immediately because they are big eaters!" Konnie says. "As long as I keep my 17 to 20 feeders filled with black-oil sunflower seeds, the grosbeaks will be with me every morning from daybreak until noon, from early December to mid-April."

Konnie usually feeds around 100 grosbeaks daily, but has had as many as 250 of the birds in her backyard at one time.

"They also like water," Konnie says. "That's why I keep a heated bowl of water on my deck. They can't bathe in it, but they drink a great deal."

A few years ago, while I was working on the PBS special *Birds of the Backyard*, there were no grosbeaks at my feeders in southeastern Wisconsin. I knew exactly where to go to find them, though.

The crew and I moved farther north to Rhinelander to work for a couple of days at Konnie's home. When we arrived at her doorstep, the first light had just appeared in the sky. We looked up over our heads. Hundreds of evening gros-

BIRD-WATCHER'S SECRET

Don't let the name fool you. Even though this bird is called an evening grosbeak, it's actually more active in the morning hours. It often settles down for the day by mid-afternoon.

beaks were already in the trees above her house, calling "clee-ip, clee-ip, clee-ip."

They were noisy, but relatively tame, as they are very social birds. They let us photograph them eating and drinking, which was a great addition to our video.

Check-Up Paid Off

I'll never forget my first sighting of evening grosbeaks while sitting in the dentist's chair. I had dreaded that December appointment for weeks, but it turned out to be a memorable one.

Though I've long forgotten the pain of the appointment, the sight of those birds against a blanket of fresh snow lives on with me today.

Backyard Birding Bio

Common Name: Evening grosbeak.
Scientific Name: *Coccothraustes vespertinus*.
Length: 8 inches.
Wingspan: 14 inches.
Description: Chunky, with a large head and large, pale, conical bill (a "gross beak"). Male has a yellow forehead, black crown, black tail, olive-brown back, yellow underparts and black wings with white secondary feathers. Females are grayish to yellow with black on their wings.
Voice: Song is a short, uneven warble reminiscent of the notes of a purple finch. Its chirping "clee-ip" notes are similar to a common house sparrow, but more shrill and harsh.
Nesting: Nests are 20 to 60 feet above the ground in a conifer. The female builds a frail cup of twigs, interwoven with moss and lichens. The three to four blue-green eggs are blotched with brown, and the female incubates them for 12 to 14 days before hatching. Young remain in the nest another 2 weeks.
Diet: Mostly insects in summer; seeds and buds in the winter.
Backyard Favorite: Sunflower seeds at a tray feeder.

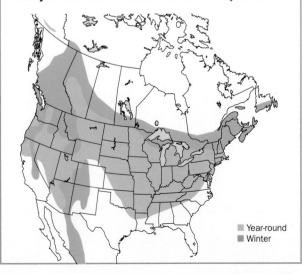

■ Year-round
■ Winter

Randall B. Henne/Dembinsky Photo Assoc.

73

70

58

67

76

No. 1

GREEN THUMB

How Her Garden Grew   54

Painting a Garden   58

Flower Man   61

From Sea to Shining Sea   64

Teamwork Equals Treasure   67

Arkansas Rain Forest   70

Neighborly Gardening   73

Backyard Metamorphosis   76

Life on the Beach   79

Living a Garden Dream   82

Lifetime of Gardening   85

How Her Garden Grew

Grew

Twenty years of trial and error created a blooming hideaway.

Story by Ann Wilson, Geneva, Illinois; photos by Irene Jeruss

While driving down a rural Redding, Connecticut road, Dennis and Nancy Pelz-Paget spotted a cozy cottage that issued an irresistible siren's call. Although both the 200-year-old home and its surrounding site needed work, the New York couple bought it and set about updating the home and landscape.

That was over 20 years ago, and since then, Nancy has developed a passion—and a talent—for gardening.

"We thought the house was just what a little country house should be," Nancy says. "But, there weren't any gardens—just a few daylilies around the foundation and a couple of apple trees. The area behind the house was like a desert.

"I wasn't a gardener when we bought the house. Now

COUNTRY COZY. Nancy and Dennis Pelz-Paget's garden is tucked along a rural road. Above right, cosmos, petunias and marigolds welcome visitors at the foot of the drive. Above, pink peony-like tulips and balloon flowers are bold and beautiful.

gardening is one of my greatest joys! When we're up here, I don't sit down much. I can spend up to 12 hours at a stretch just working in the gardens."

Nancy's not exaggerating. Since the couple only spends half the week in Connecticut, she makes the most of her time in her lushly growing beds and borders. Long after the sun goes down, this diehard hobbyist is still planting, weeding and moving plants around.

"Dennis gave me a miner's helmet with a light on it because he was getting tired of holding a flashlight while I worked," Nancy says with a laugh.

Nancy, a self-taught green thumb, caught the garden-ing bug when a friend gave her a carload of lily and aster divisions from her own garden. Nancy took a shovel to the backyard's hardscrabble earth to create holes for her newly acquired bounty.

About 10 years ago, the gardening got a lot easier when the backyard was excavated to make way for an addition to the home. Stone pathways, a water feature and patio were installed, and amended soil was brought in to create planting beds.

Today, those patio-side borders overflow with a lively, colorful array of perennials that bloom from late February into November.

"I started with nothing but have inched my way around the house," Nancy says. "I've become a 'mad' gardener—I never draw a plan. I imagine how it's going to look and in-vent my gardens as I go along."

Nancy has picked up gardening ideas and techniques

No. 1 Green Thumb

MIXING IT UP. You won't find a lack of variety in Nancy's large garden. With all the different blooms in her backyard, it looks like a beautiful and colorful quilt full of flowers. Above, hyacinths, scilla, daffodils and violas line a stone wall. At left, nasturtiums mingle with petunias for a rich scene. Above left, a mix of pink ranunculus and violas provide soft pastel hues.

from her trial-and-error endeavors, gardening books and visits to notable gardens, both here and abroad, including Monet's famous Giverny gardens, which inspired the yard's overall look.

She has become much more selective when choosing plants, seeking out hardy, long-blooming varieties with attractive dark-green, variegated or silvery foliage that maybe, just maybe, will survive onslaughts from foraging deer, voles, squirrels and woodchucks.

"I wasn't a gardener when we bought the house. Now gardening is one of my greatest joys!"

She opts for flowering plants with beautiful leaf structures, such as coral bells, lady's mantle and bishop's caps (*Epimedium*), that endure after blossoms fade. She also discovered that massing plants makes an impressive statement in the overall picture.

"You don't get enough impact with one plant," Nancy says. "I'm after that immediate pleasure of colorful blooms. In early spring, I buy inexpensive quart-size perennials at home centers, and I go to every major garden-club sale. I hit those like crazy because I can find inexpensive and different types of plants. Then I smoosh them together.

"By summer, the plants are large enough to put on quite a show. At the end of the summer, I think about what I need to fill out the beds and purchase half-priced perennials from local nurseries."

As October and November roll around, Nancy is hard at work preparing spring-blooming bulbs for planting.

"I like to plant three different bulbs in a hole, such as a tulip, a hyacinth and an allium," Nancy says. "If I'm lucky, they'll all come up together like a pretty bouquet. When you put all the effort into digging a hole, you might as well put in more than one bulb!"

Making the Most of Bulbs

Nancy achieves her nosegay-like effect by placing the largest of the three bulbs at the bottom of the hole, covering it with a layer of soil, and adding a medium-sized bulb and another layer of soil. She places the smallest bulb on top and fills in the hole.

Nancy says she's especially fond of the peony-like tulips in her garden, such as 'Angelique,' scarlet 'General Eisenhower' tulips, soft-yellow 'Mrs. John T. Scheepers'

"I learned that you can move plants like you can move furniture," Nancy recalls, "so I transplanted leftover plants and divisions out to the front beds. I like to jam-pack the flowers in around the house because I want to see something gorgeous blooming from every window when I'm inside."

Blooming Patchwork

In the front beds, white and purple tulips repeat the color of the magnolia blooms overhead. Yellow daylilies, purplish-blue nepeta, asters and zinnias line up in front of a cedar-branch fence, a dry-stacked stone wall, an antique apple tree and billowy shrub roses.

Closer to the house, a circular border of nasturtiums supplies a distinctive foliage of cottage charm. Pots of pansies, miniature iris, primroses and tulips spill from beds situated inside old stable doors that double as a gate between the roadway and front path (left).

Out back, a riotous but harmonious array of blooms showcases some of Nancy's favorite plant combinations. Pink and yellow bishop's caps nod below daffodils, and blue salvia front yellow-orange Mexican sunflowers (*Tithonia*). Blankets of blue forget-me-nots anchor yellow and pink tulips.

Nancy also tucks lungwort, campanula, lamb's ear, corydalis, perennial geranium, black-eyed Susan, bleeding heart, aster and autumn joy sedum throughout her borders.

The plants flourish thanks to Nancy's green thumb and techniques she's developed while tending her bountiful beds.

Nancy gives all her plantings a healthy start by loosening the soil in the bottom of each hole with her most essential tool—a garden claw.

Once the soil is ready, she places each potted plant, container and all, in a bucket that holds a mix of water and growth-promoter powder. Nancy soaks the plant until there are no more air bubbles, then removes the container and continues the planting process.

"I never plant without amending the soil," Nancy says.

Her secrets are simple. She adds her own mixture of topsoil, dried manure and homemade compost in every planting hole.

She also uses a slow-release fertilizer, like Osmocote, and throws in some Hydrosource water-absorbing pellets to help the soil retain moisture.

Nancy and Dennis, who is in charge of heavy-lifting tasks and wears a cap that proclaims him the "Under Gardener," help the plants survive by spraying their gardens with a variety of repellents. These are meant to deter the sometimes pesky, and always hungry, critters that frequent their wooded area.

The couple enjoys the fruit of their labors morning, noon and night. When the weather permits, they eat all their meals on the patio and take in verdant views that change from week to week and year to year.

"Each year I have a different garden," Nancy says. "Winter may have killed something, or I may find new volunteer plants growing.

"Even after all these years, I still plant things too close together. I just can't get over my need for immediate color gratification. But extra is always better. That's my theory of life!"

tulips and 'The Works,' a deer-proof daffodil collection she gets from White Flower Farm.

Like most gardeners, Nancy leaves no open area untouched. With her backyard beds flourishing, she turned toward the front yard and a stretch of land along the road.

GREEN THUMB TIP

You don't have to do a lot of work to improve the soil in your backyard. Just use a little slow-release fertilizer, dried manure or homemade compost. It's a simple idea, and the results are well worth it.

—Nancy Pelz-Paget, Redding, Connecticut

Painting
a Garden

This young couple uses plants and flowers as their multihued, artistic palette.

By Julie Dvornicky, Broadview Heights, Ohio

EDITOR'S PICK
Annual
Paradise
2008

You don't have to work with paint to be a painter. My husband, Greg, is one of the best artists I know. You won't find his work hanging on a wall or in a gallery, though. Instead, his masterpieces grace the outdoors.

It's been nearly 10 years since I first met Greg. It was a chilly November evening when our friends orchestrated a blind date between us. Our relationship quickly blossomed, and now we've been married for 7 years. (That's the couple at left.)

Prior to meeting Greg, I rarely took an interest in gardening—at least not anything beyond a pot of begonias on my shady apartment patio. We moved into our modest (and slightly tattered) bungalow shortly after we tied the knot. The home belonged to a long-time family friend, and we got an offer we couldn't refuse.

Mold It into Shape

Greg always admired the home because of its sprawling yard, and he couldn't wait to dig in. I didn't quite share his enthusiasm. To me, the house looked more like a throwback to the 1960s.

Greg tried to convince me that the entire setup would be like molding clay in our naive hands. I had my doubts, but didn't stop him.

When we first moved into our home, the lawn went right up to the foundation, and it contained many more weeds than grass. There were no beds or etched rings around the trees, and though the former owner kept things neat and tidy, the yard lacked the pizzazz that comes when flowers, shrubs and trees join forces. We were eager to give the yard our own touch.

BIG IMPACT. It doesn't take rare or unusual plants to make a strong impact in a garden. Impatiens are some of Greg and Julie Dvornicky's favorite blooms. They use lots of these flowers around their patio (left) and throughout the rest of their backyard. These inexpensive annuals really work wonders.

Keeping Critters Away

In true "painter" fashion, Greg took control and started to work his magic. He has a phenomenal way of placing color, shape, size and height together to form a grand canvas of petals and foliage. It wasn't long before our yard glowed with color and personality.

Our yard's shape resembles a bowling alley, so we wanted to break it up while adding color at the same time. Our beds are not perfectly straight in any way. In fact, they deliberately curve and wander to add interest to the large space.

Most of our flower beds contain varieties that are resistant to deer and rabbits. We found that out the hard way, but now we have a pretty good system.

After most of the plantings were complete, Greg added decorative rocks, wooden American flags and little wire fences. These extras not only look cute, but they also help keep Mother Nature in all her glory contained and off the grass and driveway.

Greg starts most of his "palette" from seed. Beginning in peat pots under lights in our basement, he hardens them off. Then he moves them to our sunporch and waits for frost-free days so he can add them to his "gallery."

We save seeds from our standouts each year and plant them in the basement in late winter. We've had lots of success, as our friends and neighbors who receive bouquets and bounties will attest. We have blooms from early spring to the first heavy frost.

Greg's plants are an extension of his personality. He even has bird friends, too. We have three birdbaths, two suet cages and three tube feeders with nyjer, black-oil sunflower and safflower seeds.

ELIMINATE THE ALLEY. Julie Dvornicky says their backyard used to look as long and uninteresting as a bowling alley. Her husband, Greg, worked his artistic magic, though. Today, their yard is overflowing with beautiful blooms. The flower beds are designed to curve to add interest to the area. In turn, they attract hummingbirds, like this young red-bellied one (above).

One spring, while putting out our solar landscape lights, Greg lost one of the batteries. I assured him we would find it while weeding or raking. Two days later, a blue jay—a regular dweller in our yard—chirped and hollered until Greg finally took notice of it.

As soon as Greg looked up into the tree, the jay opened its bill, and down fell the missing battery. It was like it was sending him a message.

The battery was just as new and shiny as the day we lost it. Some may call this amazing, but I call it a connection. In this busy world of cell phones, GPS and text messaging, Greg has meshed with the most simple and rewarding thing—nature.

A Natural Lifestyle

Our love of nature has taken us down many wonderful avenues. We garden organically and utilize a vermicomposter year-round, which turns our kitchen scraps into worm castings to fertilize our yard.

This naturalistic approach in our yard has helped educate us to change the way we do things in other aspects of our lives as well. We create and produce our own line of natural skin care products, called Nature Zone Gardens.

So now, we're taking gardening to a whole new level. We still maintain the beauty in our backyard, but we also grow plants for a cosmetic beauty as well.

As we celebrate another year of living in our hand-painted oasis, I am more proud and in love with Greg than I have ever been. He is a visionary of God's beautiful, rainbow-colored Earth.

I've never had so much appreciation for the scent of a flower or the sound of a bird singing. Greg once told me that God has provided him with so many blessings, and in turn, he wants to make Him proud. I certainly go through each day admiring Greg's perseverance and the beautiful world. I can only imagine the view of our yard from Heaven!

EDITOR'S PICK
Gardener
with Heart
2008

Flower Man

Green thumb happily shares his "Garden of Eden."

By Lewis Chollman, Knoxville, Tennessee

My flower-filled yard definitely is open to the public—and guests rarely leave empty-handed. I give a bouquet of fresh-cut blooms to just about everyone who comes to see my yard, which I've dubbed my "Garden of Eden."

Visitors aren't the only folks who receive flowers I've grown. I deliver arrangements to a number of local businesses on a weekly basis, too. I try to include clippings of rosemary in each bunch because of the herb's crisp, clean scent.

This habit of giving arrangements away might seem unusual, and it has earned me the nickname "Flower Man."

But there's a good reason behind it. After all, cutting flowers from my yard encourages even more buds to emerge!

"It's My Turn"

Gardening has long been in my blood. I worked at a nursery for many years, then maintained other people's yards for a while. When I retired a little over 10 years ago, I finally had enough time to focus on my own property, which consisted mostly of grass.

My first project was modest—a simple flower bed around a dogwood tree. But the results were pleasing, and that prompted me to continue.

The following year, I enlarged that first flower bed. And then I started adding a few more beds in different locations.

Each spring after that, I continued to expand and add beds to the area. I didn't create rigid rectangle or square gardens. Instead, I constructed them according to the way the land was sloped, or the direction that the flowers in established beds were growing.

PICKED JUST FOR YOU. Lewis Chollman's friends call him the "Flower Man" because he often takes colorful bouquets from his garden to share with area businesses. He has lots of blooms to spare, like bee balm (left), sunflowers and daylilies (above).

Natural Curves

Since I don't want the plantings to look crowded, I "listen" to the gardens and let them tell me where to expand. If flowers seem squeezed together, I round out that side a few feet, rather than uniformly increasing the size of an entire patch.

That's why you won't find any straight lines in my yard. Everything curves and gently flows together because I let the gardens unfold naturally.

What little lawn is left now forms grassy paths that wind between planting beds. And, thanks to our mild climate, those beds blossom almost 10 months a year!

For the most part, I've had lots of luck with the plants I chose. But that doesn't mean I did not encounter a problem or two along the way.

The biggest issue cropped up as the gardens increased in both size and number. Watering the plants during the hot summer months—especially at the edges of the yard—became a bit tricky.

After doing some research, I had water sprinklers installed at strategic locations around the property and found imme-

diate relief. I no longer have to drag around heavy hoses.

Mulching also has helped, keeping flower roots moist and weeds under control. I tend to add more around new plants and less on those that are established, because the mature bloomers have deeper root systems and are more resilient.

Most of the flowers in my gardens are perennials, bulbs and shrubs. I like that they come back year after year and don't require a lot of attention. You'll also find daylilies, irises, purple coneflowers, black-eyed Susans and much more gracing my gardens.

Year-Round Blooms

Annuals, like marigolds, salvia and sunflowers, also are part of the mix. By blending a variety of plants together, I wind up with something different in bloom almost all year long.

To get new ideas for plantings, I often wander through local garden centers until something catches my eye. Before I pull out my wallet, though, I read the label and decide if it will work in my yard and where I can use it.

I like to give these newbies plenty of room to grow so I don't have to cut them back later. The only ones I don't

GREEN THUMB TIP

You don't have to spend hours standing around with your water hose. Tackle dry areas in your yard by adding extra mulch or installing a sprinkler.

—Lewis Chollman, Knoxville, Tennessee

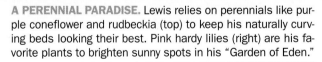

A PERENNIAL PARADISE. Lewis relies on perennials like purple coneflower and rudbeckia (top) to keep his naturally curving beds looking their best. Pink hardy lilies (right) are his favorite plants to brighten sunny spots in his "Garden of Eden."

plant myself are the sunflowers—I let the birds decide where those should go!

In Search of Ideas

Inspiration also springs up on daily walks through the neighborhood, and from my desire to pick plants that benefit wildlife, such as butterfly weed that attract butterflies and red sage (salvia) for hummingbirds.

Gardening in harmony with nature is important to me. I include birdbaths, houses and feeders so the birds have shelter and food during the winter. In return, these beauties help by taking care of insects each summer.

I enjoy keeping things simple and taking care of God's creatures and flowers. Everyone who stops by loves the view…and I feel like I'm giving something back to God.

No. 1 Green Thumb

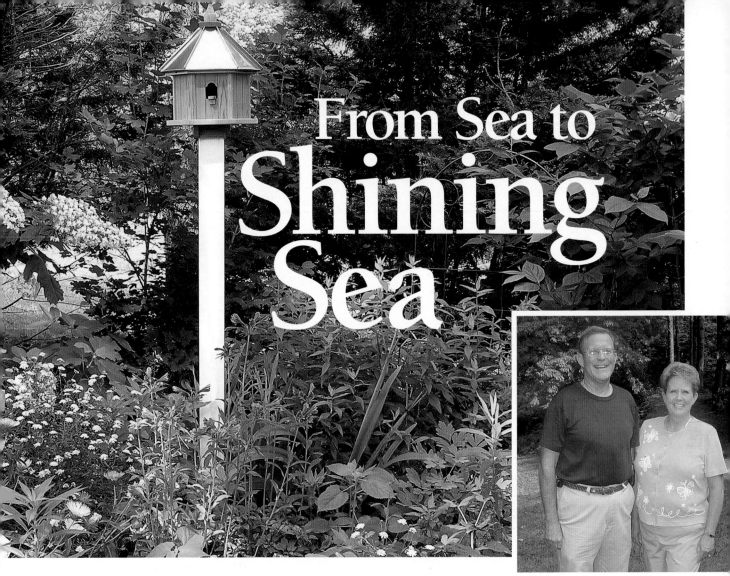

From Sea to Shining Sea

This Mississippi couple fill their garden with blooms from across the country.

By Laura Cartwright, Booneville, Mississippi

Carolyn and Cliff Cartwright have a unique way of acquiring new plants for their garden. They run!

Actually, it's Cliff who does the running. He's my son and a family doctor here in Booneville, Mississippi. Cliff started running marathons nearly 25 years ago while doing his residency in Jackson, Tennessee. Since then, he's run more than 240 races in 38 states. His goal is to eventually hit all 50 states.

Carolyn travels with Cliff for all of the marathons, but during their trips, she has a different goal in mind. She likes to buy flowers and plants from all over the country.

They plan their trips so Cliff can compete in marathons while Carolyn scouts the local nurseries.

She doesn't randomly buy plants, though. Carolyn studies the area's climate and growing conditions, carefully choosing shrubs and flowers that will do well in their own garden. In other words, she's a woman who knows what she wants!

If you drive by Carolyn and Cliff's home, you'll see that the plants they collect in their travels go to good use. Carolyn insists she is always happier when she's outside with her hundreds of different flowers and shrubs. Their beautiful gardens fill the front, side and back of their 71-acre property.

You wouldn't know their expansive, beautiful plot is actually in city limits. They like to think that they have the best of both worlds with their "city farm" filled with blooms.

Up for a Challenge

As far as flowers and shrubs are concerned, Carolyn probably knows more about them than some professionals. She grows plants for butterflies, bees and birds—especially hummingbirds—and can tell you which ones they like best.

With dozens of flower beds, you would think Carolyn

UNCOVERING TREASURES. Carolyn Cartwright (at left with husband Cliff) loves to collect plants and garden art (like the kind pictured on this page) from all over the country. While Cliff runs marathons, she searches for unique treasures to add to her backyard. One of Carolyn's favorite finds is the red alstroemeria (above right) plant she picked up in South Carolina.

meticulously plans out each plot. She doesn't, though. She says she follows her heart, starting with a few favorite plants in each area and then adding a little at a time.

As Carolyn brings back plants from her trips, she says it's fun to try new varieties—even if they are considered challenging for her area. She knows about hardiness zones and understands recommended growing conditions, but she says it's fun to push the guidelines every once in a while.

"I love to experiment," she says. "For instance, I found a beautiful dark blue salvia in Mobile, Alabama. It's not a plant common here in northern Mississippi, but I tried it anyway. With a little tender loving care, it's now thriving!"

Her secret to success is simple. Carolyn mulches her flower beds with 1 to 2 inches of pine bark in spring. Then in fall, she rakes 2 to 3 inches of leaves over the beds to give it additional protection for winter. She says this improves her soil and increases her chances of success with challenging blooms.

Pretty Flowers, Pretty Pictures

Carolyn uses the same method to grow a jacobinia plant that she got from North Carolina and an alstroemeria plant from South Carolina. Jacobinias are native to South America and are usually used as houseplants. Alstroemerias can also be tricky. But they both grow strong, thanks to her green thumb.

Carolyn does most of the gardening work herself, but every once in a while she manages to rope Cliff in, too. In particular, he likes magnolia, which is Mississippi's state flower. He has planted more than 20 of them along the side of their house, with several different varieties in the mix.

Carolyn likes to believe she has Cliff interested in flowers almost as much as she is, but the truth is, he's really in it for the photos more than anything. He loves photography, and her flowers make perfect subjects for him to practice with.

ROOM TO ROAM. You'll find plenty of interesting garden items around the Cartwrights' 71 sprawling acres, including, from above: azaleas, pink ceramic mushrooms and vibrant irises.

It's not just flowers that Carolyn likes to collect around the country. She also looks for unique yard art and birding items. Some of her favorite finds include a ceramic pink mushroom from Nebraska, a painted ladybug rock from Missouri, and all the unusual birdhouses she's picked up from across the country, including Colorado, North Carolina, New York and Iowa.

Keep on Running

It doesn't look like Cliff plans to stop running marathons anytime soon, which is fine with Carolyn. She's happy to tag along on the trips, discovering new gardening plants and treasures along the way. There's no telling where their travels will take them next. Thirty-eight states down…12 to go!

GREEN THUMB TIP

Add a little personality to your yard. We collect garden plants and art from the different states we visit. Nearly every item in our garden has a story. It's a great way to build a collection full of personality.

—*Carolyn Cartwright, Booneville, Mississippi*

Chapter 2

Teamwork Equals Treasure

This couple put heart and soul into their garden.

By Carol Martz
Acme, Pennsylvania

My husband, Jim, and I live in a beautiful area known as the Chestnut Ridge, about 50 miles south of Pittsburgh. Over the years, we have planted hundreds of different trees, plants and shrubs to fill up our once bare backyard. It's quite a bit different from the four plain deciduous trees and a single pine that greeted us when we moved here more than 30 years ago.

As our daughters grew, so did our interest in gardening. While the girls splashed about in the aboveground pool, Jim and I began planting and tending flowers. We learned a lot by trial and error and worked together to get through many brutal winters. Those winters taught us what would really survive, regardless of what the plant hardiness zone maps said.

New Discoveries

Some of the best flowers we've grown have come from unexpected places. Years ago, I was weeding when I discovered an unusual grass with blue flowers.

I love blue blooms, so I dug it up and planted it toward the front of the flower bed. Later, when Jim came in, he told me that I had missed a prominent weed among the flowers, so he yanked it out for me and dumped it into the compost.

I immediately went out to the compost and dug around until I found my new flower. I put it back in its spot and scolded Jim. Thanks for the help, but hands off, buddy!

Today, we have several of these carefree little plants, which I now know as blue-eyed grass (*Sisyrinchium angustifolium*).

I love seeing how our garden has evolved over time. Several years ago, we added a sunporch and brick patio with an arbor on the back of the house. A purple wisteria has now completely covered the top. The shade is a welcome relief from the hot summer sun.

A Christmas gift of a small pond and fountain kit from Jim inspired our next backyard project. Soon, we had plans to add a large pond. We worked out a work-sharing deal with a landscaper to eliminate some of the expense. A friend dug out the pond with his digger, and then the landscaper laid the pond. To save even more money, we gathered stones and small boulders from one of our farmer friends instead of buying them.

In the end, we created a very natural stream and pond. It is now home to goldfish, koi and various water plants.

Three months after we completed our pond, the swimming pool collapsed. On a cold January day, a huge block of ice slid through a split in the sidewall and traveled down the yard on a wall of water.

After tearing down the remainder of the pool, we had a large, bald spot in the yard. I thought it would be a great place for a gazebo, but Jim wanted to plant grass.

The gazebo won, and it is now the focal point of the

TOPSY TURVEY. Add a little whimsy to your garden by making the Martzs' creative flower planter (right). It's easy to do. Take a metal rod and run it through the drainage holes of several pots, including the bottom one, which is bigger overall. Anchor the rod in the soil, and then plant your favorites flowers. It's that simple!

backyard. The first couple of years we planted lots of annuals for color, but now perennials are taking over. My favorites are purple coneflowers, black-eyed Susan, 'Goldilocks' rudbeckia and Virginia bluebells.

It seemed logical to put another small pond and waterfall near the gazebo. This time, Jim and I did the digging with shovels, and we used a preformed pond.

Sharing the Yard

A couple summers ago, we had the honor of hosting our nephew's wedding ceremony in the backyard. My assignment was to keep all the flowers alive and beautiful for the big day. Ironically, our part of the country was in the middle of a drought that year, and temperatures were in the 90s.

The backup water tank was empty, and it was the first time Jim and I had to buy water for the pond since we in-

Chapter 2

GONE FISHING. When Jim Martz isn't gardening with his wife, Carol, you may find him relaxing by their large garden pond...perhaps even jokingly getting out his rod and reel. At left, a trickling waterfall flows into a smaller pond surrounded by blooms.

I save all my identification tags from everything I buy so I can review what did well and what to skip buying next year.

Since Jim's retirement, we spend most days outside. It might seem like a lot of work to some people, but it is our hobby, and we both love having little projects to keep us busy.

Our loving families must be responsible for our passion in flower and vegetable gardening. Perhaps it is that love that helps all the flowers grow so well!

stalled it. The water truck arrived just as the rehearsal ended, and Jim and I went into gardening mode. We watered everything that night and again in the morning.

About 125 guests attended the ceremony, and we received many wonderful compliments on our gardens. The bride and groom weren't the only smiling, happy couple on that special day!

Strategies in the Off-Season

Since trees surround the pond, it creates a problem in autumn when the leaves fall. We devised a solution, though.

We surrounded the pond and stream with a woven plastic snow fence. The netting catches the leaves before they can drop onto the water, and it is easy to shake the leaves off the netting.

Our vegetable garden also gets "put to bed" during winter. I use six or seven sheets of newspaper and then cover that with layers of herbicide-free grass clippings, compost and shredded leaves. That way, underneath all those "blankets," the busy earthworms chew up the good stuff.

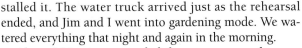

GREEN THUMB TIP

For a great blue bloom, try growing blue-eyed grass (*Sisyrinchium angustifolium*) in your garden. This carefree plant makes quite a statement.

—*Carol Martz, Acme, Pennsylvania*

No. 1 Green Thumb

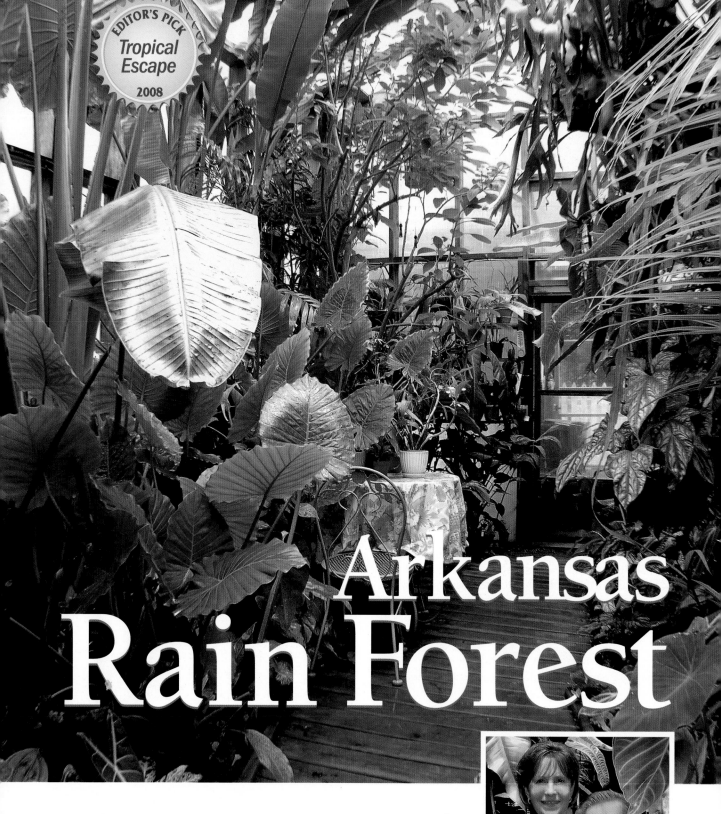

Arkansas Rain Forest

It's always summer in this tropical backyard garden.

By Steve Lucas, Siloam Springs, Arkansas

You don't have to look very far to find a hint of the tropics in Steve and Janice Lucas' yard. This red *Megaskepasma erythrochlamys* (below left) and 'Black Magic' hybrid orchid (below right) are just two of many exotic blooms.

Years ago while living in Florida, I told my friend Tom White that if I ever moved, I was going to build my own tropical rain forest under glass. He laughed.

Tom owns a tropical plant nursery called Zone 10 in Homestead, Florida. I had been buying plants from Tom for quite a while, and he knew how nuts I was about exotic things that climb, grow and flower.

I had my entire yard in Miami landscaped as a "rain forest." Of course, that was easy in Miami. It rarely got cold enough to hurt anything that grew outdoors. I had my yard filled with exotic vegetation, three ponds, a stream and very little grass. (I hate to mow.)

Pack Your Bags

In 2000, my wife, Janice, told me that it was time to leave Florida after almost 24 years in the sunshine. She wanted to live closer to our grown children and her own family in Arkansas. I reluctantly agreed, but I had one condition: I wanted to take my plants. To my surprise, she approved.

In the summer of 2001, we purchased an old colonial home in the extreme northwestern part of the state. We hauled hundreds of exotic plants with us, including an orchid collection of nearly 400.

Fortunately, the house already had a small greenhouse attached to it. But I had bigger plans.

Today, we have a 24-foot square atrium in our backyard, complete with 12-foot walls and a 17-foot ceiling. The winter temperature never dips below 55°, even if there's snow on the ground.

Before we planted anything in the greenhouse, we prepared the soil. We wanted it as close as possible to the soil conditions tropical plants love. It had to be very porous, quick draining, fertile and hold moisture without staying soggy.

My problem was I lost both of my legs early in 2002, so digging was out of the question. That's where Janice earned her keep and my deep respect.

I wanted the majority of the big plants to be planted directly in the ground. Only the rarest specimens could be in pots. Janice dug holes and placed almost every single plant! And she mixed huge amounts of peat, perlite, sand, humus and numerous other additives to make it tropical in nature.

In the center of the greenhouse, we wanted a 3,000-gallon pond. Don't worry; Janice did not have to dig it. We hired someone to do it, but then Janice did carry and lay almost all of the big rocks that line

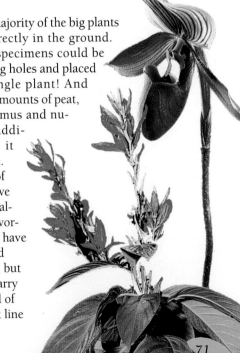

BLUE BACKYARD. Many of Steve's plants have unique and colorful leaves, like the iridescent blue tones of *Colocasia esculenta* (above) and *Microsorium thailandicum* (above right).

the pond and its interior. By the way, she's only 5 feet tall and barely weighs 100 pounds!

Once the plants were in the ground, they grew like crazy. I love plants that are truly exotic and tropical. My love for them stems form my professional days. I spent my business life as a commercial photographer and writer. I was fortunate to travel to gorgeous locations all over the world.

As a result, I've been all over the tropics and have seen a lot of rain forests from those in the Caribbean to ones in South America, Africa, Asia and the tropical Pacific and Indian Ocean regions.

That's where much of my love for exotic plants started. In 1986, I had an assignment that took me to Singapore and onto the Indian Ocean for 2 weeks. While there, my host asked if I'd like to visit the national orchid collection. After one visit, I was hooked! To this day, I still love orchids, and my collection is always growing.

In late 2005, I started getting the itch to share our rain forest with others. I decided to build my own Web site. With it, my goal from the beginning has been to write the material in such a way that anyone—regardless of their knowledge level of plants—could easily understand what I was saying and use the information. Apparently I'm doing something right because my Web site gets several thousand hits each week. (You can see it for yourself it by visiting *www.exoticrainforest.com*)

GREEN THUMB TIP

Don't be afraid to try something different. Exotic plants aren't just for the tropics. Try growing one indoors to see how much it can brighten the area.
—Steve Lucas
Siloam Springs, Arkansas

If you like exotic plants, you'll find lots of interesting photos and reading on my site. I love to collect rare specimens such as *Cercestis mirabilis*, the African embossed plant.

It's one of the most beautiful in my collection. The leaves appear to have had a fern painted on them with an interesting embossed effect.

We also grow a large number of rare anthuriums and philodendrons. Most of our species don't even have common names because they are so rare. I'm always trying to learn, though. I'm in touch with two of the world's top botanists on almost a weekly basis.

The Rare and Beautiful

A couple of my favorite anthuriums include 'Equitoriana 106,' which is unique because of its heart shape. Then there's *Anthurium vetchii*, with leaves up to 6 feet long.

Of the many different philodendrons we grow, one of my favorites is the *Philodendron hastatum*—a plant that is quickly becoming endangered in Brazil.

Then there are the true oddities in our garden. We have a rare fern from Thailand, known scientifically as *Microsorium thailandicum*. It has fronds that turn iridescent blue if grown in low light. Another interesting plant we have is from Borneo. It's a type of pitcher plant (*Nepenthes ventricosa*). It has little "pitchers" on the ends of its leaves that in the wild will actually help it catch insects!

In one corner of our garden, we have tree-sized banana plants that really produce fruit. Some people have told us that they are some of the sweetest bananas they have ever tasted.

So, believe it or not, there really is a rain forest in Arkansas. No matter what season it is, my backyard is always warm and blooming.

So, by the way, Tom—I really did it. I finally have my own tropical rain forest under glass, and it's spectacular!

Neighborly Gardening

I remember the first time I discovered the garden of Diane Gustus (below). I was walking through my neighborhood when I noticed an immaculate cottage-like home on south Nicollet Avenue. I couldn't help but stop to admire the artistically designed landscape and colorful flowers.

Soon, the street became a permanent fixture during my walks. I loved to soak up the beauty of her gardens and looked forward to seeing what was new. Most times, Diane would be outside, tending to her plants.

It wasn't long before I started chatting with her on a regular basis. She was always more than willing to stop what she was doing to answer my questions and show me around the yard.

Today, her garden is one of the best hidden gems in our metropolitan area, located just outside of the Twin Cities. I like to think of it as the secret garden of Bloomington. Nearly every day, Diane has visitors who stop to admire her work. They come in ones, twos and even tour groups!

Keeping It Small

Diane is quite humble when it comes to her yard. She first caught the gardening bug more than 15 years ago when her youngest child graduated from high school.

"I needed a hobby," she says. "I wanted to keep it small, so I planted a few seeds in the back left corner of my yard and let them grow."

*Gardener happily welcomes
visitors into her yard.*

By Sharon Storholm, Bloomington, Minnesota

The keep-it-small plan didn't last long. As the years passed, her fascination for plants grew, and her love for nature became evident in the ever-growing size of her garden. Slowly, she transformed her backyard into a masterpiece, reminiscent of an English garden.

Climbing roses, ornamental grasses, peonies, brick walking paths and colorful lawn furniture all come together to create a wonderful, relaxing atmosphere. Birds love her yard, too. Diane has birdbaths and unusual bird feeders tucked in every corner so she can enjoy the beauty of nature in a peaceful, quiet setting.

In addition to being a neighborhood "tourist attraction," Diane's garden serves as a getaway for her and her husband.

"We have a couple of secluded seating areas where we enjoy having coffee and snacks," Diane says. "It gives us a chance to relax and enjoy the garden."

Patio Accessories

The main area Diane is referring to has a royal blue patio table and chairs (below). Off to the side, there are three baker's racks with a variety of interesting plants and blue glassware. On sunny days, the rays of the sun produce magical dancing effects on the glassware collection.

"People have told me that the glassware could be damaged since it sits outside in the weather, but not a single one has been affected," Diane says. "Plus, it's one of my favorite parts of the garden."

LOCAL ICON. Diane Gustus' yard has quite a reputation in Bloomington, Minnesota. In summer, new visitors stop by every day to admire and discuss the plants in her garden.

The second seating area is located at the back of Diane's yard, and offers protection from the sun with a canopy of vines and flowers. Some of Diane's favorite flowers are her magnolias.

"When you're desperate for blooms in spring, they're a breath of fresh air," she says.

Another one of her favorite plants is 'Disco Belle' hibiscus, a perennial with large pink blooms that lights up the yard throughout the summer.

Though Diane's yard is full, she loves browsing greenhouses, looking for unusual plants to add to her yard. There's only one catch, though. If she buys something new, then something old has to go.

"I don't have anymore room in my garden, so if I buy a new plant, I have to remove an old one," she says. "I try to give plants away to neighbors or friends. I also belong to a garden club, so they never go to waste."

Diane jokes that her neighbors help her in other ways with her garden, too.

"Every fall, they donate hundreds of bags of leaves, which I run through my leaf shredder and then use to insulate my plants over winter," she says. "You should see my son and me as we drive around the neighborhood stuffing my car full of leaves. It's quite a sight."

Backyard Sanctuary

I'm amazed at what Diane has accomplished in our city. We could all learn from her example.

She shows us that we don't need to go on vacation or to a fancy secluded getaway to enjoy a beautiful sanctuary. We can create our own unique place for enjoyment and relaxation right in our own backyards.

A TOUCH OF BLUE. You'll find lots of blue blooms in Diane's yard (like those above and at left). Some of her favorite blue accents aren't even flowers. Below, her collection of blue glassware sits among blooms on baker's racks on her patio. On sunny days, Diane says the glassware "dances" in the sun.

GREEN THUMB TIP

Don't be limited by only using flowers to brighten up your yard. Garden accessories like statues and even glassware can really add color and life to the area.

—*Diane Gustus, Bloomington, Minnesota*

*Gardening
for butterflies
helped couple
transform yard.*

By Betsy Moll Lancaster, New York

Backyard
Metamorphosis

My husband, Robert Thill, and I have been planning and cultivating gardens around his childhood home for more than a decade. Our original plan has evolved over the years, and happily, we've had more gardening successes than failures.

Now, with our landscape rejuvenation project in its 11th year, we feel we're finally getting it right. And our garden really took flight last year, when we began attracting monarch butterflies.

Before we launched into that project, however, we spent many years on the rest of the property. We added perennial borders, vegetable plots, and a line of shrubs that separates our yard from our neighbor's drive. We planted ivy, clematis and spring-blooming deutzia to camouflage a chain-link fence.

Today, a vine-covered pergola (above) shades our south-facing terrace and links the patio and perennial beds. The hydrangeas we planted—including peegee, 'Nikko Blue' and 'Snowball'—offer spectacular blooms at different times during the season. A rose of Sharon reliably blooms from August to October at the entrance to our back patio.

But, alas, some of our original plant and placement choices weren't as winning. Six viburnums succumbed to record snowfalls and foraging viburnum beetles. And after

"GROWING" BUTTERFLIES. Betsy Moll often collects some of the monarch caterpillars from her garden for a closer view. She places the caterpillars in glass jars (left) and feeds them daily. Once they have formed their chrysalises, she hangs them upside down until the adult butterflies finally emerge (above).

our first season of stunted tomatoes and sickly broccoli, we discovered that toxins from nearby black walnut trees adversely affected the plants' growth.

Like all gardeners, we learned from those mistakes. We replaced the viburnums with weigela and Japanese maple, and moved the vegetables away from the walnut trees into raised beds we designed. (We also learned that the 6-foot width of the beds makes it difficult to reach in for weeding and planting—4 feet would have been better.)

Butterfly Season

Although our gardens are always works in progress, last year we hit the nail on the head. We revised our plans to make way for migrating monarchs, and had our most rewarding and magical gardening season so far.

As a result of our research and labors the previous year, monarch butterflies flocked to our 2006 gardens to feed and reproduce. In the fall of 2005, I read *Four Wings and a Prayer* by Sue Halpern. The book's spellbinding tales of the multigenerational monarch migration and the people dedicated to the monarch's survival inspired me. I knew I had to participate.

I decided to create our own monarch-friendly habitat, which meant growing milkweed plants—the primary food source for the monarch caterpillar. Monarch caterpillars eat only milkweed leaves, which contain toxins that don't harm the caterpillars, but make them distasteful to predators.

That September, I scouted local nurseries and found three white swamp milkweeds (*Asclepias incarnata* 'Ice Ballet'), which I planted near the back patio. I had concerns about growing this swamp plant in well-drained soil, but with regular watering the plants have done well.

In spring, Robert set up fluorescent lights, trays and peat pots in our basement so I could start milkweed varieties that would do well without such careful watering. I chose some yellow and orange butterfly weed (*Asclepias tuberosa*). I also started pink swamp milkweed from seeds sent to me by my daughter-in-law Mary, who maintains a butterfly garden at a Minnesota elementary school.

While I was at it, I started other butterfly magnets, including 'State Fair' and 'Scarlet King' zinnias. By June, the

FLORAL BUFFET. Butterfly favorites like rudbeckia (top left) fill Betsy and Robert's backyard. Above right, hanging bas-kets accent the porch with a medley of nectar-rich blooms.

tiny plants, then in 3-inch pots, were ready for hardening off and planting in the garden. The nectar was all set to flow.

More Than Milkweed.

And flow it did! It was a banner year for monarchs. They had visited our gardens in previous years, but in 2006 they stayed around.

Our milkweed hosted monarch eggs, provided food for the caterpillars, and supported the developing chrysalises. By adding zinnias and cosmos in the raised beds, we attract-ed masses of nectar-seeking monarchs and other butterflies as well.

With all these monarchs to watch, I started an "exhib-it" on our front porch, which has attracted guests of the two-legged variety.

I pick the tiny caterpillars—banded in yellow, black and white—from where they hatch on milkweed leaves and place them in sterile canning jars equipped with paper-tow-el lids. I clean the jars daily and add pieces of freshly har-vested milkweed.

GREEN THUMB TIP

If you want to host monarchs in your backyard, then Monarch Watch is one of the best resources that you can use. Go to www.monarchwatch.org to learn more. —Betsy Moll, Lancaster, New York

Front-Row Seat

When the caterpillars pupate, I hang the emerald-green chrysalises where we can watch them, awaiting the day they break open to ever-so-miraculously reveal the or-ange-and-black butterflies nestled within.

Because of our efforts, we were able to certify our yard as a Monarch Waystation through the Monarch Watch Web site. The abundant sunlight and quality soil in our yard helped us meet the certification requirements. Also, we had plenty of dedicated garden areas, which we easily achieved in our backyard, since an effective waystation only requires 15 square feet of space.

It Was Meant to Be

Looking over our original garden plan, we realized that we were on the way to meeting these requirements before we even decided to attract monarchs.

We had already been growing butterfly attractors such as purple coneflowers, phlox, butterfly bush, sedum and bee balm. Our six raised beds, once used primarily for vegetables, now also display milkweeds and cascades of nectar-rich annual flowers.

What's next for our landscape? We've been experi-menting with common milkweed (*Asclepias syriaca*). And, I understand that swallowtails like fennel and parsley.

Hmm…maybe I could grow those and see what flits in and stops over next year!

Chapter 2

Life on the Beach

This creative gardener brings beach living to her northern backyard.

By Marion Manley, Peterborough, Ontario

Gardening and the beach. To me, there's never been a better combination.

I like to think of myself as a seasoned gardener beach bum. I love the beach and I love gardening, so the two naturally go hand-in-hand.

I grew up on Lake Huron in Sarnia, Ontario, and the Great Lakes are in my blood. My husband and I can't really move to the lake, so I try to bring as much of the beach as I can to our backyard.

I don't have a lot of room to work with ever since we became empty nesters and downsized our home. We have a small lot that is 41 feet wide and narrows in the backyard. It doesn't stop me from packing as much beach and garden into the space as possible, though.

Get It Under Control

Since our home faces east, we quickly discovered grass wouldn't grow on one side of our house. No problem! Instead of grass, we now have a lush area filled with hostas, spirea, Solomon's seal, columbine and lily-of-the-valley.

Lily-of-the-valley can often be aggressive, so I didn't take any chances. I planted it in a large plastic flowerpot and

deliver it to our backyard. I jumped at the chance! Now we have a beautiful, huge rock in our yard, which our grandchildren love to climb.

A Natural Fit

At the same time of the boulder delivery, the excavator also dumped several buckets of topsoil in our backyard. We amended it with manure and peat moss, which I believe is the key to my thriving garden.

As you look around our garden, you'll see more natural treasures from the Great Lakes. I have large, weathered tree roots that washed up on the shores of Lake Superior. I use them for decoration, along with driftwood signs and

ODE TO THE GREAT LAKES. Marion Manley grew up on Lake Huron and was determined to bring some of that atmosphere to her garden. Below, a lighthouse stands tall in her flower beds, and a nautical cutout on her wooden gate welcomes visitors.

then buried it in the ground. Every spring, I have a perfectly round bunch of lily-of-the-valley with no fear of them spreading and taking over the garden. I've been doing it this way for about 10 years now, and it works perfectly.

As soon as you walk through our wooden gates, you immediately get the sense of the Great Lakes. We have a lighthouse cutout on the gate, and a flagstone path meanders through the garden.

We had a low-lying area in our backyard that was difficult to maintain, so we turned it into a Great Lakes beach area instead. We put landscape fabric down and filled the space with several inches of beach stone, which we got from Lake Erie, Lake Ontario, Lake Superior and Lake Huron.

I love stone. When we built our home, the excavator offered to load up a huge boulder in the neighborhood and

GREEN THUMB TIP

I believe recycling can do wonders in the garden. I use old tomato cages to make trellises for my vines.
—*Marion Manley*
Peterborough, Ontario

beach ornaments that I picked up from Lake Ontario and Lake Erie shores.

One of my favorite pieces is a precast gull I bought near Lake Superior. When I first purchased it, I used concrete paint, and in 7 years, I've never had to redo it.

I'm lucky to have lots of help with my garden from my family. My talented son, Michael, built a lighthouse and English-cottage style shed for us. He's always willing to help improve our garden area. He's working on plans for a small pergola right now.

As far as flowers go, my garden is filled with various lilies, sedum, clematis, peonies, coneflowers and many more perennials. I even have a prickly pear cactus planted under the overhang of my upper deck. Here, it's somewhat protected from our harsh winters, and it has lovely, bright yellow flowers in early July.

Several years ago, we installed a 6-foot wooden fence, along which we now grow holly, calla lilies, Virginia creeper, climbing roses and Russian sage—my favorite bloom.

Another one of my favorite plants is rose of Sharon. My shrubs have both single and double blooms in many different colors including white, light pink and purple. They grow 5 feet and bloom from August through October. I was afraid these beauties wouldn't bloom well in my area, but all it took was a little mulch and they've done just fine.

Bringing It All Home

Since our yard is too small for a compost pile, my biggest challenge is to keep the flower beds edged and to dispose of excess sod. I top most of my beds with 4 inches of pine

mulch to help keep out weeds.

One of our biggest challenges is to find evergreen shrubs that will survive in large containers throughout winter. We get several feet of snow each year, so I'm always looking for ways to add greenery to my garden during those cold months.

I have wonderful memories of Lake Huron with my mom and dad, and I'm glad I can re-create some of that today. I often take time to sit back in our Adirondack chairs and count my many blessings. After all, I have the beach and gardening all at my fingertips. What more could you want?

SAY IT WITH STONE. Marion loves using stones throughout her yard. She borrowed the idea for this particular structure (right) after seeing it along roadsides in northern Ontario. The design means "Have safe travels and a happy day." Below, Marion's winding stone path brings her entire garden area together.

Living a
Garden Dream

Colorful retreat grew with years of practice and patience.

By Dale Jarrett, Montgomery Village, Maryland

Gardening has always been part of my life. For as long as I can remember, I've been around people who loved their yards and took good care of them.

Working in the garden was one of my chores as a boy growing up in Jacksonville, Florida. Everything grew fast in the warm, humid climate, so I was constantly learning how to grow and tend plants.

From experienced gardening neighbors, I also learned there is more to gardening than planting. They taught me how to display plants, shrubs, perennials and annuals with a sense of depth, dimension and color.

Now, after 3 years of gardening at my new home in Maryland, we have a great foundation to continue building upon. I love the relatively mild seasons and weather extremes, which allow for a seasonal display of color.

The previous home owner planted a lot of native and natural-looking plants, a variety of ferns, perennials like black-eyed Susans, and different types of purple coneflowers and hostas. I started by redefining the beds and bordering them, rearranging what I had inherited, and then began to fill in the blanks.

Yard Comes Alive

I've been working on making the yard friendly to birds and butterflies by adding feeders, a birdbath and fountains.

The birdbath is popular, especially in the morning and

late evening. The birds even jump into the fountain! I've counted 15 species of birds, including an occasional red-tailed hawk and great blue heron, scoping out the goldfish pond for a free meal.

I have a vision of what I want the garden to look like. It really feels like the opportunity to paint on a canvas!

The biggest challenge when it comes to planting and laying out our garden is visualizing the heights of flowers to help create a dimensional look. I don't want my shorter liatris to disappear behind my giant iris bed!

A Tall Order

Instead, I place taller plants along the fence, including bee balm, dahlias, purple coneflowers, daisies and cannas, as well as vines like morning glory and cardinal climber. In front of there, I love plants like daylilies, Asiatic lilies, Lucifer lilies and liatris. The resulting combinations are like a beautiful flower arrangement in the yard.

Finally, it's great to bring in some long-lasting color with annuals. I've had to learn what will grow best in the different spots of sun or shade in the yard. Begonias, petunias, cosmos, marigolds and zinnias do well in most areas.

For the hot, sunny areas, I prefer vincas, while impatiens fill in the shade. I've even had a lot of impatiens volunteer themselves from last year's plantings. And boy, did that fill in the nooks and crannies of the garden this year!

I'll admit I'm still learning, so I often have to move plants. I want to display them nicely and give them enough space to spread out.

Gardening on a budget has been another challenge. Costs are a factor to consider when fulfilling and building my garden vision, so it helps to be patient. I've learned how to be frugal and shop smart when it comes

COLORFUL VISION. Purple coneflowers and Asiatic lilies (below) attract birds and butterflies like the black swallowtail. Below left, Dale peeks through some tall, green foliage. He says planting tall flowers next to shorter ones helps create depth.

to fixing up and replenishing our garden. You don't have to spend a fortune, you just need to know where and when to shop.

In late summer to early fall, most garden centers begin to reduce the prices of their perennials. Sometimes the plants look a little tired, but don't let that stop you. They'll thrive over the next seasons.

GREEN THUMB TIP

Take advantage of "bargain days" at your local garden center or nursery. Late summer and early fall are some of the best times to pick up inexpensive perennials for the next season.
—*Dale Jarrett*
Montgomery Village, Maryland

GONE FISHING. Dale's pond has koi and plants like water lilies and water hyacinths. The area is a great spot for birds to visit. Once, it even attracted a great blue heron looking for a meal!

The Great Divide

Also, as the perennials grow and thrive, you can eventually split and spread them all over the place. You can even share them with your friends and neighbors. And perhaps some friends will share from their gardens. In fact, sharing plants has added some personal connections with friends to my garden.

People often ask me how I know what to plant. My answer is that I observe what grows nicely in other people's yards or in magazines. To find out plant names, I take pictures and show them to garden experts at the nursery or whomever I can to get answers.

So, take notice of what you like elsewhere, and you, too, can create a colorful retreat. That's how I did it!

Lifetime
of Gardening

Retired horticulturalist has been growing plants for more than 70 years.

By Elizabeth Smith, Lancaster, Ohio

My life as a gardener began when I was 6 years old. I remember helping my father plant tomatoes in our backyard in East Aurora, New York that summer. My two older sisters and I had the chore of weeding the garden. They grumbled, but I loved it!

My attraction to gardening didn't stop there. I worked at a greenhouse through high school, and then I went to study horticulture at The Ohio State University.

That is where I met my husband, Richard. We were a perfect fit—he wanted to start his own business, and I wanted to run a flower shop. Once we married, Richard and I moved to his hometown of Lancaster, Ohio, where we

bought a garden store. We were young and happy, raising a family and spending our days among flowers.

Taking a Break

Richard and I ran a successful business for more than 20 years, but after his untimely death in 1978, I decided to take a break.

I had been giving people gardening advice for years. It was time to apply some of that same advice to my own yard. After all, we did live on a 92-acre farm that seemed to be begging for some fresh landscaping.

My biggest challenge was the sheer size of it all. I had no idea where to start. I knew I needed something to break up the landscape, so I built a wooden fence, which is now the focal point of my yard.

The first plants I put along the fence were oriental lilies ('Casa Blanca' is my favorite). These low-maintenance beauties grow 6 to 7 feet tall and have gorgeous blooms, 6 to 8 inches wide. In spring, I use a 5-10-10 fertilizer on my lilies and other perennials. This keeps my garden looking its best throughout the year.

Around the lilies, I planted perennials and shrubs like Korean lilac, tree peonies, Christmas ferns and cleome. Soon, I ran out of room, so I extended the bed 4 feet wider and kept right on planting.

It wasn't long before I ran out of room again and had to dig up the other side of the fence. Here, I planted kousa dogwood, butterfly bushes, hostas, heliopsis, ornamental

GARDEN FAVORITES. The centerpiece of Elizabeth's garden is the Amish playhouse that she bought a couple years ago (it's pictured on page 85.) She has plenty of other garden favorites that come in the form of blooms, too. Below, cleome line the split-rail fence. Left, 'Mona Lisa' lilies surround the gazebo, and Wave petunias (top) spill out over an old stump.

Chapter 2

grasses and more.

In front of my flower beds, I grow dwarf daffodils. They put on a stunning show in spring, and best of all, the deer dislike them.

I love using annuals to fill in my garden. Wave petunias are my absolute favorite. They bloom until late frost, and there's no deadheading required. Best of all, you can collect the seeds in fall to plant next year.

To do this, let your petunias brown and die. Then simply crumble the petals in your hand to reveal the tiny seeds inside. I've been doing this for years. My petunias always look great, and it saves me a lot of money!

Adding Personality

Once I finished planting flowers along my fence, I moved on to the areas closer to my house. I spent an entire summer laying a brick patio. It was a lot of work, but I can proudly say that I did it all myself.

A couple of years ago, I found an old playhouse in Amish Country. It's now my "garden house" where I keep my tools and supplies. I plant wildflowers around it, and it's one of my favorite places in the garden.

Over the years, one of my best gardening finds has been the kousa dogwood. I've always loved dogwoods, but dogwood anthracnose has made them endangered in our area. The Kousa variety, however, is resistant to this disease. The blooms are a beautiful white, and the birds love the seeds. I have four in my yard, and they look amazing in spring.

Family Business

I did eventually reopen the garden store that my husband and I started. My eldest daughter, Peggy, helped me manage it. Our family ran the store for 38 years until I retired.

When people heard I was going to retire, they said to me, "Now you can do what you really want."

I always smiled at this because I knew I was already doing exactly that.

With more than 70 years of gardening under my belt, I'm happy to see how the hobby has evolved over time.

When I was growing up, only the wealthy or elderly had flowers. Nowadays, everyone wants a garden, and I think it's wonderful! Flowers make you happy, no matter what your age!

GREEN THUMB TIP

There's always room for more, if you ask me. Don't let your full flower bed stop you from adding more blooms to your garden. It's easy to grab a shovel and add a few inches here and there in front of an established bed to get in a lot more plants. —*Elizabeth Smith, Lancaster, Ohio*

104

100

108

96

BACKYARD BIRD HAVEN

92

A Perfect Pair   90

Setting the Table   92

Little Trees, Big Benefits   96

Home Tweet Home   100

More Birds, Less Work   104

Fantastic Feeders   107

Berries for the Birds   108

107

90

Photos: above, Kathy Adams Clark/KAC Productions; opposite page, waxwings, Maslowski Productions; goldfinch, Francis and Janice Bergquist; warbler, Jim Simek/Nature's Images

BIRDS AND BLOOMS:
A PERFECT PAIR

By George Harrison
Contributing Editor

Birds and blooms are a natural duo, depending on each other for survival.

Birds not only eat flowers, but they also consume the fruits, berries, nuts and seeds that flowers produce. In return, birds pollinate flowers and spread their seeds.

I recently watched a pair of cedar waxwings eat the flower petals off an apple tree in full bloom. They had built a nest on a branch of the same tree, so they had plenty to eat without leaving home.

Waxwings are just one of the birds that look to blooms for survival. Hummingbirds are among the most common winged visitors to flower gardens. The nectar of red geraniums, petunias, impatiens, fuchsias and cardinal flowers draw passing hummingbirds like a magnet.

Any plants that produce berries also are popular among our feathered friends. American highbush cranberry, elderberry and American mountain ash will all attract birds, such as gray catbirds, American robins, northern cardinals, cedar waxwings and northern mockingbirds.

Seed-producing plants are a hit, too. These flowers will attract a variety of birds, including finches, chickadees, titmice, nuthatches and buntings. Rudbeckias, coneflowers, liatris and sunflowers are some top choices.

Thistle plants are also valuable to seed-eaters. American goldfinches even delay their nesting season until the blue-flowering bull thistles go to seed. The birds use the thistle down to build their nests and the seeds to feed their young.

The next time you're preparing your garden, keep the birds in mind when selecting the plants you want to grow. You can add color and feathered friends to your yard with the right blooms.

Readers share some of their favorite plants and sweet blooms for attracting more feathered friends to their yards.

Liatris

Since I started planting perennial **bachelor's buttons** and **purple coneflowers** in my yard, I've seen more American goldfinches than ever before. —*Jill Hersch*
Ayr, North Dakota

We've had a lot more hummingbirds in our backyard since we added **bee balm**, **cardinal flower** and **'Dropmore Scarlet' honeysuckle**. The honeysuckle blooms early spring until frost. —*Barbara Mohr*
Elkhorn, Wisconsin

I've found hummingbirds love my **columbine, coral bells** and **red** and **purple salvia**.
—*Georgia Stewart*
Field Editor, Hebron, Illinois

My **honeysuckle** doesn't stop attracting birds when its flowers fade. Its succulent berries are great for attracting cedar waxwings later in the season. Be careful to select only non-invasive species.
—*Gary Clark*
Knowlton, Quebec

Honeysuckle

Kathy Adams Clark/KAC Productions

I have had more visitors at my hummingbird feeders since I planted **butterfly bush** and **trumpet vine** near them. —*Marianne La Fountaine, Fremont, Ohio*

I plant **hollyhocks** and **cannas** to attract hummingbirds.
—Sandra Voss, Granville, Iowa

Hollyhock

I often see American goldfinches flocking around my **cosmos**—especially in autumn as the plants go to seed. I've counted at least a dozen finches bouncing from one stem to another in search of seeds. —*Cherie Boulton*
Hayward, California

Plant **geraniums, rose of Sharon** and **rhododendrons** to attract more hummingbirds to your backyard. They are great plants all summer. —*Tina Jacobs*
Wantage, New Jersey

Donna and Tom Krischan

I've found two types of purple flowers that attract lots of winged activity—**stokesia** and **liatris** (sometimes called blazing star or gayfeather). Stokesia, also called stokes aster, looks like an annual aster with narrow purple petals extending upward. Liatris produces long spikes of blooms with green leaves shooting out from the main stalk.
—*Gloria Meredith, Harrington, Delaware*

To attract orioles to your yard, plant nectar-producing flowers like red-hot poker.
—Allison Schott, Brantford, Ontario

Plant pink and red **azaleas, petunias** and **daylilies** to attract hummingbirds. Their funnel-shaped, nectar-producing blooms and bright hues will invite the winged jewels to your backyard. —*Laura Horning*
Miffletown, Pennsylvania

After years of planting flowers for birds, I've developed a good list of my favorites. For blue jays, try planting plumed **cockscomb, marigolds, sunflowers, four-o'-clocks** and **hibiscus**. For hummingbirds, plant **morning glories**, orange and red **gladiolus**, perennial **sweet peas, lantana** and **turkscap lilies**. —*Marsha Melder*
Field Editor, Shreveport, Louisiana

I'd discovered **mountain bluets** and **zinnias** provide food for American goldfinches. The birds bend the drying flower heads to the ground as they land on them, then pull out the seeds with their bills. It's fascinating to watch.
—*Charlene Margetiak*
Norwalk, Ohio

Buntings and finches really love the tall spikes of blooms that appear on our **common mullein**. This wildflower is perfect for our feathered friends.
—*Marcia Sinclair, Marion, North Carolina*

Hummingbirds seem to prefer the nectar of my **cypress vines**. As soon as the vines start blooming, the birds ignore my sugar-water feeders and spend all their time at the flowers instead. —*Josephine Ayers*
Aiken, South Carolina

Setting the Table

Tips to transform your yard into a bird haven.

Yarn Goes a Long Way

Every year when I volunteer at a children's camp, we play a game called friendship web. You start with 20 to 30 children in a circle and give each one a different ball of yarn. They tie one end around their waist and then throw it to another child across the circle. After several tosses, we have a colorful, tangled pile of yarn.

In the past, we would always just throw the yarn away, but recently, I started a new tradition. I bring it home and cut it up with scissors to make hundreds of smaller pieces. Then I scatter them around my yard.

Within a few days, my feathered friends take all the pieces for their nests. As I walk around my yard, I see colorful strands of yarn hanging from trees and poking out of birdhouses. I love nesting season, and I'm glad I'm able to help out a bit!
—*Richard Unangst, Orangeville, Ohio*

Towering Birdhouses

I have an easy way to make multiple birdhouses (right) that are always used during nesting season. I start with long pieces of 4-inch-thick PVC pipe, then construct a wooden system of dividers to insert inside the pipe, each creating a nesting cavity. This makes them easy to clean after nesting season.

One of my towers is for bluebirds, and the other is for wrens. True, both birds are territorial, but the male wrens often prepare several nest sites for the females to choose from. So my tower gives the birds lots of choices
—*Alphonse Hoernig, Perryville, Missouri*

Fan Favorite

EDITOR'S PICK
High-Flying Idea
2008

"When my daughter and son-in-law replaced ceiling fans at their home in Roswell, New Mexico, I kept trying to figure out how to make them useful instead of just throwing them away," writes Joe Laky of Jamestown, Louisiana. "Here's the result (above). We love to sit on our porch and watch the hummingbirds. It swings in the wind, but it doesn't matter. They love it so much that we refill at least three of the feeders a day."

Hang It Up

I was tired of watching the European starlings and common grackles harass the black-capped chickadees during nesting season, so I decided to take action. I knew I had to create an obstruction to deter predators from the birdhouse entrance, but it couldn't get in the way of the chickadees.

The solution turned out to be simple. I took the wire from old coat hangers and shaped several around the front of the nesting box. I set them about 1-3/16 inches apart (roughly the same size as the entrance). Now chickadees can get in, but intruders stay out!

Another benefit of the design is that it keeps red squirrels away, too. They used to chew and damage the entrances of my birdhouses, but now they can't get at them.
—*Derek Rolfe, Ontario, Canada*

Tried-and-True Suet

I've been using this suet recipe for years, and it's a favorite among the woodpeckers in my area. Here are the ingredients:

1 cup crunchy peanut butter	1 cup lard
2 cups quick-cooking oats	1 cup flour
2 cups cornmeal	1/3 cup sugar

Melt lard and peanut butter in the microwave, and then stir in the remaining ingredients. Pour into square containers and store in the freezer. Makes 6 to 8 cakes.

—*Joseph Nye, Canandaigua, New York*

Increase in Traffic

My husband, Merle, attached a yellow plastic bucket to the bottom of our finch feeder to catch the hulls and dropped seed. To our surprise, doing that attracted even more birds to eat in our yard.

Before, we had lots of American goldfinches, but now the northern cardinals feed, too. They land in the bucket or on the wooden perches at the bottom of the feeder. Then they lean down to eat the dropped seed. In the beginning, only a female cardinal ate from the bucket. But now a male has joined in.

It's fun to see goldfinches and cardinals eating from the same feeder. It takes more food to keep the feeders full, but it's worth it.

—*Joyce Haddock-Kolbus
Mattoon, Illinois*

Bottled Up

We have lots of oak trees in our area, and unfortunately, that means a lot of squirrels, too. Our bird feeders are prime targets for these critters, so I wanted to stop them from stealing all of our birdseed.

I took five plastic bottles and drilled 1-inch holes in the caps and bottoms. Then I slipped them onto the pipe that holds our feeder (right). The squirrels no longer steal my birdseed, and they have yet to figure out how to climb the bottles!

—*La Motte Brindley
Lorain, Ohio*

Secret Ingredient

Here's a suet treat I make that the birds love. First I line a 13-inch by 9-inch pan with foil. Then I mix together oatmeal, peanut butter and melted fat.

Now this might sound like ordinary suet treat, but this is where the secret ingredient plays a part. I add raspberry seeds.

I like to make seedless raspberry jam, so when I strain the seeds, I save them to use with my suet recipe. After I add those, I put the pan in the freezer and cut the suet into squares when it's set. Then I put a few pieces into a mesh bag and hang it from the spruce tree near our deck. The birds enjoy the treat, and we love watching them.

—*Ruby Winspear, Wyoming, New York*

Attracting Orioles

In the past, I've had limited success using oranges to attract Baltimore orioles. Then I discovered grape jelly.

For years, people had told me it's the best thing to attract and keep orioles coming to your yard. Now I believe them.

When I first decided to offer jelly, I saw a nice copper and glass feeder at the store. It was too expensive, though, so I went to my husband instead. I drew a picture of the feeder and described it him. Within a few hours, we developed this homemade version (right), made from twisted copper and a short, simple glass.

Now the orioles visit us 50 to 100 times a day. So take it from me—you don't have to spend a lot of money to keep orioles coming back to your yard. With a little creativity and grape jelly, you too can have your own feeder.

—*JoAnne Dellacona, Hyannis, Massachusetts*

EDITOR'S PICK

Pest-Free Diner

2008

Take It Up a Notch

"My brother Tom (above), who lives in northern Wisconsin, has been battling squirrels and bears at his feeders for years," says Kent Thurston of Timonium, Maryland. "His solution is a 4-inch-square steel tube with feeders he can raise and lower. The squirrels cannot climb it, and the outriggers attached to the bottom are buried 3 feet into the ground to keep the bears from pushing it over. Now the birds can eat in peace."

Leftovers for the Birds

I keep trimmed fat from pork chops, beef steaks, roast chicken skin and even soup grease to make my suet. I simply store it in a container in the freezer. When I have enough collected, I throw it all into a slow cooker overnight. The next morning, I cut up the pieces that didn't melt and throw in a few black-oil sunflower seeds. Then I pour it into cardboard milk cartons.

Once it cools and hardens, I slice the carton to the size of our suet feeder, peel off the cardboard and serve. This recipe is a favorite with my hairy and downy woodpeckers.

—*Alice Wohlgemuth, Riding Mountain, Manitoba*

Music to My Ears

For added birding enjoyment during the winter months, we place a baby monitor among our feeders. It is amazing how clearly you can hear all of the interesting bird sounds, particularly pecking at sunflower seeds.

We keep the monitor in a plastic bag outside so it always stays dry, and then we bring it in each night. Now we get to hear and see the birds like this tufted titmouse (above) all at once! It has given us a whole new experience in bird-watching.

—*Rosalee Schwartz, Indianapolis, Indiana*

Cheep Eats

For an inexpensive suet feeder, put a block of suet inside a nylon hair net. Once you tie the top and hang it, you have an instant feeder. The birds love it, and it's very "cheep."

—*Sara Sundby, Thief River Falls, Minnesota*

Mourning Snack

I designed this critter-proof feeder for mourning doves. Our property is near an 18-acre forest with squirrels, raccoons and foxes, so it was a challenge to figure out a way to keep all of those critters away.

To make the feeder, I took a wooden frame and covered it with 1/2-inch hardware cloth. Then I added a green, porous plastic cloth on top of that. Finally, I added side frames and intermediate crosspieces to support another level of 1/2-inch hardware cloth (below).

I put safflower seed in it for the doves. The critters can't get to the seed, but the birds can reach in with their bills. When the squirrels tried, I think they soon gave up because their noses got sore!

—*Max Eckhart, Alexandria, Virginia*

Seeing Red

It's easy to attract northern cardinals to your backyard. To keep them happy year-round, set out black-oil sunflower seeds. It's their favorite. And for even more traffic, install a birdbath.

As spring rolls around, you'll have plenty of cardinals. Here's one of the red beauties (below) that was in our backyard one year. We snapped this picture just as it finished dining on sunflower seeds. —*Robert Greene, Acworth, Georgia*

Martin Maintenance

We love having purple martins nest in our backyard in spring. We get a lot of traffic, but that doesn't mean it has to be a lot of work.

I build my birdhouses (above) out of fiberglass and have them on a pulley system, so I can raise and lower the houses with just a few cranks. Then I put a hinge on the side of the door so it swings open for easy cleaning. I have four houses in my yard, and all the homes are filled at nesting time. Then when the birds are finished nesting for the season, it's easy maintenance. —*J. Wayne Bockholt*
Rosenberg, Texas

Quantity and Quality

If you want to make a big batch of suet at one time, then this is the recipe for you.

In a large bowl, mix together 2 pounds of melted lard, 3 pounds of wild birdseed, 5 pounds of yellow cornmeal and 1 large jar of crunchy peanut butter.

This makes 20 to 30 containers of suet. The birds love it—we have a pair of pileated woodpeckers that never fail to let us know when their feeder is empty. —*Carrie Vadnais*
Millerville, Minnesota

Rolled in a Pie

Homemade pie dough is a favorite of woodpeckers, nuthatches and chickadees. In fact, I whip up a special batch just for them. Here's the recipe:

Use any pie dough recipe and add peanut butter, nuts and seeds. I sometimes include dry dog food (a good source of protein) and meat drippings.

When finished, roll the mixture into balls and place in onion bags. During warm weather, the balls will melt, so be sure to hang it where it won't leave a greasy mess.

—*Joyce LaBellee, Onaway, Michigan*

Make Your Own Tree

This might be my husband's most innovative idea yet. Bill retrieved an old branch that had fallen from one of our trees. Then he set up a metal fence post in our backyard and attached the branch to it.

It instantly became our feeder tree. We added peanut butter in several holes that the branch already had. As you can see, it didn't take long for the birds to feel at home (right). We often see them feeding by the dozens!

This was inexpensive and easy to make. We've been enjoying the visitors to the "tree" outside our patio doors for nearly 3 years.

—*Barbara Waller, Woodlawn, Illinois*

Backyard Bird Haven

LITTLE TREES, BIG BENEFITS

Attract birds to your yard with dwarf conifers.

By Kris Wetherbee, Oakland, Oregon

When it comes to attracting birds, there is a guaranteed recipe for success. Birds are more likely to flock to a backyard that provides the tempting trio of food, shelter and nesting sites.

And what's a great way to offer all three? Conifers!

Seed-filled or berrylike cones offer food, while dense branches provide four-season refuge as a place to nest or hide from predators. Problem is, if your yard doesn't already boast a few conifers, you may not have the space to grow a full-sized fir or large Colorado blue spruce.

That's where dwarf conifers come in. These compact versions of the large trees offer beauty, versatility *and* the qualities birds love.

With sizes ranging from low-growing ground covers to small globe shapes to pyramidal trees growing 5 feet tall, dwarf conifers easily fit into yards of all sizes. And, in addition to making your place more bird-friendly, their small stature and interesting colors and needle textures satisfy a broad range of landscape needs.

Different Definitions of "Small"

"Dwarf conifer" is a somewhat relative term. While they are slower growing and smaller in stature than their full-size counterparts, the rate of growth and the ultimate height depend on your climate, site conditions and characteristics of the particular species.

Dwarf conifers offer a wide range of colors, shapes and textures, making them a great choice for scaled-down landscapes. Color options go beyond your typical shades of green to include yellows and oranges, soothing tones of blue, or variegated needles or scales.

Certain conifers even change color with the season—whether as contrasting shades of new spring growth, the fall foliage of deciduous conifers like larch, or the interesting plum color that appears with cooler weather on trees like false cypress and many juniper ground covers. Showy cone-like flowers on certain species of fir, spruce and pine provide spring color in hues of pink, purple, lavender and red.

The more diminutive dwarf conifers don't provide much benefit to birds as shelter, though these ground covers can complement other plants or provide cones for food. The key is to select trees that serve birds, yet still fit the size and style of your landscape.

For shelter and nesting purposes, select trees with an upright or drooping growth habit. If you're unsure how they'll grow, check the plant information. There also may be clues in the tree's botanical name. Upright cultivars often contain the words *Fastigiata* or *Columnaris*, while *Pendular* means it has drooping branches.

Beauty and Function

Conifers that grow in attractive mounds or are shaped like pyramids make great structural accents. Two examples are dwarf western hemlock (*Tsuga heterophylla* 'Thorsen's Weeping') and dwarf Sawara false cypress (*Chamaecyparis pisifera* 'Curly Tops'). Dwarf columnar species, such as common juniper (*Juniperus communis* 'Compressa') or eastern arborvitae (*Thuja occidentalis* 'Degrott's Spire'), provide intriguing exclamation points of interest in perennial beds or borders.

The selection of conifers that provide food is quite broad. The seed-filled cones of spruces, firs, pines and many others appeal to nuthatches, finches, grosbeaks, chickadees and other seed-eating birds. Junipers and yews provide a feast of berrylike cones for species like waxwings, robins, bluebirds and sparrows.

When looking for a dwarf conifer, start with your local nursery. The increasing popularity of these small trees means many garden centers have at least a few varieties.

For a larger selection, try a specialty nursery like Rich's Foxwillow Pines Nursery in Woodstock, Illinois, which focuses on dwarf conifers. Or, check with Monrovia, a national wholesaler that provides a list of plants it carries along with local outlets on its Web site.

The best time to plant conifers is during the cool days of fall or anytime the ground is not frozen. Areas with milder

PERFECT PARTNERS. Dwarf conifers are a good way to get the benefits of evergreens without taking up much room (plus, they look great in groups, at left). Birds might seek refuge in the dense branches (like the male bay-breasted warbler below) or eat seeds from the cones.

climates can plant anytime from October through March. Most conifers grow best in slightly acidic soil in a sunny, well-drained site. Give the trees a bit of afternoon shade in the hot, southern regions of the country.

For the most part, yews (*Taxus*), hemlocks (*Tsuga*) and some species of false cypress (*Chamaecyparis*) also do well in partial shade. However, there are certain cultivars in nearly all conifer types that will tolerate some shade.

As a general rule, conifers also prefer moderately moist soil for best results. However, junipers, pines and true cedars (*Cedrus*) easily adapt to dry conditions once they are established.

Once planted, the trees don't require much care. Soils of average or less fertility actually help encourage the dwarf characteristics, so applying a thin layer of organic mulch, such as compost, pine needles, shredded bark or leaves, once a year is plenty.

Imagine the Possibilities

Conifers are a great way to cultivate your creativity. Just open the windows to your imagination.

For example, varieties with interesting shapes or forms can be used in place of garden statues. Use columnar types as evergreen "pillars." Or create carpets of color on a slope by combining low-growing or mounding varieties in various colors.

Ornamental grasses or shrubby perennials like artemisia, lavender or Russian sage add height to a hillside of low-growing conifers.

However you arrange your plantings, it's important to think of dwarf conifers as companion plants and accent pieces rather than as singular trees. Smaller species look best when planted in groups, and combinations of different textured conifers with existing shrubs and perennials create interesting landscapes.

With a little planning and patience, you'll find dwarf conifers are more than a guaranteed recipe for attracting birds to your backyard. They're also a recipe for beauty.

SEVEN TOP PICKS FOR BIRDS

These conifers may be dwarf in size, but they all provide giant benefits to birds in the way of seeded cones, insects and year-round shelter.

1 **Creeping juniper** (*Juniperus horizontalis* 'Mother Lode'): Attractive ground cover with bright, golden-yellow foliage that turns plum in winter. Berrylike cones. Zones 3 to 9.

2 **Dwarf Canadian hemlock** (*Tsuga canadensis* 'Cole's Prostrate'): Low, spreading habit with cascading branches. Dense shelter for ground-feeding birds like towhees and juncos. Zones 4 to 8.

3 **Dwarf Colorado spruce** (*Picea pungens* 'Montgomery'): Intensely blue, dense mound that becomes pyramidal to 5 feet tall when mature. Favored by chickadees and grosbeaks. Zones 3 to 8.

4 **Dwarf Korean fir** (*Abies koreana* 'Starker's Dwarf'): Dwarf nest-form tree, grows 3 to 4 feet tall. Zones 4 to 6.

5 **Dwarf mugo pine** (*Pinus mugo* 'Slowmound'): Dense, dark-green foliage, grows 3 to 5 feet tall and wide in 10 years. Zones 2 to 7.

6 **Golden eastern arborvitae** (*Thuja occidentalis* 'Rheingold'): Orangish-gold, globe-shaped tree with soft young foliage. Grows to 4 feet in 10 years. Zones 4 to 7.

7 **Sawara false cypress** (*Chamaecyparis pisifera* 'Curly Tops'): Silvery-blue foliage with distinctive curled needles. Pyramidal habit, grows 5 to 8 feet tall. Zones 4 to 8.

Home Tweet Home

Readers share their most creative birdhouses.

Beach Retreat

"A few years ago, I built this birdhouse (below) to help raise money for Habitat for Humanity," says Peter Moehrle of Orlando, Florida. "I designed it to resemble a traditional Malaysian home. I hope it makes the perfect bird retreat in someone's backyard."

Tea with the Birds

"I made this teapot birdhouse, complete with hanging cups, for my wife," writes James Sevenich of Wheaton, Illinois. "She loves to sit on our front porch and drink tea with her friends. Now she can watch the birds at the same time."

Adorable Adobe

"This adobe-style birdhouse reflects my love of the Southwest and our beautiful state," writes Virginia Stanbrough of High Rolls, New Mexico. "My husband, Bill, made it and cut out the wood figures. I made the chilies, Indian corn, bowl and other decorations out of clay. Once everything was painted, the scene really came to life."

Mother Goose Special

"I love incorporating broken ceramics and other found objects into art," writes Elinor Nield of Soquel, California. "I call this birdhouse design 'Mother Goose' because of its whimsical storybook shape. It's a great place for the birds to call home, and the roof lifts off for easy cleaning, too."

Walk in the Woods

"I've been building birdhouses and other yard art in my wood shop since I retired," says Tim Kirsch of Solsberry, Indiana. "I made this log cabin design from some sticks I found in the woods. It's amazing what you can create from nature."

The Right Accessories

"My husband, Ed, and I have made several golf-themed birdhouses (above) for family and friends," writes Kathy Rogers of Huntsville, Alabama. "To complete the houses, we add plenty of golfing accessories, including tees, balls, pencils and even divot tools. On the back of the houses, we put our favorite golf saying—'Always keep your own score. Your best wood is a No. 2 pencil.' "

Fit for a Goose

"Everyone who sees this birdhouse (right) can't help but smile," says Holly Collett of Tucson, Arizona. "My grandson Tim made it for his parents' country yard in Elkhart Lake, Wisconsin. I think the entrance hole would accommodate a Canada goose!"

Leave the Water Running

"Our grandson built this birdhouse (below) for us in his masonry class," write Lee and Sherri Winter of New Castle, Pennsylvania. "We love our unique faucet house, and apparently, the birds do, too. A few weeks after we hung it up, we had a pair of wrens. We loved watching the nestlings poking their heads in and out of the hole."

House Boat

"When someone ask me to build a birdhouse for our local hospital's annual fund-raiser, I wanted to make something unique for the special occasion.," says Fred Field of Englehart, Ontario. "I designed this boat birdhouse especially for tree swallows, which are plentiful in our area. The boat's floor has hinges, allowing for easy cleaning after nesting season is complete."

Copycat Castle

"This castle birdhouse was designed after King Ludwig's castle in Germany," writes Guy Claybourn Jr. of Palacios, Texas. "This is the same icon that influenced the Disney World castle. My talented friend Vic LeFevre constructed the house almost entirely out of PVC pipe."

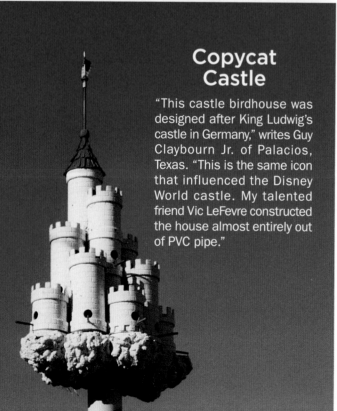

Down on the Farm

"When a friend of my daughter's needed a special gift for her father, I came up with this birdhouse," says Bill Hultz from Jacksonville Beach, Florida. "He is a wheat farmer in Ponca City, Oklahoma, so I structured this after the combine he uses on the farm."

Light 'Em Up

"Our first son was born on the Fourth of July, and these firecracker birdhouses always make me think of him," says Richard Becka of Garfield Heights, Ohio. "I constructed the two houses using an 8-inch plastic pipe for the body of the birdhouse and a rope for the fuse."

Island Getaway

"I made this Polynesian-themed birdhouse (above) from scraps of lumber and other recycled items," says Beret Dickinson of Escondido, California. "I used a straw broom for the roof, and the perch on the top is a table leg. Now it's ready for a spot on an island."

Cottage Charm

"We were surprised and delighted when our friend Ralph Schuler gave us this enormous purple martin house that he modeled after our cottage home," says Cynthia Beaubien from Middle Lake, Saskatchewan. "My husband, Paul, shingled the roof with cedar, and it looks great! Here are Paul (left) and Ralph, just before the house went up on its post. The birds are really living in style now!"

EDITOR'S PICK
Martin Mansion
2008

MORE BIRDS
Less
Work

Drought-resistant plants attract a torrent of winged activity, but require little watering.

By Kris Wetherbee, Oakland, Oregon

Birds need water. Plants need water. So it makes sense that moisture is an essential part of any backyard habitat for winged wildlife.

But keeping a garden irrigated can take a lot of work. That's why using a mix of water-wise plants is a great way to attract a deluge of birds and butterflies without spending precious time and money on watering.

A plant's drought tolerance varies, depending on your soil, climate and location. It's best to pick plants suited to your personal growing conditions. For example, hollyhocks do fine without supplemental water in areas that receive some summer rain. In regions with dry summers, however, these statuesque blooms will have a powerful thirst.

Growing conditions can also vary within your own garden. South and west exposures tend to dry out more quickly than areas facing north or east. Choose plants with a stronger drought tolerance for these hotter zones. Artemisia, cotoneaster, echinacea, rudbeckia, sedums and most salvias are good selections. These plants will also entice birds and butterflies with shelter and food.

A few shade-tolerant plants that can handle occasional drought include hostas, bear's breech (*Acanthus*), hardy geraniums, heavenly bamboo (*Nandina domestica*) and bearberry (*Arctostaphylos uva-ursi*).

As you devise your planting strategy, think vertically as well as horizontally. Choose a combination of plant sizes, and different colors, textures and seasons of bloom.

Small water-thrifty trees and shrubs add character and color. A few good choices to try in your yard are western redbud (*Cercis occidentalis*), chaste tree (*Vitex agnus-castus*), red-leaf rose (*Rosa glauca*) and strawberry tree (*Arbutus unedo*). Grapes, currants, gooseberries and other water-wise fruit-bearing shrubs and vines provide a great food source for many birds.

Herbs are also remarkably adaptable to dry conditions. Rosemary, oregano and many other flowering herbs have nectar-rich blooms that are well-suited to certain butterflies, moths and beneficial insects.

Healthy plants can get by on less water than plants that are stressed. Timely weeding and feeding are the first steps to keeping plants healthy. But adding organic mulch will always enhance the drought tolerance of most any plant.

Start by mixing a 3- to 6-inch layer of organic matter, such as compost, into the soil before you plant. Doing this increases the water-retaining capacity of the soil and creates an environment that encourages roots to grow deeper, which makes it easier for the plants to find and absorb moisture during times of drought.

Adding organic mulch like compost, shredded leaves, herbicide-free grass clippings or aged sawdust to the surface is a good idea as well. This will conserve water by preventing weeds (which waste water and nutrients) and keeping soil temperatures cooler and moisture levels more consistent, while also reducing surface evaporation.

No plant can survive without water. Even water-thrifty plants need consistent watering the first year or two as they become established. After that, the key is to water deeply and infrequently, which will promote a deeper and more extensive root system.

The best time to water is in the cool of the early morning or evening. That way, more water seeps into the soil and less is lost through evaporation.

The 12 drought-resistant suggestions that start below are a great launching pad for an easy-care garden. By growing the right water-thrifty plants and utilizing strategies that help maximize moisture, you can keep your landscape lush and winged visitors like birds and butterflies content during times of drought and beyond.

What's more, using less water to produce a downpour of color also gives you more time to sit back and soak it all in.

Editor's Note: Kris Wetherbee is the author of *Attracting Birds, Butterflies & Other Winged Wonders to Your Backyard.*

A DOZEN DROUGHT-BUSTERS

You can increase your winged population and decrease your water bill with these 12 water-wise plants. Once established in the garden, they will easily adapt to dry conditions, requiring little to no supplemental water during the dry season.

Bill Leaman/The Image Finders

RDA, INC.

Agastache *(Agastache species)* Known as hummingbird plant, licorice mint, Mexican hyssop or anise hyssop, depending on each species. Trumpet-shaped flowers attract hummingbirds, sphinx moths and butterflies. Seedheads provide food for birds. Zones 5 to 11; blooms from summer to fall.

Richard Day/Daybreak Imagery

Butterfly weed *(Asclepias tuberosa)* Flat-topped flower clusters are a nectar source for butterflies and hummingbirds. Includes milkweed, the caterpillar host plant for monarchs. Zones 3 to 9; flowers in summer.

Coreopsis *(Coreopsis species)* Nectar-rich blooms appeal to butterflies, such as skippers, buckeyes and painted ladies. Seeds provide food for sparrows, chickadees, finches and other seed-eating birds. Zones 3 to 11; summer to fall blooms.

Rick Weatherbee

Germander *(Teucrium chamaedrys)* Evergreen shrubby perennial serves as a shelter site for hibernating butterflies. Whorls of nectar-rich flower spikes attract a variety of butterflies and beneficial insects. Zones 5 to 10; blooms in summer.

MORE WATER-WISE PLANTS

Rudbeckia *(Rudbeckia species)* Daisy-like flowers provide nectar for butterflies. Birds relish the seedheads. Zones 3 to 10; blooms summer through fall.

Goldenrod *(Solidago* species) Flowers attract butterflies, including monarchs, blues and hairstreaks. Its seedheads attract varied bird species. Zones 3 to 10; midsummer to fall flowers.

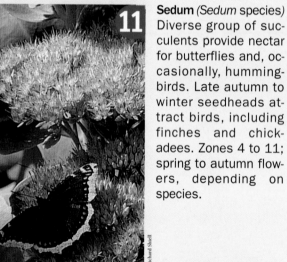

Salvia *(Salvia species)* These annuals, biennials and perennials attract hummingbirds, butterflies and moths. Perennials are hardy in Zones 4 to 11, though it differs by variety; summer blooms.

Lavender *(Lavandula species)* Aromatic flowers attract many butterflies, especially skippers, painted ladies and sulphurs. Finches and other birds dine on seedheads from early fall through winter. Zones 5 to 11; blooms in summer.

Penstemon *(Penstemon species)* Bell-shaped flowers attract moths and butterflies, such as skippers and swallowtails, as well as hummingbirds. Provides seeds for birds and serves as a caterpillar host plant for some checkerspot butterflies. Zones 3 to 10; summer flowers.

Sedum *(Sedum species)* Diverse group of succulents provide nectar for butterflies and, occasionally, hummingbirds. Late autumn to winter seedheads attract birds, including finches and chickadees. Zones 4 to 11; spring to autumn flowers, depending on species.

Purple coneflower *(Echinacea species)* Coneflower blooms offer nectar for fritillaries, skippers and viceroy butterflies, as well as hummingbirds. Late autumn seedheads attract finches, chickadees and nuthatches. Zones 3 to 10; flowers in summer.

Yarrow *(Achillea species)* Flattened clusters of tiny flowers attract hummingbirds and butterflies. Seeds appeal to many birds. Zones 3 to 10; summer to early fall blooms.

Chapter 3

Fantastic Feeders

These feeders offer birds fine dining year-round

Not by the Book

"When I gave my husband, Gene, a book on birdhouses and feeders, I had no idea he'd make all the projects in the book!" writes Sue Turner of Douglasville, Georgia. "He loves working with wood and now creates his own designs like this covered bridge feeder."

Feeder with a View

"I have worked on stained glass projects for several years and recently decided to make a stained glass bird feeder," writes Mart Barker of Eugene, Oregon. "So far, the birds have eaten more from the glass feeder (left) than the others we have."

No Coins Required

"When my husband and I saw this replica of a vintage gumball machine (below) for $5 at a garage sale, I suggested that we buy it and turn it into a bird feeder," says Linda Dinius of Ft. Wayne, Indiana. "He liked the idea and immediately took on the challenge. He made a few minor adjustments to the machine to accommodate its new purpose, and we now have a unique feeder that the birds love."

Victorian Beauty

"I designed and constructed this stately gazebo-style bird feeder entirely of western cedar," writes Don Skomsky of West Chester, Pennsylvania. "It measures 22 inches square, is 26 inches tall and is mounted on a sturdy 4-inch-square cedar post. The pyramid at the peak lifts off to allow filling of the central feeding tube, which holds nearly 2 quarts of seed."

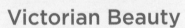

Mosaic Masterpiece

"My sister-in-law recently got me interested in creating mosaics using cut glass," says Irene Baker of Vail, Arizona. "Of course, being a bird enthusiast, one of my first projects was a new bird feeder.

"I snipped and glued the glass, included a few opaque beads for a raised texture, and finally grouted and painted it. The new addition creates a nice touch of color in my backyard."

EDITOR'S PICK
Old-Time Classic
2008

Carolina chickadee on winterberry by Richard Day/Daybreak Imagery

BERRIES FOR THE BIRDS

They'll flock to a fruitful selection of trees and shrubs.

By George Harrison, Contributing Editor

While nutritionists need to use tools like food pyramids and daily requirements to persuade people to eat enough fruit, our feathered friends need no such convincing.

For them, especially in winter, berries can mean the difference between life and death.

More and more, birds like American robins and eastern bluebirds are spending winters in the North. Although temperature changes may play a role in this, more important is that these birds are finding enough high-energy foods in northern climates to survive winters. Berries and berrylike fruit are a big part of that.

Even in the South, berries are an essential winter food

for many birds. Drive down Route 1 through the Florida Keys in winter, and you'll see northern mockingbirds defending their berry-filled feeding territories about every 100 yards along the highway.

Many Birds Eat Fruit

Elsewhere, species like northern cardinals, chickadees, waxwings, woodpeckers, finches, nuthatches, grosbeaks and titmice include fruit in their winter diets.

Like feeders and birdbaths, berries are a big draw for birds in fall and winter. Adding a selection of berry-producing plants will provide both food and natural cover for birds.

The best fruit-producing trees and shrubs are native

16 "Berry Good" Choices

1. **Barberry** (*Berberis* species), Zones 3 to 8; invasive in some areas

2. **Chokecherry** (*Prunus virginiana*), Zones 2 to 8

3. **Coffeeberry** (*Rhamnus californica*), Zones 7 to 9

4. **Crabapple** (*Malus* species), Zones 3 to 8

5. **Highbush cranberry** (*Viburnum trilobum*), Zones 2 to 7

6. **Manzanita** (*Arctostaphylos* species), Zones 8 to 10

7. **Mountain ash** (*Sorbus* species), Zones 2 to 7

8. **Mulberry** (*Morus* species), Zones 4 to 8

9. **Pagoda dogwood** (*Cornus alternifolia*), Zones 3 to 7

10. **Serviceberry** (*Amelanchier* species), Zones 2 to 9

11. **Southern waxmyrtle** (*Myrica cerifera*), Zones 7 to 9

12. **Spicebush** (*Lindera benzoin*), Zones 4 to 9

13. **Sweetbay** (*Magnolia virginiana*), Zones 5 to 9

14. **Virginia creeper** (*Parthenocissus quinquefolia*), Zones 3 to 9

15. **Washington hawthorn** (*Crataegus phaenopyrum*), Zones 3 to 8

16. **Winterberry** (*Ilex verticillata*), Zones 3 to 9

Readers Share Their Favorite Picks

The berries of my mountain ash are a favorite of cedar waxwings. After the leaves fall, the regal birds flock to my tree, staying until all the fruit is gone. —*Bettie Pierce, Slaterville Springs, New York*

Nothing brings in the birds like our crabapple trees. Northern mockingbirds, American robins, cedar waxwings and others eat the fruits. —*Charlotte Clark, Glenpool, Oklahoma*

We've planted a variety of trees and shrubs in our yard, but the birds' favorites are the blueberries, hazelnuts, huckleberries and dogwood fruits. —*Shirley Van Mechelen, Everett, Washington*

Berry-loving birds are sure to flock to a mulberry tree. We planted ours in the backyard where its abundant fallen leaves and flower petals wouldn't bother our neighbors. It's worth the mess, however. Birds gather to eat the plentiful mulberries that form in summer. —*John and Eula Henline, Sioux City, Iowa*

Chokecherry and cherry trees are popular picks for American robins. I often watch as they pluck the ripe fruit (right), then wash it in my birdbath! —*Anne Fauvell, Rapid City, South Dakota*

Scarlet tanagers, indigo buntings, flocks of cedar waxwings, northern cardinals, house finches and American robins simply adore my serviceberries and dogwoods. —*Bev Dennison, Crandon, Wisconsin*

My neighbor's Washington hawthorn (right) is ideal for birds. Its red berries provide winter nourishment, and its thorns deter cats. —*Jo Ann Sheldon, Arkansas City, Kansas*

plants. Select species that will thrive in your climate and soil, and fit the space you have.

The Choice Is Yours

The number of shrubs, vines and small trees that produce fruit birds will eat is extensive. The list above is a good place to start (to find out your Zone, see the Plant Hardiness Zone Map at the end of the book). You can also check with your county Extension or a garden center to learn the best plants.

And if you don't have berry-producing plants in your yard, and a hungry bluebird or robin shows up this winter, there are a few impromptu options.

Try placing fruit like blueberries, raspberries, chopped apples, raisins, grapes or orange or grapefruit halves on a tray feeder. The birds should eat up your offerings…no convincing needed.

116

120

118

130

126

122

CHAPTER 4

FLYING FLOWERS

Pearl Crescent   112

Meadow Fritillary   114

Monarch   116

Anise Swallowtail   118

Milbert's Tortoiseshell   120

Spring Azure   122

Question Mark   124

Hummingbird Clearwing   126

Aphrodite Fritillary   128

Orange Sulphur   130

Spicebush Swallowtail   132

Hackberry Emperor   134

Photos: spring azure at left, Roland Jordahl; opposite page from top left: monarch, Larry Dech; Milbert's tortoiseshell, Warren S. Greene, orange sulphur, John and Gloria Tveten/KAC Productions; hummingbird clearwing, Richard Day/Daybreak Imagery, anise swallowtails, Francis and Janice Bergquist

PEARL CRESCENT

You have to look closely to discover these hidden treasures.

W ant to catch sight of this dainty little butterfly? Look down! The pearl crescent flies low to the ground through grasses, flowers and weeds, relying on vegetation to hide it from predators.

Its diminutive wingspan—ranging from 1 to 1-1/2 inches—also plays a protective role, making it almost inconspicuous. But the pearl crescent's vibrant markings are anything but subtle.

Viewed from above, the wings are a luxurious, golden orange with a wealth of sable patches and black zigzag markings, including a prominent row of dots rimming the bottom portion of each lower wing. The females tend to have more black markings than the males. The wing edges of both are a dark brown.

Underneath, the pearl crescent's wings are much lighter, typically golden with delicate orange scallops and a few dark circles. The undersides of each wing also bear a single white, moon-shaped mark, the "crescent" that gives the butterfly its name.

One of the most common meadow butterflies in North America and a member of the large brush-footed family, the pearl crescent can be found throughout much of the United States and into southern parts of Canada.

Keeping a Low Profile

It prefers open areas and can often be spotted alternately flapping and gliding through meadows, weedy fields, open streams, sunny gardens and roadsides. Look for it in areas that contain asters, purple coneflowers, goldenrods, ironweeds and zinnias, all favorite sources of nectar for this butterfly.

Although it depends on its low-flying habit to shield it from birds and other hunters, the male pearl crescent is quite aggressive when it comes to finding a mate.

The male generally perches on grass or branches with wings outspread to watch for females. When anything—whether it is a butterfly, bird or even a human—enters the pearl crescent's territory, it immediately takes flight to investigate and chase away the competition. It isn't unusual for a male to swoop at a bird...and wind up as a meal.

Attractive Asters

The asters adult pearl crescents use for nectar serve another purpose as well. Females lay clusters of eggs on the leaves of the plants, which provide food for pearl crescent caterpillars.

In northern climates, pearl crescents produce one to two broods between May and October. In the South, the butterflies are active year-round and may produce five to six broods.

The caterpillars that hatch 4 to 10 days after the eggs are laid are very distinct. They have black heads and pale brown bodies highlighted with brown branched spines and a white to yellow lateral stripe.

The offspring stick together and feed in a group, al-

MOONSTRUCK. Catch a glimpse of a pearl crescent with its wings folded, and you'll understand its name. A white crescent is on the underside of each wing (see above right).

Photo at left: Richard Day/Daybreak Imagery

Flying Flower Facts

John and Gloria Teeter/KAC Productions

Common Name: Pearl crescent, pearly crescentspot.
Scientific Name: *Phyciodes tharos*.
Family: Brush-footed.
Wingspan: 1 to 1-1/2 inches.
Distinctive Markings: Top of wings are a rich, golden orange with a patchwork of dark brown or black marks. Underneath, there is a pearl-colored crescent mark near the edge of each wing.
Distinctive Behavior: Pearl crescents fly low, darting through vegetation. Males are quite territorial and will aggressively investigate any intruders.
Habitat: Fields, meadows, gardens, roadsides and other open spaces.
Caterpillar: Pale brown with black head; brown branched spines and a white to yellow lateral stripe.
Host Plant: Asters.

■ Range

though they aren't voracious or considered a pest to their host plants. After 3 weeks of munching, each caterpillar forms a yellow, gray or brown chrysalis, which may bear stripes or patches of other colors as well.

Anywhere from a week to 12 days later, the adult pearl crescents emerge and launch right into flying, feeding and finding a mate. They don't have time to waste—their lifespan is a mere 4 to 10 days.

BUTTERFLY BIT

Try planting asters, purple coneflowers, goldenrods, ironweeds and zinnias to lure these butterflies to your backyard.

MEADOW FRITILLARY

Keep an eye out for this petite, quick-moving field butterfly.

I f your backyard borders are overrun with rampaging violets, wild daisies and dandelions run amok, take a moment and count your blessings. Your unruly landscape is the perfect habitat for a small, but mighty pretty, visitor.

Violet leaves are the primary food source for the caterpillars of the meadow fritillary, one of the lesser fritillaries that are found across sections of the northwestern and northeastern United States.

The reddish-orange meadow fritillary looks quite similar to two of its western counterparts in the West and North, the Pacific and Frigga fritillaries. All three of these species are smaller than most of the greater fritillaries, including the widespread great-spangled fritillary.

Regardless of their petite stature, the meadow, Pacific and Frigga fritillaries are still lovely sights, whether they are flitting through a Rocky Mountain pass or alighting on a wildflower in an Illinois prairie.

Home Range

Meadow fritillaries are found in the eastern half of North America and are seen in greater numbers than the two western species. They've also become established across a larger section of the country.

They visit meadows, hay fields, bogs and pastures from eastern British Columbia through southern Canada and from the northern United States to Newfoundland. They are also found in eastern Washington, central Colorado, the Midwest and as far southeast as North Carolina.

In the Northwest, Pacific fritillaries are the most widespread of the lesser fritillaries. Their territory ranges from central British Columbia and southwestern Alberta south through central California and Idaho.

Pacific fritillaries inhabit open, moist areas along roadsides and in mountain forests, seaside marshes and meadows.

Frigga fritillaries, on the other hand, are a more north-

John and Gloria Tveten/KAC Productions

GREAT COLOR. No matter how you look at it, the meadow fritillary has great color. Its rich orange wings are speckled with unique patters of black (left) while its undersides have purple and gold (above). At right, an adult emerges from its chrysalis.

ern species. They inhabit an area from Alaska southeast to northern Quebec and Ontario and south to British Columbia, Colorado and Michigan. They seek out willow and alpine bogs.

Identifying Features

Meadow fritillaries may be hard to spot, as they rapidly zigzag through open fields, roadside meadows and flower beds, but they take their time when sipping nectar.

Unruffled by humans' presence as they feed on blooming black-eyed Susans, sunflowers, clover, dandelions and daisies (and sometimes dung!), they allow observers an up-close look at their eye-pleasing colors and patterns.

The meadow fritillaries lack the silver markings of their greater fritillary relatives, but they make up for the lack of luster with a lively pattern of black dashes, dots and swirls on the upper sides of their tannish-orange wings. Orange, gray and purple swirls mark the undersides of their hind wings.

Angular, clipped forewings help distinguish the meadow fritillary from other fritillary relatives.

In the Beginning

Meadow fritillary caterpillars are equally colorful.

They will produce two to three broods from May through September. The females lay white or greenish-yellow eggs on twigs and plants (in the vicinity of violet host plants) from which the caterpillars eventually emerge.

Meadow fritillary caterpillars have yellow-mottled, purple-black bodies with black spines.

The caterpillars will feed on violet leaves until they transform into yellowish-brown, gold-marked pupae. Within a few weeks, these chrysalises will open to release another crop of these beauties into the world.

And, if you leave those pesky dandelions or violets standing, meadow fritillaries may fly right into your backyard!

Flying Flower Facts

David Cavagnaro

Common Name: Meadow fritillary.
Scientific Name: *Boloria bellona*.
Family: Brush-footed butterflies.
Wingspan: 1-1/4 to 1-7/8 inches.
Distinctive Markings: Reddish-orange wings with heavy black dashes and dots. This butterfly's squared-off angular forewings and its lack of silver markings distinguish it from other fritillaries.
Distinctive Behavior: They fly low to the ground in a rapid, zigzagging pattern. Males may be spotted during the day flying low over wet areas and meadows as they search for mates.
Habitat: Moist meadows, hay fields, pastures, roadsides and bogs. They will also visit gardens.
Caterpillar: Purplish-black, sometimes mottled with yellow, with branching spines protruding from brown bumps.
Host Plant: Violets.

■ Range

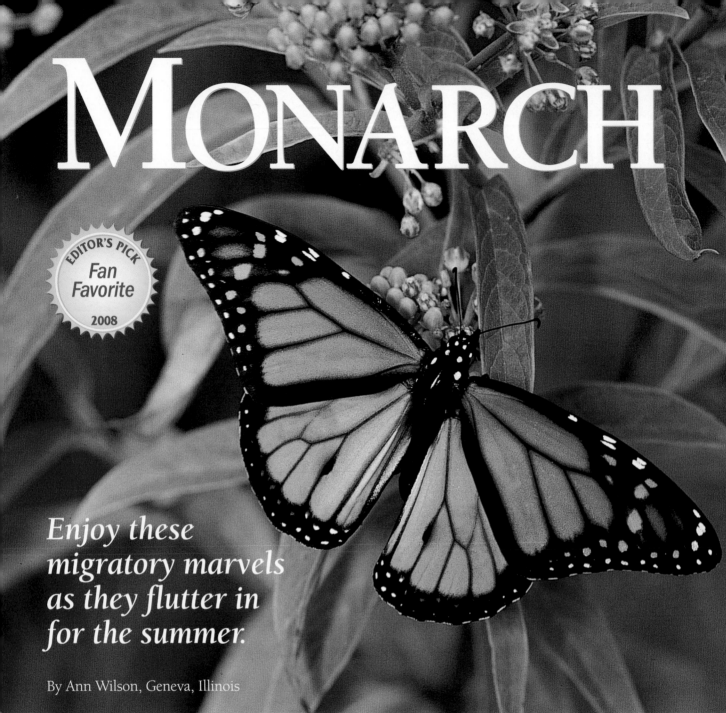

MONARCH

Enjoy these migratory marvels as they flutter in for the summer.

By Ann Wilson, Geneva, Illinois

EDITOR'S PICK
Fan Favorite
2008

Richard Day/Daybreak Imagery

Whenever monarch butterflies sail through my gardens, I stop whatever I'm doing to watch their graceful journey. The orange-and-black silhouettes cast a mesmerizing spell as they flutter amid my trumpet vines, purple coneflowers and sedums.

My admiration is part childlike wonder and part appreciative awe. When I was a kid, the monarch was the first butterfly I learned to identify. Now, I also respect them for their amazing migratory prowess.

The ever-regal monarchs are indeed sovereigns of the sky, traveling thousands of miles each fall as they journey south from Canada and the United States to Mexico and coastal California. During the following spring, the butterflies' offspring make the return trip north, stopping in milkweed-rich prairies, fields and butterfly gardens to continue the breeding cycle.

Across North America, summer-migrating monarchs will mate up to seven times to ensure the species' survival. Unfortunately, a monarch's lifespan is short—they're likely to live for only 2 to 6 weeks.

With 4-inch wingspans, monarchs are easily spotted as they glide through the landscape. They even boast distinct characteristics that allow perceptive observers to differentiate the sexes.

Male monarchs have raised black dots on their hind wings (like the one above) that store pheromones to attract females. Males also have thinner black veins than female monarchs. Because of their less-pronounced veins, males in flight will appear to be brighter in color than their duller-orange mates.

Larry Dech

EAT FOR GOOD HEALTH. Plant milkweed to attract monarchs. As caterpillars (right), monarchs dine on milkweed, which has bitter toxins that protect both caterpillars and adult butterflies from hungry would-be predators. At left, you can recognize a male monarch by the two small black dots found on its hind wings.

Catch the Metamorphosis

To attract monarchs to your garden, cultivate stands of milkweed (*Asclepias* species). Milkweed is the primary host plant for monarchs and supplies developing caterpillars with food. The plant also possesses bitter-tasting toxins, which protect both the caterpillar and adult monarch from predators.

The egg-to-butterfly process spans about a month, but may progress more quickly in warmer climates. A female monarch will lay nearly 400 creamy-hued eggs on the underside of milkweed leaves. Yellow-and-black-banded white caterpillars emerge from the eggs to feed on milkweed leaves.

The caterpillars eventually hang upside down on twigs and turn into gold-dotted, jade-green chrysalises that develop into butterflies, which in turn sip milkweed nectar.

Monarch Watch, an organization dedicated to the preservation of the monarch, suggests people dedicate at least 15 square yards of sunny garden space to monarch-friendly plants to accommodate both their breeding and feeding needs.

Flowers They'll Love

In addition to cultivating milkweed plants, pack your borders with pink, purple, yellow, red and orange flowering perennials and annuals that supply nectar.

Twelve good monarch-magnet plants include: Joe Pye weed (*Eupatorium purpureum*), meadow and prairie blazing stars (*Liatris ligulistylis and Liatris pycnostachya*), blue floss flower (*Ageratum houstonianum*), purple coneflower (*Echinacea purpurea*), Mexican sunflower (*Tithonia*), black-eyed Susans (*Rudbeckia*), verbena, zinnia, cosmos, bee balm (*Monarda*), butterfly bush (*Buddleja*) and viburnum. (For additional information on monarchs, you might

Flying Flower Facts

Bill Campbell/KAC Productions

Common Name: Monarch.
Scientific Name: *Danaus plexippus.*
Wingspan: 3-1/2 to 4 inches.
Distinctive Markings: Bright orange with black veins; black margins speckled with white.
Habitat: During migration, they're widespread and found in cities, suburbs and rural areas. When breeding, they're found in weedy fields and meadows near milkweed plants.
Caterpillar: White with black and yellow stripes with black thread-like projections at each end.
Host Plants: Milkweed.

■ Winter
■ Summer

want to check out the Monarch Watch Web site at *www.monarchwatch.org.*

Create a truly hospitable haven by adding a few other butterfly amenities.

Give monarchs a place to drink with a ground-level watering trough. (A small plate or a pile of sand with a shallow depression in it works well). And place flat stones amid plants to provide roosts for sun basking.

Then, just sit back and enjoy the monarch's colorful visits—this summer and for numerous years to come!

Flying Flowers

ANISE SWALLOWTAIL

This sizable beauty spices up western gardens.

Look about the open garden areas of the western U.S. and Canada, and you'll likely spot an anise swallowtail.

It easily is the most abundant butterfly in these parts—and the most adaptable, since it lives anywhere from sea level to mountain plateaus. Dense forests are the only places you won't find these creatures.

Although it resembles its swallowtail cousins, including the giant, western black, desert and Oregon, the extra-wide bands of yellow crossing the middle of its 3-inch-wide wings distinguish the anise swallowtail.

Additional small yellow scallops highlight the black edges of each wing, and the lower wings bear splashes of blue that point toward rusty orange eyespots. Its ebony body is accented with a bold yellow stripe down each side.

While both genders are strong fliers, the male anise swallowtail tends to glide toward any elevated spot on the horizon. Called "hilltopping," this behavior allows the male to take advantage of lofty spots to locate potential mates.

Males also typically are more aggressive in flight, actively identifying and confronting intruders of all sizes, while females bob about open areas in search of sustenance and host plants. Prime targets for food include aster, yarrow, butterfly bush, zinnia, verbena, mint, oregano, coreopsis and scabiosa.

There's no question the butterfly prefers anise, too, especially since it's the host plant for its offspring. Females also will lay their cream or yellow eggs on fennel, cow parsnip, carrots, parsley, angelica and citrus trees.

Upon hatching, the caterpillars are small and dark and resemble bird droppings. As they voraciously munch on the leaves, stems, buds and flowers of their host plants, the larvae grow rapidly and change color, eventually becoming green or greenish-blue with black stripes and yellow dots.

To protect themselves from predators, anise swallowtail caterpillars will project a pair of orange horns, called osmeteria. Not only do these horns look threatening, they

---

GOLDEN WINGS. Named for its host plant, the anise swallowtail also dines on other nectar-rich flowers. You can distinguish it from other swallowtails by the wide, yellow bands on its wings.

Flying Flower Facts

Common Name: Anise swallowtail.

Scientific Name: *Papilio zeliacon.*

Family: Swallowtail.

Distinctive Markings: First of all, look for wide, yellow bands across its wings. It also had blue marking and orange eyespots on hind wings.

Distinctive Behavior: Males dart across the landscape to investigate potential mates or confront intruders. Females are found bobbing around in open area.

Habitat: Found west of the Rockies at all elevations, from tidal areas to mountains. Prefers open fields, deserts, canyons, roadways and forest clearings.

Caterpillar: These crawlers are green or greenish-blue with thick black stripes across their bodies and distinct orange dots.

Host Plants: Anise, sweet fennel, parsley, carrots, cow parsnip, citrus trees and seaside angelica.

■ Range

Photo opposite page: Francis and Janice Bergquist

also emit a terrible odor and effectively chase away hungry hunters.

After several weeks of gorging on vegetation, the caterpillars achieve maturity and begin to form light-green or brown chrysalises.

Typically, each caterpillar remains in its chrysalis over the winter. And, as metamorphosis advances, the casing may darken to a rich cocoa or vibrant emerald before the fully developed butterfly emerges.

Milbert's Tortoiseshell

Warren S. Greene

There are two sides to this dramatic butterfly.

By Kirsten Sweet, Editorial Assistant

When its wings are open, the bright, vibrant colors of this butterfly make it hard to miss. In addition to its obvious vibrant orange and yellow bands, small iridescent spots of blue outline the hind wings of the Milbert's tortoiseshell.

Add that to the beautiful dark chocolate-brown that paints the wings closest to the body, and the Milbert's is a real eye-catcher.

It isn't always a striking sight, however. When its wings are folded, this member of the brush-footed family looks a lot like a dry leaf. Its underside is an array of drab brown colors that help it blend with its surroundings. So keep an eye out. You could be staring right at this butterfly without even noticing.

Anywhere Is Home

With a wingspan of only 1-3/4 to 2 inches, the Milbert's tortoiseshell is quite small, so if you want to see one, it helps to know where to look. They inhabit much of Canada and the northern half of the United States.

You'll typically find the Milbert's near dry streambeds and canals, riversides, beaches, meadows and rocky alpine areas. Although they prefer the cooler climes of northern areas and higher latitudes, these butterflies are quite versatile and will occupy lowlands if the temperature is right.

The brisk-weather butterflies may even emerge from hibernation on a warm day in winter in temperate regions.

Nettles are their host plants, so look for them in areas where these flowers are abundant. You might also spot the butterfly perched on stony banks, logs or hillsides. These likely are males watching for females. Selecting a perch rather than patrolling in flight may help them conserve energy.

Common Name: Milbert's tortoiseshell.

Scientific Name: *Nymphalis milberti.*

Family: Brush-footed.

Wingspan: 1-3/4 to 2 inches.

Distinctive Markings: Bright orange and yellow outer bands, with faint blue dots on the margins.

Distinctive Behavior: Adults often feed on sap from tree stumps or broken branches.

Habitat: Prefers higher altitudes, but they can be found in all types of temperate habitats within its range.

■ Range

Caterpillar: Black, spiny caterpillars have small white flecks, and a green and yellow stripe on each side.

Host Plants: Nettles.

"EYE" SEE YOU. Though you might notice a pair of "cat's eyes" on the Milbert's tortoiseshell (left), these marks aren't part of its defense mechanisms. Instead, these butterflies rely on camouflaged wing undersides (top and right) to disguise themselves, while the caterpillars (above) hide in curled leaves.

Growing Up

Females will lay their pale-green eggs on nettles. They lay the eggs in batches of several hundred at a time. In areas with mild weather, there usually are two broods per year. The summer brood becomes dormant (called estivation) during hot weather and then becomes active again in fall. This often makes people think there are three broods annually instead of two.

The caterpillars are black and spiny with small, white flecks and a green and yellow stripe on each side. At first they live in groups in silken nests, before emerging to continue to feed and grow on the nettles. Then they create a chrysalis that is grayish or greenish tan and thorny.

The last brood of the year will seek shelter and hibernate as adult butterflies, sometimes in small groups.

There are several other tortoiseshell species, including the Compton and California. The three share some characteristics.

The tips of their forewings are squared off, rather than pointed like many butterflies. They also have the brown and orange markings that resemble a tortoise's shell. The Milbert's has the brightest hues, though.

Keep your eyes peeled for this beautiful flying flower. You might spot a Milbert's tortoiseshell feeding on sap from tree stumps or broken branches, or it's favorite, flowering nettles.

SPRING AZURE

This gem signals the return of warm weather.

Roland Jordahl

Just as its name implies, this blue jewel of a flier graces the landscape as soon the first spring blooms appear. Keep your eyes open on sunny days, and you'll likely see a spring azure or two flitting about blossoming dogwoods, flowering herbs and even dandelions.

Though the butterfly only has a petite 1-inch wingspan, it's not difficult to spot. Its rich, violet-blue wings are outlined in black with delicately fringed edges, making the creature stand out against the soft green of up-and-coming plants and grasses.

The undersides of the wings—typically a pale grayish-white with dark dots spattered across the surface—aren't as noticeable. And, like so many species, the females tend to be duller in color overall compared to the males, often appearing more white than blue with a much broader black border.

The blue coloring of these butterflies does not fade away when spring turns into summer. However, spring azures that fly early in the season sport wings with deeper hues than those that come from late-spring and summer broods.

Out in the Open

A member of the gossamer wing family, the spring azure is most at home where it has room to roam. It prefers to flit about spacious forest glades, along roads and in open fields throughout much of Canada and the U.S., with the exception of Texas and southern Florida.

This beauty flies slowly but steadily and often low to the ground, searching for nectar-filled flowers or mud puddles from which to draw water and minerals (like the group of blues puddling at top right). Males actively patrol for mates, stationing themselves near dogwoods, viburnums, blueberry bushes and other specimens that serve as host plants.

Females lay pea-green eggs in open flowers and on buds of host plants. The larvae that hatch 3 to 6 days later

Chapter 4

TINY DANCER. Spring azures have blue topwings (like the female above right). Top, the butterflies gather at puddles. Above, caterpillars adjust their colors to their surroundings.

range in color from cream to yellow and pink to brown, depending on the population. Many of the caterpillars will assume the color of the host flowers or buds as a form of protection.

Attractive to Ants

The caterpillars routinely have dark lines running down their backs or green slashes lining the sides of their bodies. They spend the next 2 to 3 weeks doing what most caterpillars do—consuming their host plants and growing rapidly.

Spring azure larvae do have an unusual habit that provides important protection from predators. They secrete a sweet, protein-filled substance called honeydew that attracts ants. The ants slurp up the secretions, and in turn prevent other insects and parasites from making meals out of the caterpillars.

Mature caterpillars form plump tan or brown pupas that vary in color, depending on the time of year. In spring,

Flying Flower Facts

Common Name: Spring azure.
Scientific Name: *Celastrina ladon.*
Family: Gossamer wing.
Wingspan: 3/4 to 1-1/4 inches.
Distinctive Markings: Wings of adult males are a silvery violet-blue from above, and grayish-white with black markings and outer edges from below. Females are duller in color with more white and a broad black border on the topside.
Distinctive Behavior: The spring azure caterpillar secretes a sweet substance (honeydew) through glands on its abdomen. This protein-rich substance attracts ants, which not only eat the substance, but also help protect the caterpillar from flies, wasps and other predators.
Habitat: Open roadsides, clearings, forested areas and brushy fields.
Caterpillar: Colors vary from cream to yellow-green and pink to brown. They are often marked with darker patterns on the back and sides.
Host Plant: A wide variety of woody and herbaceous plants, including viburnum, dogwood, blueberries, meadowsweet and wax flower.

■ Range

chrysalises are on the pale side, while those that form later tend to be darker. You can usually find the pupas attached to the stems of host plants or on the ground among leaves that have fallen off the plants. Because of their small size, they are very difficult to find.

The last brood of caterpillars stay snug inside the chrysalises over winter, waiting to transform into blue-winged wonders as soon as mild breezes begin to blow again.

QUESTION MARK

Kathy Adams Clark/KAC Productions

*Butterfly punctuates
wooded areas
with subtle beauty.*

By Kathleen Zimmer-Anderson
Waukesha, Wisconsin

Curious about how this earth-toned beauty got its name? Take a close look at the undersides of its wings, and you'll have your answer. Located on the lower portion of each hind wing is a small, silvery white comma and dot. Together, they appear to form a question mark.

The coloration on the rest of the question mark's underwings is a mixture of grays and browns. On top, the wings are more distinctive, a velvety combination of rich mocha and orange.

This member of the anglewing family, a subgroup of the much larger brush-footed clan, is also called a "violet-tip," a reference to the lavender that edges the angular wings on top. Underneath, the question mark's wings bear a wash of gleaming purple, especially during spring and fall. Its wingspan is modest, about 2-1/2 inches across.

Paul M. Butler/The Image Finders   David Liebman; eggs (below), David Liebman   Tom Allen

IF THE NAME FITS. A small "question mark" on the underside of its wings (opposite page) gives this butterfly its name. The caterpillars (above) look a bit intimidating. Above right, a chrysalis mimics the appearance of a curled-up leaf.

leaf, allowing it to escape the attention of hungry hunters.

Adult butterflies emerge a week or two later. Those that transform in autumn will tuck themselves into a woodpile or another protected site and wait until spring. The question marks that appear earlier spend 6 to 20 days brightening the landscape as they search for food and mates.

Favorite Hangouts

Look for the question mark along open roads, in wooded areas and orchards, and near sunny riverbanks and stream edges. The beauty also flits about open fields, but it's not a frequent visitor in gardens. That's because it doesn't survive on nectar.

Instead, the butterfly sips on rotted fruit, tree sap and even manure. To attract them to your backyard, set out a plate of fruit or position some pieces on a tree branch. You can also spray water on a large rock or on the pavement to provide a fluid and mineral source they can't resist.

When a question mark feels threatened, however, you'll have a hard time finding it. These butterflies are especially good at hiding…and they can "disappear" in plain sight.

It often perches upside down on a tree trunk and holds its wings closed. The mottled brown coloring of its underwings, combined with the wings' irregular edges, help it blend in and make it nearly invisible. The creature will also pose on a branch, positioning itself so it looks like a dead leaf.

Distasteful Disguise

The question mark's offspring are easier to spot. Their long stack of green eggs, which can be found on elms, nettles, hops or hackberry trees, stand out, whether they're laid singly or in vertical towers (left).

And from the moment they hatch, the caterpillars make a statement. With bodies covered in bristling spines, the orange, black and cream-colored creepers look unappetizing, even painful, to potential predators.

After a month of steady munching on the foliage of its host plants, each caterpillar has matured to its full length of 1-5/8 inches and is ready to go into hiding. It crafts a grayish-brown chrysalis that hangs from a branch and is a dead ringer for a spent

Flying Flower Facts

Common Name: Question mark.
Scientific Name: *Polygonia interrogationis.*
Family: Brush-footed.
Wingspan: 2-3/8 to 2-5/8 inches.
Distinctive Markings: A silvery question mark on the undersides of its wings.
Distinctive Behavior: To hide, the question mark will perch head-down on a tree trunk and fold up it wings, exposing the undersides that blend in with the bark. They dine on rotted fruit.
Habitat: Open woods, fields, parks, roadsides, orchards and sunny streamsides.
Caterpillar: Its blackish body is covered with white dots and yellow or orange lines, as well as bristle-like orange spines. The spines closest to the head are black. At maturity, it measures 1-5/8 inches.
Host Plant: Nettles, hops, hackberries and elms.

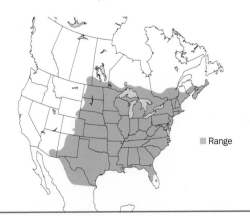

■ Range

This look-alike's identity is often mistaken.

By Kirsten Sweet, Editorial Assistant

HUMMINGBIRD CLEARWING

A tiny clear-winged creature hovers next to a flower then quickly rolls up its feeding tube and flies away. A hummingbird? Close, but no. It's a hummingbird clearwing moth.

When Cindy Wells of Alliance, Ohio spotted a hummingbird clearwing moth, at first she thought it was a baby hummingbird.

"I was extremely excited, so I went and got my camera and snapped a few pictures of it," Cindy writes. "It wasn't until I developed the photos that I realized it was a hummingbird moth instead."

Although the differences between the bird and the moth become blurred while they're in motion, in photos or up close, the distinctions are quite evident. The hummingbird moths have antennae and their bodies are spindle-shaped.

Same Taste for Flowers

Part of the sphinx moth family, the hummingbird clearwing moth closely resembles hummingbirds in feeding habits. It uses a coiled tube that it extends out of its mouth to feed, then rolls back up and out of the way. Hummingbird moths use the tube to extract nectar from flowers like honeysuckle, bee balm, lilac and snowberry.

"One of the most beautiful flying insects is the clearwing hummingbird moth," says Tom Dukes of Gerrardstown, West Virginia. "I was lucky enough to be standing next to a large thistle in full bloom when a hummingbird moth dropped in for a free lunch."

A distinct attribute is in its name—the clear wings. The wings of this moth start out as a solid red or brownish color with veins and borders a reddish-brown as well.

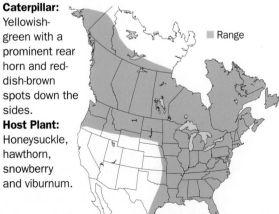

DOUBLE TAKE. The hummingbird clearwing moth resembles its namesake, especially while hovering over a flower. Reader Jack Terres spotted two of the moths (above) in his garden.

The inner portion of the wings lack scales and are clear.

Hummingbird moths, scientifically known as Hemaris thysbe, have a wingspan of about 1-1/2 to 2 inches. Unlike other moths, which fly at night, the hummingbird moth flies during the day, usually in meadows, forest edges and flower gardens.

Typically, hummingbird moths will stay at one flower for a very short time before darting off to the next one.

Jack Terres of Bethlehem, Pennsylvania was lurking in his butterfly garden with a camera when he was joined by not one, but two hummingbird moths.

"I was startled by the sight of two hummingbird clearwing moths," he writes. "While they seemed to be trying to stare each other down (above), they actually dined peacefully on a butterfly bush."

Life Story

Female hummingbird moths lay small, green eggs on the undersides of leaves in early spring. They hatch into larvae that have a prominent horn on the rear (above right).

The caterpillars feed on cherry or plum trees, honeysuckle, snowberry and hawthorn.

When they're ready, the caterpillars form dark-brown cocoons in the leaf litter. Some spend winters like that, but others in the South, where there is a second brood, appear again in late summer or fall.

The hummingbird moth is sometimes associated with the tomato hornworm moth, another member of the sphinx moth family. But while tomato hornworms have a negative reputation due to their appetite for eggplant, potato and green pepper plants, the hummingbird clearwing stays away from such garden fare.

Instead, hummingbird moths are a delightful sight in the garden—hardly a pest.

Flying Flower Facts

Common Name: Hummingbird clearwing.
Scientific Name: *Hemaris thysbe.*
Family: Sphinx moth.
Wingspan: 1-1/2 to 2 inches.
Distinctive Markings: Clear wings surrounded by red or brown hues. Body is olive-green with reddish bands on lower half.
Distinctive Behavior: Flies quickly from flower to flower and hovers almost motionless while feeding.
Habitat: Meadows, forest edges and flower gardens.
Caterpillar: Yellowish-green with a prominent rear horn and reddish-brown spots down the sides.

Range

Host Plant: Honeysuckle, hawthorn, snowberry and viburnum.

Flying Flowers

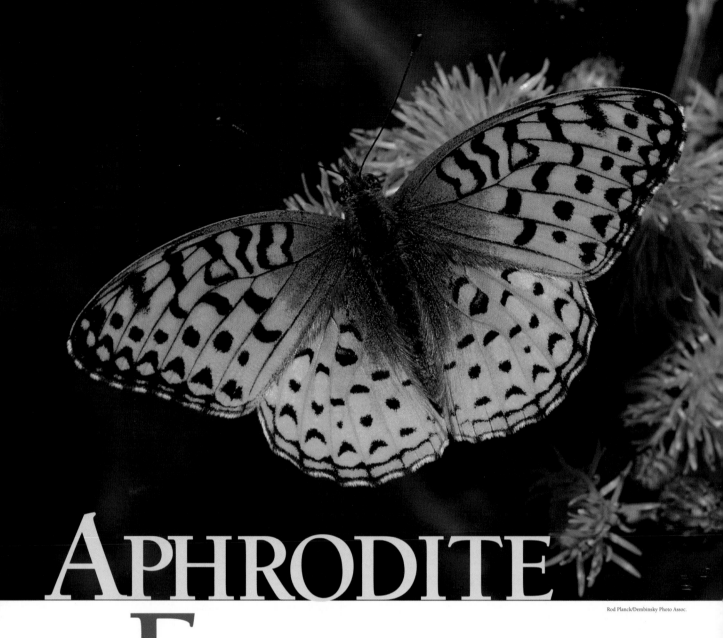

APHRODITE FRITILLARY

This beauty lives up to its mythological moniker.

Like the ancient Greek goddess of love, the Aphrodite fritillary is both beguiling and gorgeous. The mythological character gave this graceful flier its name, and it's quite fitting. It's not hard to become infatuated with it as it flits through fields and meadows in the northern tier of the U.S. and southern Canada.

Seen from above, its rich, tawny orange wings and striking array of brown or black markings stand out among greenery and flowers alike. Underneath, the butterfly's forewings are lighter in color with similar dark dashes and dots.

The hind wings, on the other hand, are distinctly dif-

ferent. They feature a warm, cinnamon shade, covered with eye-catching iridescent silver dots that are more triangular in shape near the outer margins.

Mistaken Identity?

As pretty as an Aphrodite's wings are, they bear a strong resemblance to two close cousins, the great spangled fritillary and the Atlantis fritillary. These butterflies all use the same territory. This makes identification tricky.

You can distinguish among these members of the brush-footed family partly by size. The wingspans of the

Aphrodite and Atlantis range from 2 to 3 inches in width, while the great spangled's can reach 4 inches. This is especially true for females, which tend to be bitter. Male great spangled fritillaries, on the other hand, may be the same size as the other two species.

The best way to tell them apart is to look at the undersides of the wings when one of these butterflies pauses to sip nectar. On the great-spangled fritillary's hind wings, there are broad bands of yellow-tan separating the silver spots from the outer margins.

These bands are missing or nearly invisible on the Aphrodite fritillary, and are very narrow on the Atlantis. Also, the undersides of the Aphrodite's wings are reddish brown, while those of the Atlantis are a darker brown with a greenish cast.

The Aphrodite begins making appearances in late June, as does the great spangled fritillary. In addition to meadows and fields, it prefers tall grass prairies, forests and foothills where it can find thistles, rabbit brush, dogbane and other wildflowers.

It isn't unusual to spot Aphrodites congregating by the dozens in areas where plenty of nectar is available.

Female Aphrodites wait until the end of summer to lay their eggs—and they do so haphazardly in select places where violets will bloom the following year.

Searching for Violets

What's interesting about this habit is that by the time they're ready to lay eggs, the violets are dying back for the winter.

Although the butterflies know where violets typically grow, that doesn't mean the plants are easy to find after the flowers have faded. So the eggs are usually laid randomly in violet-prone areas.

The cream-colored eggs the females lay turn a steel gray before hatching a week or so later. The caterpillars that emerge are brown with black bands and dark spines. They eat the eggshells, then immediately seek shelter under nearby leaves until the next spring, a common behavior among fritillary larvae.

When warm weather returns, the caterpillars come out to gorge on newly sprouted violets. They continue to grow and munch until mid-June.

The caterpillar then forms a chrysalis among the plants in a loosely formed shelter. The chrysalis is reddish-brown in color and is usually darker toward the tail.

So try planting violets in your garden next season for these beauties. With a little bit of luck, the goddess of love just might pay you a visit! ✦

Flying Flower Facts

Common Name: Aphrodite fritillary.

Scientific Name: *Speyeria aphrodite.*

Family: Brush-footed.

Wingspan: 2 to 3 inches.

Distinctive Markings: Tawny orange wings, accented with a splattering of dark brown or black spots and dashes and crescents. Underneath, the forewing is lighter with similar markings, except for a band of shiny silver spots along the edge. The hind wing sports a richer cinnamon hue and a multitude of silver spots that become more triangular away from the body.

Distinctive Behavior: Females lay eggs near patches of violets that have already bloomed and died. Eggs are laid haphazardly and at random in those areas. Females actually lay the eggs on the dying leaves.

Habitat: Wooded areas, tall-grass prairies, foothills and mountain meadows.

Caterpillar: Spiny brownish-black with black spines.

Host Plants: Violets.

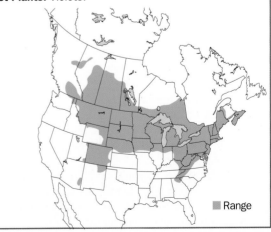

■ Range

Rick and Nora Bowers/KAC Productions

ORANGE SULPHUR

Take a close look to identify this beauty next door.

By Julie Warner, Milwaukee, Wisconsin

The orange sulphur may be common, but that doesn't mean this citrus-hued beauty is easy to pick out of a crowd. Though it shares the sulphur-yellow underwings of many of its cousins, sneaking a peek at the characteristic orange topside is a challenge.

That's because the orange sulphur sunbathes with its wings closed, instead of spreading them open like most other butterflies. This practice is called lateral basking. The orange sulphur warms its body by turning to mirror the sun with its folded wings.

About the only time you'll see an orange sulphur with flat wings is in flight, or when the female rejects a male.

If you do catch a glimpse of its orange upper wings, you'll see a broad, black border marking the edges and a black spot on each forewing, along with a faint splotch of orange on the hind wings. On female butterflies, that black border is paler and often interrupted by patches of yellow.

Great variation exists in the coloring of orange sulphurs, which range from vibrant orange to golden yellow.

Underneath, they appear incredibly similar to its oft-confused cousin—the clouded sulphur. Though the differences are difficult to pick out as they flit around a garden, in photos, you'll notice that the orange sulphur's underwings are truer yellow, while those of a clouded sulphur have a greenish hue.

Orange sulphurs expanded from their original range in the West and South in the 1930s as agriculture practices

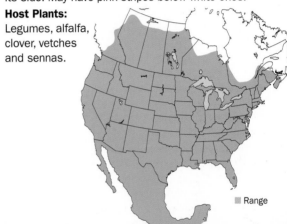

Flying Flower Facts

Common Name: Orange sulphur, alfalfa butterfly.

Scientific Name: *Coliaseurytheme.*

Family: Sulphurs.

Wingspan: 1-1/2 to 2-3/8 inches.

Distinctive Markings: There's always some orange present, whether it's the hue of the wings or a splotches on the top or underside of the hind wings.

Distinctive Behavior: Gathers at puddles or wet ground to sip nutrients (called "puddling," like the butterflies at left). Basks in the sun with wings closed.

Habitat: Various open spaces: farm fields, prairies, yards and roadsides.

Caterpillar: Small, grass-green caterpillar is covered with tiny, white hairs. White stripes edged in black run along its side. May have pink stripes below white ones.

Host Plants:
Legumes, alfalfa, clover, vetches and sennas.

■ Range

spread. The caterpillars feed on alfalfa and various legumes, so you're likely to find these butterflies flying in fields of these crops. This is also why some people call these fliers alfalfa butterflies.

In fact, the caterpillars' voracious appetite for these crops makes them a pest to some farmers.

Extremely common throughout most of North America today, orange sulfurs will inhabit nearly any open space, including fields, gardens, lawns, roadsides, deserts, prairies, foothills and mountain meadows. You may even find them gathered together to indulge their penchant for sipping minerals from mud puddles.

Though there are many other yellow butterflies, female orange sulphurs are able to select an orange sulphur mate by detecting the amount of ultraviolet light reflected by the male's wings.

Still, these two species sometimes crossbreed, mostly in areas with dense populations of both, such as a field of alfalfa.

The butterfly's long, white eggs, which turn scarlet prior to hatching, can be found slightly scattered on either the tops or bottoms of leaves of various legumes, indicative of the female's hurried nature and disregard for particulars.

The caterpillars that emerge (above) are dark green with thin, pale racing stripes and velveted with tiny, white hairs. It grows to about 1-1/2 inches when mature.

There typically are three to five generations from early spring until fall. The last brood overwinters in the chrysalis, which is green and peppered with yellow and black. Then these butterflies emerge in time for spring. Each generation lives for only 4 to 6 weeks.

Now, "orange" you glad this sulphur is so common, after all?

SPICEBUSH SWALLOWTAIL

This dramatic creature is like a breath of fresh spring air.

Chapter 4

Standing out against a field of green or a multihued swathe of perennials, the spicebush swallowtail truly captures the eye. Its obsidian wings, dusted with a haze of greenish-blue, bright-orange spots near the body and a string of creamy-white dots along the edges, are stunning.

Like other members of the swallowtail family, the spicebush sports distinctive tips, or tails, at the bottom of its wings. It's also quite sizable, measuring 3-1/2 to 4-1/2 inches across.

If you catch sight of this beauty when it's perched and its wings are closed, you'll see the same velvety black-brown tone highlighted by a less brilliant silver-blue mist between double rows of orange spots on the lower wings.

Aside from being pretty, these markings on the undersides of the wings provide protection, too. They mimic those of the pipevine swallowtail, a relative to the spicebush that leaves a bad taste in predators' mouths. In fact, it's so foul that one glimpse of the orange and blue pattern will cause birds and other hunters to fly in the other direction.

While this beauty is a common guest in suburban gardens, where it eagerly dines on honeysuckle, butterfly bush, Joe Pye weed, purple coneflower and common zinnias, it also frequents forest edges, fields and meadows. This is where its favorite host plant, the spicebush, grows. It is also where the butterflies are most likely to lay eggs.

Females will also lay eggs on sassafras and bay plants, with those living in northern regions producing two broods, and those in the South producing three.

When the larvae emerge from their pale-green eggs, they resemble bird droppings more than anything else. But as they grow, these caterpillars transform into striking offspring.

Each one turns dark green with menacing dark-centered orange eyespots on both sides of its oversized head. The eyespots and big noggin make it resemble a small snake, an appearance reinforced when the caterpillar rears up as if to attack a predator.

For additional protection, the spicebush swallowtail caterpillar will curl itself up in the leaf of a host plant, effectively camouflaging itself while it rests and feeds. And if that doesn't keep it safe, the creature has a forked gland, called an osmeterium, hidden behind its head that will emerge and release a foul odor.

After a month of eating and growing, the caterpillar—now about 1-1/2 inches long—forms a chrysalis. The chrysalis is green in spring or brownish-gray if formed later in the season.

Late-season caterpillars will spend winter in their chrysalis. Come spring, these inky fliers will emerge, stirring up interest around the country.

Richard Day/Daybreak Imagery

Flying Flower Facts

Rick and Nora Bowers/KAC Productions

Common Name: Spicebush Swallowtail.
Scientific Name: *Papilio troilus.*
Family: Swallowtail.
Wingspan: 3-1/2 to 4-1/2 inches.
Distinctive Markings: A gentle wash of greenish-blue on the lower wings, and a pair of orange dots stands between the distinctive tails.
Distinctive Behavior: Both males and females flutter wings slowly when sipping nectar from flowers.
Habitat: Forest edges, meadows, gardens and fields.
Caterpillar: Initially, the larva is small. As it grows, it turns green and forms a set of rimmed orange eyespots on either side of its head.
Host Plants: Spicebush, sassafras, redbay and other bays.

■ Range

Richard Day/Daybreak Imagery

NOW YOU SEE ME, NOW YOU DON'T. Eyelike markings make the spicebush swallowtail caterpillar stand out. As they mature, they may hide in leaves before entering their chrysalis.

David Liebman

HACKBERRY EMPEROR

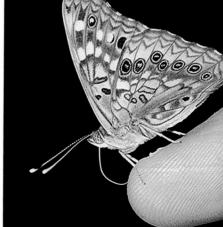

Richard Day/Daybreak Imagery

The hackberry emperor is one congenial critter. This friendly insect may hitch a wing-resting ride on unsuspecting humans, or land to sip salt from the sweat of a gardener's brow (or any other exposed body part).

This acrobat of the sky briskly and erratically flits amid a forest's canopy or along a river's shore, only to gently dive downward to drink from wet roadways, streams and mud puddles. When they are finally ready to take a break from their antics, they rest upside down on tree trunks.

The hackberry emperor—found from Colorado east to Massachusetts, in southwestern mountainous regions and in northern Mexico—boasts a wingspan of 1-3/8 to 2-1/4 inches. Its coloring varies by region, but the wing's upper sides generally range from grayish- to reddish-brown and feature darker-colored tips.

Take a Closer Look

Rows of white spots and black dots decorate the upper wings, while the undersides showcase a distinct row of yellow-outlined black eyespots splashed with blue along with a smattering of fuzzy white dots. The female's color palette is usually lighter and more vibrant than the male's.

It's not hard to know where to look for this butterfly. The hackberry emperor larva only feasts on the leaves of the hackberry tree and its relatives, the sugarberry tree and dwarf hackberry. Wherever these host trees are present, hackberry emperors are sure to be soaring about.

Richard Day/Daybreak Imagery, Two photos at right, David Liebman

LET'S BE FRIENDS. The hackberry emperor is a friendly flier and will often land on humans to get a taste of salt from their sweat. Don't forget to look for the caterpillars of these butterflies through fall and winter, too. In October, the caterpillars prepare to hibernate as groups in curled-up leaves.

Searching for a Snack

The hackberry emperor is a butterfly with an affinity for woods, water and waste. The butterfly makes its home near hackberry trees, whether they're growing in woodlands, along roads and rivers and in neighborhoods.

A scavenger of sorts, the hackberry butterfly passes over nectar-rich flowers to search for rotting fruit, such as fallen crabapples or berries too long on the branch, dung, carrion and tree sap. A favorite stopover of these butterflies includes muddy manure piles, where they can dine and drink at the same time.

Producing one to three broods from May through October, hackberry emperors lay clusters of ridged, yellowish-white eggs on hackberry leaves. Flattened green caterpillars patterned with horizontal stripes and dots in yellow and chartreuse emerge from the eggs.

Two branched horns sprout from the caterpillar's head, while two taillike projections jut from its rear. The caterpillars feed in a group on hackberry leaves until they morph into a pale green, two-horned chrysalises .

Caterpillars hatching late in the season shade to brown and overwinter as a group inside dried, curled-up leaves. As temperatures warm during the following spring, the caterpillars shade back to green, feed on leafing out hackberry trees, and launch the metamorphic cycle again.

Flying Flower Facts

Common Name: Hackberry emperor.

Scientific Name: *Asterocampa celtis.*

Wingspan: 1-3/8 to 2-1/4 inches.

Distinctive Markings: Upper sides of wings range from grayish- to reddish-brown. Wings have dark tips, distinct white dots and dark spots. Undersides of wings boast yellow-outlined dark eyespots splashed with blue.

Distinctive Behavior: Flies quickly in an erratic manner; rests upside down on tree trunks; often lands on humans to sip the salt from their sweat.

Habitat: Wherever hackberries grow, including moist woodlands, riversides, city parks and neighborhoods.

Caterpillar: 1-1/4 inches long, green with yellow and lime stripes and dots; forked horns at both ends.

Host Plants: Hackberry trees (*Celtis* species), sugarberry (*Celtis laevigata*), dwarf hackberry (*Celtis tenuifolia*).

■ Range

158

150

144

138

152

Chapter 5

BLOOMING BEAUTY

Lavender	138
Coral Bells	140
Pansies	144
Crocus	147
Asters	150
Oriental Poppies	152
Gladiolus	155
Pentas	158
Zinnias	160
Yucca	163
Snapdragon	166
Amaryllis	168

Photo this page: gladiolus, Jim Baron/The Image Finders; opposite page, clockwise from top left: pentas, Richard Shiell; asters, Donna & Tom Krischan; pansies, William H. Johnson; poppies, Faith Bemiss; lavender, Mark Turner

155

Lavender

This traditional favorite is a multisensory treasure.

You'll always find weeding more of a pleasure than a chore when you grow English lavender. This bluish-purple bloom rises in charming clouds to enrich gardens with heavenly scents.

With the brush of a gardener's hand, the plant's spiky flowers and needlelike leaves release a heady fragrance that is part spice, part floral and all together soothing. Fragrance aside, there are numerous other reasons to give lavender a whirl. The easy-to-grow plant is beloved by bees and butterflies, but shunned by deer and rabbits.

A shrubby, woody perennial, lavender bears beautiful silvery-green foliage that provides a pretty foil for colorful flower companions. Its unique grayish leaves also make it a standout in evening gardens that are designed to shine in the moonlight.

Quite a Reputation

Employed by modern herbalists to wash away one's worries, early Romans used lavender to cleanse their hands and bodies. In fact, the plant's name derives from the Latin word *lavare*, which means to wash.

Ancient cultures believed that snakes made their homes in clumps of lavender and so deemed the plant a symbol of distrust. Lavender has also been dubbed "Good witch's herb" because its purple flowers were thought to protect against evil.

Throughout time, lavender has been considered both calming and curative. People add it to bathwater for a spa-like experience or tuck lavender sachets under their pillows to induce peaceful slumber.

Lavender has also been used to mend injuries, thwart

'Grosso'

Mark Turner

'Munstead'

Mark Turner

Plant Profile

Common Name: English Lavender.
Botanical Name: *Lavandula angustifolia.*
Bloom Time: Summer to fall.
Hardiness: Zones 5 to 9.
Height: 1 to 2 feet.
Spread: 1 to 3 feet.
Flower Colors: Lavender to deep purple and whitish pink.
Flower Shape: Whorled flowers on the ends of long, graceful spikes.
Light Needs: Full sun.
Soil Type: Quick-draining, prefers slightly alkaline.
Planting: Spring is the preferred planting time for northern areas of hardiness; or if you live in a warmer area, you can plant this beauty throughout the season.
Prize Picks: 'Munstead,' 'Hidcote,' 'Buena Vista,' 'Graves,' 'Nana Alba' and 'Royal Velvet'; *L.* x *intermedia* cultivars: 'Hidcote Giant,' 'Provence' and 'Grosso.'

disease, and reduce the itch and soreness of sunburn and bee stings. And there's a very good reason for tucking lavender sachets into drawers and closets: It's already a natural moth repellent.

English lavender requires a sunny site and good air circulation. In fact, too much watering can result in rotting crowns and roots.

In colder zones, plant lavender by early summer so it has plenty of time to set down roots before frost. Gardeners in mild climates can plant lavender into fall.

Lavender won't grow in heavy or clay soils. Create lighter and better-draining soil by amending the planting bed with compost, peat moss or other organic material. Mulch plant bases with a layer of sand or pea gravel to keep plant crowns and foliage dry.

Throughout the summer, cut flowering stems to encourage vigorous plant growth and continued blooms. In spring, after plants begin producing new growth, remove dead growth and cut back old growth by one-third. This will rejuvenate the plants and give them a tidier appearance.

Hang It Out to Dry

English lavender is the most cold-hardy, compact and aromatic of all lavender—numerous cultivars are harvested for their fragrance, flavor and perfectly dried forms.

Lavender is one of the easiest perennials to dry. Harvest lavender stems in late morning after the dew has dried. Turn the bundle upside down, and secure the stem ends with a rubber band. Slide a paper clip through the band to use as a hook.

Hang the bundles upside down from nails, clotheslines or drying racks in a dry, dark space with good air circulation. Leave the bundles in place for a week or so. They'll be ready use in crafts and arrangements when the bundle's innermost stems have thoroughly dried.

Mix It Up

Lavandin cultivars (*L.* x *intermedia*) combine the best characteristic of English lavender and spike lavender (*L. latifolia*) to produce hybrid cultivars with fragrant blooms on long stems. 'Grosso' (above left) is a favorite for drying.

Plant lavender in clumps or rows of three to five plants to showcase their flowers and fragrance. You might also consider interplanting them with herbs, annuals and perennials, such as oregano, rosemary, pentas, gazania, coneflowers, salvias and sedums, that thrive in hot, dry soil.

Tuck them in as specimen plants in rock gardens or in terra-cotta containers filled with a lightweight potting mix. Marshal taller varieties along your heat-reflective driveways, sidewalks and concrete patios where you're sure to breathe in their engaging aroma every time you stroll by. All in all, you can't go wrong with this appealing, multisensory beauty.

Rick Wetherbee/The Image Finders

EDITOR'S PICK
Perfect Combo
2008

CORAL BELLS

With this flower, it's the colorful
and textured leaves that sing.

By Ann Wilson, Geneva, Illinois

More than 4 decades have passed since I first noticed the coral bells blooming in my mom's garden, but I can still picture those coral clouds that billowed, seemingly unanchored, amid daisies and bee balm. Upon closer examination, I noted the plants' wiry stems, which, alas, dispelled the free-floating illusion.

But coral bells still cast a magic spell for me. The sight of the airy pink sprays always conjures up memories of lazy summer days spent watching my mom putter in her backyard flower beds.

Sightings of old-fashioned coral bells are fewer now. Today's cultivars are definitely not your mother's flowers.

Plants featuring purple, red, black, silver, amber, orange and bronze leaves have taken center stage. Leaves, ranging from heart-shaped to deeply ruffled, showcase contrasting veins or attractive mottled patterns. The latest introductions are often chosen more for their distinctive evergreen foliage than their sometimes insignificant whitish blooms.

Flower lovers will be happy to note that horticulturists have turned their talents to creating cultivars that combine surprisingly shaded leaves with eye-catching blossoms in shades of hot pink, bright white and vivid red.

"I've been a fan of the new fancy-leafed coral bells," says plant expert Melinda Myers. "I like their attractive foliage, but have missed their outstanding flowers. Luckily, growers have come up with varieties like 'Plum Pudding' that give you both attractive foliage and good-looking flowers on one plant." (For other varieties that "have it all," see the list on pages 142-143.)

Background Check

Coral bells are herbaceous, clump-forming perennials that are native to North America. They flourish in a variety of habitats, from western rocky hillsides to southwestern canyons, midwestern woodlands or eastern seashores.

Also commonly known as alumroot, this plant's botanical name is *Heuchera*, which comes from 18th-century German botanist Johann Heinrich von Heucher.

Taking the best traits from wild Heuchera species, growers have developed hundreds of garden-worthy cultivars. Since the introduction of 'Palace Purple' in the early 1990s, coral bell hybridization has been proceeding at a fast and furious pace.

In fact, there are so many cultivars, it may be hard for the average gardener to sort through them all. The reason behind this coral bell boom is simple, says Richard Hawke, a plant evaluator at the Chicago Botanic Garden.

"Heucheras produce lots of seeds and are easy to propagate," he says. "As people see the new cultivars, excitement grows and growers introduce more plants."

Richard is well acquainted with the wide variety available. He spent 5 years evaluating more than 60 different coral bell species and cultivars.

With new coral bells being introduced every year, Richard recommends doing some research before picking plants for your yard.

Talk to folks at local garden centers to find out what cultivars they've carried for a couple of years and have grown successfully. Call your county Extension service or botanical garden to find out what cultivars they recommend for your area.

"Take time to study a plant's track record," Richard advises. "Just because it's a brand-new plant doesn't mean that

Plant Profile

Common Name: Coral bells.
Botanical Name: *Heuchera.*
Bloom Time: Varies by cultivar, but most coral bells bloom from late spring into early summer. A few varieties bloom from August into October.
Hardiness: Zones 3 to 9.
Height: 8 inches to 3 feet.
Spread: 12 to 24 inches.
Flower Colors: White, whitish-green, pink, coral and red.
Flower Shape: Bell-like.
Leaf Colors: Purple, red, black, silver, amber, orange and bronze.
Light Needs: Partial shade to full sun.
Soil Type: Moist, rich and well draining.
Planting: Plant in early spring.

GARDEN RINGERS. Varied foliage, versatile growing conditions and dainty flowers make coral bells a sure winner for just about any yard. Try planting these to add interest in your garden.

Mark Turner

Blooming Beauty

FLOWERS, FOLIAGE OR BOTH?

Don't know where to start with coral bells? We've sorted through the most popular cultivars and grouped them by the different features they offer.

Take your pick from varied foliage types and flower colors. Or select from our favorite category, "Best of Both," for varieties that combine unusual foliage and vibrant blooms.

ORANGE-SHADED FOLIAGE: Peach Flambé, Marmalade, Caramel, Ginger Ale and **Amber Waves** ▲

SILVER-FROSTED OR VEINED FOLIAGE: Cinnabar Silver, **Cathedral Windows** ▲, Frosted Violet, Color Dream and Montrose Ruby

THE BEST OF BOTH: Vesuvius, Tango, Hollywood, Fandango, Monet, **Plum Pudding** ▶, Fantasia, Hercules and Silver Veil

RUFFLED FOLIAGE: **Chocolate Ruffles** ▲, Sashay, Purple Petticoats, Amethyst Myst and Black Bird

it's necessarily a better plant than those that are already out there."

Cultivating Coral Bells

Because of their mounding habits, coral bells work well when placed in the front of perennial beds, in just about any combination. Depending on the variety, they can be used in rock gardens, massed as ground covers, left to naturalize or even grown in containers.

Coral bells look best when planted in sweeps of three or more plants, but some of the larger fancy-leaved cultivars easily stand alone as specimens.

In general, coral bells grow best in well-drained, lightly shaded sites that have humus-rich soil. Depending on type, some coral bells will thrive in full sun if the soil is kept moist, not soggy. In southern zones, coral bells do best in sites that don't receive afternoon sun.

Since the plants are shallow rooted, they may heave out of the ground during winter's cycle of frost and thaw. Richard says if heaving problems occur, immediately push plants back into the soil. Even in warm-weather climes, the woody-rooted plants may rise from the soil and need to be replanted every few years.

In colder areas, it's best to plant or divide coral bells in the spring so plants' roots have time to take hold before the snow flies. In temperate zones, plant coral bells in spring or fall.

"Heucheras are fairly adaptable," Richard says. "Give the plants a site with good winter drainage and enriched soil, and just set them in the ground and leave them to grow."

My friend Pam Hamilton has had wonderful luck with the coral bells in her garden. She knows how to mix and match for the best combination. She uses 'Purple Palace' as an edging for her deck-side perennial border, which she

RED-SHADED FOLIAGE: Sparkling Burgundy, Midnight Rose, Pink Marble and **Can Can** ▲

VARIEGATED OR MOTTLED FOLIAGE: Dale's Strain, **Snowstorm** ▲, Frosty, Crown Jewel and **Green Spice** ▶

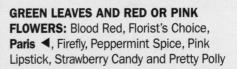

DARK-PURPLE TO BLACK FOLIAGE: **Obsidian** ▲, Molly Bush, Palace Purple and Cappuccino

GREEN LEAVES AND BRIGHT-WHITE BLOOMS: White Cloud and **Autumn Bride** ▲

GREEN LEAVES AND RED OR PINK FLOWERS: Blood Red, Florist's Choice, **Paris** ◀, Firefly, Peppermint Spice, Pink Lipstick, Strawberry Candy and Pretty Polly

plants with spring-blooming bulbs, cheddar pinks, thread-leaf coreopsis and rudbeckia for a multi-textured tableau.

"The purple color is beautiful against the other foliage," Pam says. "The ruffled leaves soften the edges of my borders, and the low-growing mounds contrast nicely with the fernier leaves of the coreopsis and pinks.

"I love to use coral bells with tulips and daffodils because the coral bells look pretty right away in the spring, and as they grow, they hide the bulb's yellowing foliage."

Shade or Sun

Pam knows the importance of giving coral bells the right place to grow. Following the directions on the plant tags, she planted red-flowering coral bells in the shade, but found they didn't thrive.

So, she moved the nearly dead plants to a site where they get afternoon sun. Now, they're flourishing and supplying a lively contrast at the base of her blue-flowering spirea (*Caryopteris*) shrubs.

Other perfect partners for sun-loving cultivars include ornamental grasses, daylilies, catmint, daisies and bee balm. Shade-tolerant plants, such as hosta, ferns, veronica, campanula and forget-me-nots, make fine companions for coral bell cultivars that prefer life on the shady side.

Try using cultivars with vibrant-hued foliage to underscore a garden's color scheme. Plant maroon or purple varieties beneath red-leafed Japanese maples and barberries; interplant frosted-leaved coral bells with like-hued artemesia for silvery still lifes that brighten walkway edges.

With more and more cultivars being introduced every year, you're sure to find an array of coral bells that will complement any color palette and suit almost every planting site.

🐦

Blooming Beauty

PANSIES

William H. Johnson

Fresh-faced flowers evoke the promise of spring.

By Ann Wilson, Geneva, Illinois

What's not to like about a pansy? Appearing in garden centers by early April, colorful flats of the perky-faced flowers banish my winter blues. Pansies, which tolerate light frost and even a dusting of snow, are one of the first plants I tuck into beds and containers each spring.

The cool-weather-loving plants kick-start my growing season, and sometimes stage an encore after taking a break during summer's hottest months. When my pansies don't make it through the heat, I just head over to the home center to replenish my stock.

There's a lot to love about pansies. In addition to being simple to grow and problem free, the plant's flowers are edible, easily pressed for craft projects and attract butter-flies like crazy. Since each flower grows on its own stem, pansies make stalwart additions to bouquets.

I don't think I've ever met a die-hard gardener who did not appreciate these fresh-faced beauties. Friends of mine who live in warmer areas applaud the pansy because it perfectly carries their gardens through winter. And, in regions with temperate summers, pansies happily bloom from spring until frost.

Depending on the planting zone, pansies are considered short-lived perennials, biennials or annuals. But whatever the growing zone, pansies supply gardeners with an array of options.

Take Your Pick

Pansies can be planted to edge sunny or shady borders, to fill rock-garden pockets, add color to seasonal containers and window boxes, or to hide the yellowing foliage of tulips and daffodils. And, because they're inexpensive, you won't feel badly about replacing them with hot-weather annuals like impatiens or petunias.

Wherever you choose to plant the pansy, its charmingly mustached countenance will make you smile and fall in love all over again with this ever-popular darling of the cool-weather garden.

Love, Legends and Lore

Love is a word long associated with the garden pansy. Introduced in 1839, the common garden pansy (*Viola x wittrockiana*) was a labor of love for English gardener William Thompson, who spent nearly 30 years hybridizing a garden-sized viola by cross-breeding smaller, wild species to include Johnny-jump-ups (*Viola tricolor*), horned violets (*Viola cornuta*), mountain pansies (*Viola lutea*) and blue-flowering violets (*Viola altacia*).

The resulting hybrid featured the pansy's now-familiar face and was originally only seen in shades of white, purple and yellow.

Over the course of history, the adorable flowers and heart-shaped leaves gave birth to a number of romance-related legends.

The word pansy comes from the French word *pensee*, which means "thought." Some folks believed that the sight of pansies could spark thoughts of the person who loved the viewer. The Celts conjured up love potions by brewing dried pansy leaves into a tea, and ancient cultures thought the plant's leaves could be used to mend a broken heart.

Knights of the Round Table employed pansies in a she-loves-me, she-loves-me-not fashion. If a pansy petal had seven lines, love would be constant. Eleven lines were not as lucky—it signified love lost.

Even Cupid is connected to pansies. A myth tells that all pansies were white until pierced by Cupid's arrow, which caused some pansies to produce yellow and purple blooms.

The potent love connection also brought about some cleverly conceived nicknames for the pansy. Amorously inclined gardeners have dubbed them tickle-me-fancy, call-me-to-love-you, love-in-idleness, heartsease and kiss-her-in-the-pantry.

Those with a more practical bent responded to the pansy's funny facial features and called them monkey flower or three-faces-in-a-hood.

Modern-Day Varieties

Today, nearly 300 varieties of garden pansies are available to the home gardener. During the past 6 decades, horticulturists have developed heat- and cold-tolerant cultivars, solid-hued strains, winter-blooming types and plants that bear extra-large blooms.

Take time to check seed packets and plant labels to find the type that suits your needs. If you want larger pan-

sies that make a colorful impact in the garden, look for cultivars in the Allegro Series, Bingo Series or Swiss Giants Hybrids. For early-blooming varieties, check out the Color Festival Hybrids and the Forerunner Series. Cultivars in the Velours Series bloom with tiny, delicate flowers that are ideally suited for nestling in the front of a window box.

Cultivars such as 'Icicle,' 'Second Season' and 'Sub Zero' will survive rigorous winters and can perform like short-lived perennials. Flowers in the Imperial Series, Maxim Series and Universal Series are good choices for gardeners who want heat-tolerant cultivars that will continue blooming into the summer.

When purchasing pansies, buy transplants or potted plants that have healthy-looking foliage, stocky forms and numerous unopened buds. It's best to pass on annuals that are already in flower. These blooming plants look pretty now, but they're using precious energy to produce flowers instead of putting it toward the roots.

If only flowering plants are available, pinch off the blossoms before putting the plants in the ground. (I've always hated breaking off the flowers, but the petal plucking does result in overall healthier plants.)

Pansies can be planted in early spring after the soil has dried and again in the fall. Although they're easy to grow, pansies do have a few planting and growing requirements

---

COLORFUL CONTAINERS. With an array of hues, pansies are great for perking up containers, whether planted alone or with other blooms. And because they thrive in the cool temperature of spring and fall, they mix with flowers from either season.

GREEN THUMB TIP

Pansies can bring splashes of color to dreary winter days. Try growing 'Icicle,' 'Second Season' and 'Sub Zero' cultivars in your winter garden or containers. They are specifically designed to withstand cold temperatures and perform like short-lived perennials.

Plant Profile

Common Name: Pansy.

Botanical Name: *Viola* x *wittrockiana*.

Bloom Time: Varies by cultivar. Most types flower in the cooler weather of spring and autumn. In warmer climates, some varieties will grow as winter annuals.

Hardiness: Zones 4 to 8.

Height: 6 to 9 inches.

Spread: 9 to 12 inches.

Flower Colors: Purple, white, yellow, orange and red. Bi-color flowers with a face-like pattern are the most common.

Flower Shape: Five overlapping petals, some with ruffled edges.

Light Needs: Full sun to partial shade.

Soil Type: Moist, rich and well draining.

Planting: Plant transplants in early spring. To grow from seed, start indoors in January or February in northern climates. In warmer areas, plant in late summer for blooms the following spring.

Prize Picks: Imperial Series, Maxim Series, Universal Series and 'Springtime' are heat-tolerant choices, while 'Icicle' and 'Second Season' will tolerate cold weather.

that you should keep in mind.

They're happiest when planted in well-drained, compost-enriched soil and benefit from applications of a balanced fertilizer throughout the season. Pansies are sun lovers, but will grow in partial shade. In areas with hot summers, plant pansies in light shade to extend their flowering time. In cool-weather climates, place pansies in sunlit beds.

Good companions for pansies include spring-blooming bulbs, cool-weather annuals such as sweet alyssum, dianthus, stock, snapdragon, sweet pea, decorative kale and chrysanthemum. Interplant pansies with early perennials such as hellebores, forget-me-not, columbine and coral bells. Or employ pansies as ground covers in front of hostas and ferns. They'll keep things interesting until the foliage plants leaf out later in the spring.

Summer Vacation

When the plants quit flowering and start looking shabby, prune them back to just a few inches tall. As temperatures fall in the autumn, the plants will revive and bloom once again.

Plan on picking plenty of pansies while they are in bloom. Regular cuttings will help keep the plants producing new flowers.

Combine pansies with dwarf daffodils, grape hyacinths and dwarf irises for nostalgic nosegays. Use them in crafts and cooking. Ranging from mild to minty in flavor, edible pansy flowers visually and tastefully pep up salads, soups and honey. Garnish cakes or cocktails with flowers or petals.

Or, try preserving their beauty by pressing the flowers in a book for a couple of weeks. Once they've dried, you can frame the pressed pansies for perennially charming artworks that will keep springtime pleasures always in view and on your mind. 🐦

FACE IT, pansies are a fun flower that really brighten spring yards. They originated as a hybrid of species like Johnny-jump-ups (lower right), and now come in hundreds of forms, from those with "faces" to All-America Selections award winners.

Jim Hays/Unicorn Stock Photos

CROCUS

Small but showy, this flower heralds the start of spring.

By Kathleen, Zimmer-Anderson, Waukesha, Wisconsin

When it comes to crocus, they're always worth the wait. Even my 5-year-old daughter agrees. Abigail helped me plant a bunch of crocus on a crisp fall day last year and listened patiently as I told her that the flowers need to sleep over the winter, then they'd bloom when spring returned.

She nodded, smiled and patted the mulch we'd layered over the soil—and I took pride in my parenting capabilities, and the fact that I was nurturing a gardening genius.

A few days later, the truth came out. I saw Abigail squatting in the garden among yellowed hostas and dying daylilies, looking intently at the spot where we'd planted the crocus before plunging her fingers into the shredded bark and dirt.

"Where are those flowers, Mommy?" she asked, perplexed. With a sigh, I explained the process again. In fact, I had to repeat that explanation a few more times before March arrived and the beauties pushed through the mulch and began to bloom.

What was Abigail's response to her first crocus sighting? "Finally!" she proclaimed.

A Colorful Past

These natives of the Mediterranean, Spain and northern Africa have been rewarding gardeners' patience for thousands of years. The cup-shaped bloom shows up in art dating back to 1500 B.C., as well as in a tale of unrequited love in Greek mythology.

The crocus arrived in England in the 1500s, where it quickly became popular and was mentioned by such noteworthy figures as William Shakespeare and Francis Bacon.

The plant has been cherished over the centuries for more than its beauty. The long, red styles of *Crocus sativus* (opposite page), the oldest cultivated species, provide the herb saffron.

While saffron was widely used in both food and medi-

BEAUTY IN NUMBERS. For the greatest impact, plant crocus in large groups, like the purple and white varieties (above). For best results, select a sunny site. These flowers open in bright light, but will close at night or under cloudy conditions.

cine, its rich golden color was also considered valuable. The herb was the main ingredient in the dye that colored fabric worn by aristocrats and royalty in Europe and Asia. The name of the flower, which is Latin for saffron, acknowledges its importance.

Still prized in modern times, saffron has become the world's most expensive flavoring agent, due to the fact that it takes roughly 2,333 blossoms to make a single ounce!

Gardeners' Favorite

Today, there are about 80 species of crocus and numerous hybrids, ranging in height from 2 to 5 inches and in hues from purple, yellow and orange to blue, white and striped varieties. The sizable cup-shaped flowers burst open in bright sun, but close at nightfall or under cloudy conditions.

These popular perennials are available with different bloom times, allowing gardeners to cultivate a display of color that lasts throughout spring. There are also varieties that flower in fall and winter.

The Dutch or common crocus (*Crocus vernus*) is the easiest to find at garden centers and home stores. They typically produce the biggest blooms and flower from February to April, depending on where you live. Popular hybrids include the 'blue Enchantress', purple and white striped

GREEN THUMB SECRET

Don't let squirrels and other critters steal your bulbs. Plant *Crocus tommasinianus*. This pretty spring bulb is one of the few crocuses pests won't touch.

Chapter 5

'Pickwick' and 'golden Yellow Mammoth.'

Sweet-smelling *Crocus chrysanthus*, or snow crocus, are a great choice for southern climates. 'Cream Beauty' and 'Bluebird' are lovely solid color varieties, while 'Zwanenburg Bronze' is a striking yellow flower with rich, reddish-brown shading.

Crocus tommasinianus, a pretty spring bloomer, is a great choice if your garden is beset by squirrels and chipmunks. This is one of the few crocus that these critters don't like, and they will leave the corms alone.

For autumn color, try the lilac-colored saffron crocus. Or turn to *Crocus speciosus*, a variety that produces long, showy blooms in shades of blue and violet.

Cultivation Is Carefree

With crocus, it's easy to add a blast of intense color to your garden. They're a breeze to grow, and have few problems or pests.

Most spring-blooming varieties require a cooling period to bloom, making them ideal for northern gardens. Those who live in the South can mimic these conditions by placing corms in a refrigerator for 8 weeks before planting. If you have questions about what species is right for your area, check with your local garden center or your county Extension agent.

Fall bloomers can be planted in summer and then will bloom in the same year.

To ensure the best results, choose a planting site that receives lots of sun—and plan to plant the flowers in masses of 15 or more for the greatest impact. They look especially nice under trees, in rock gardens and even naturalized into the lawn.

Crocus prefer well-draining soil, but they will perform under less-than-ideal conditions. If your soil has a lot of clay in it, improve drainage to prevent root rot by adding peat moss, compost or other organic material.

Place crocus corms, which look like small, slightly flattened bulbs, into 3-inch-deep holes spaced about 4 inches apart. Cover with soil and add mulch for extra protection.

Once the corms are in the ground, they pretty much take care of themselves. Add bulb fertilizer during planting if your soil needs it, but don't overwater or you'll wind up with rotted corms instead of beautiful blooms.

Squirrels and other yard critters often dig up and eat or move crocus corms, but you can defeat them by choosing a variety they don't like. Or cover your newly planted corms with wire mesh before topping off with soil.

Once blooms have faded, let the leaves turn yellow and die. The foliage feeds the corms to help produce the next year's flowers.

After a few years, you might notice a decrease in flowering. If that happens, dig up the corms, divide and replant. You'll have another profuse show when spring returns.

Plant Profile

Common Name: Crocus.
Botanical Name: *Crocus.*
Bloom Time: Late winter to early spring; some varieties bloom in fall.
Hardiness: Zones 3 to 8.
Flower Colors: Yellow, white, orange, blue and purple; both solid and striped varieties.
Flower Shape: Cup-shaped and large in proportion to the plant. Blossoms open in sunlight.
Height: 2 to 6 inches.
Spread: 4 to 6 inches.
Light Needs: Full sun.
Soil Type: Well-draining soil.
Planting: Place corms in holes that are 3 inches deep and 4 inches apart. Plant spring-blooming varieties in fall; plant fall-blooming types in summer.
Prize Picks: Dutch crocus *(Crocus vernus)* hybrids are popular, like the purple and white striped 'Pickwick', 'golden Yellow Mammoth', 'blue Enchantress' and white 'Peter Pan.' The orange or yellow blooms of *Crocus chrysanthus* are good for southern gardens.

Alan and Linda Detrick

Richard Shiell

Alan and Linda Detrick

S'NO PROBLEM! In northern gardens, crocus can bloom through a little snow. In the South, golden snow crocus hybrids (top left) flourish. At left, saffron crocus is prized for its red styles, which are the source of the herb saffron.

149

ASTERS

Stunning beauties bring the last hurrah to fall gardens.

Just when you think your garden is finished for the season, asters bring brilliant color to autumn's harvest-hued landscape.

With blooms in pink, blue, white, lavender or red, these daisy-like blossoms seamlessly carry formal beds, cottage borders and rock gardens. The unexpected color lasts from late summer through the first hard frost, and sometimes longer!

The perennial fills in borders with shrubby green foliage in spring and summer, and then delivers a flashy finale with blooms in fall. Aside from its good looks, asters are great for your backyard visitors, too. Bees and butterflies love this late-season nectar source, and birds enjoy the plant's seeds well through winter.

Popular Aster Options

Ranging from 8 inches to 5 feet in height, aster cultivars are generally long-blooming plants that, unlike chrysanthemums, usually return year after year. With these appealing combinations, what's not to love?

The hardest thing about growing asters may be sorting through the varieties suited to one's planting zone. There are approximately 250 annual, biennial and perennial aster plants. Many are North American natives, while others hail as far away as South Africa.

Native asters can be spotted growing along roadsides and sprouting uninvited amid flower borders. But happily, hybridizers have created garden-worthy cultivars that supply the gardener with better-behaved, varying-sized plants that work from the front to the back of the border.

The most recognizable of the asters, New England asters (*Aster novae-angliae*) are hardy in Zones 4 to 8 and boast yellow-centered lavender flowers on strong stems that range from 2 to 6 feet in height. (All the aster photos on these two pages are varieties of New England asters.)

The tall, strong stems, which may require staking, make this type of aster a good option for cutting. Popular cultivars include rosy-red flowering 'Alma Potschke,' which grows to 4 feet; the more compact, vibrant purple 'Purple Dome,' which rises to 2 feet; and the 3-foot-tall, white-blooming 'Mount Everest.'

New York asters or Michaelmas daisies (*Aster novi-belgii*) are similar to their New England cousins and are hardy in Zones 4 to 8, with cultivars growing between 1 and 6 feet in height. 'Apple Blossom' is a vigorous grower with dense, pink flowers on 3-foot plants. 'Royal Ruby' boasts red-hot, semi-double flowers; 'Professor Anton Kippenberg' grows only to 12 inches and produces semi-double blue blossoms.

'Purple Dome'

Bushy asters (*Aster dumosus*) are hardy in Zones 4 to 8 and boast compact mounding forms and disease-resistant foliage. Popular cultivars include dwarf varieties such as 'Wood's Blue,' 'Wood's White' and 'Wood's Pink,' which grow between 12 and 18 inches tall and 18 to 24 inches wide.

A North American native, heath aster (*Aster ericoides*) is hardy in Zones 4 to 9 and boasts profuse sprays of small white, pink or purple flowers on plants ranging between 18 inches and 3 feet in height. Popular cultivars include 'White Heather,' which grows to 30 inches tall and 20 inches wide, and 'Blue Star,' which grows between 1 and 3 feet tall and wide and bears blue-tinted white flowers. 'Snowdrift' is a spreading ground cover aster with masses of white flowers—the plants grow only 8 inches tall while spreading to 2 feet in width.

Lore and Legend

Appropriately pegged as the flower that represents the month of September, asters also bear descriptive nicknames, such as "Goodbye-Summer" and "It-Brings-the-Fall" that spotlight its appearance in the growing season.

The word aster derives from the Greek word for star—an apt portrayal of the flower's stellar silhouettes. To the French, asters symbolize courage, and they often place them as tributes atop soldiers' graves. Early Brits called the plant "Starwort," and ancient cultures burned the leaves to shoo away snakes.

Other cultures used various parts of the plants to create curative teas, ointments and powders to treat everything from diarrhea and fever to arrow wounds and poison ivy. Contemporary fiber artists, following in the footprints of their pioneering ancestors, use aster flowers to produce golden dyes to tint textiles and baskets.

Generally, aster plants are easy to care for. Most prefer full sun, though some plants even tolerate partial shade if equipped with moist, well-drained, compost-amended soil. In hot climates, asters will perform better if they receive afternoon shade.

Get Growing

Plants should be placed in full sun and spaced between 18 and 24 inches apart, which allows for good air circulation and prevents diseases such as wilt and powdery mildew. The plant needs minimal fertilization when grown in properly aerated soil. Just divide asters every 3 years to ensure optimum flowering.

Pinching back or shearing asters' new growth through June will create sturdier plants that are less likely to fall over in wind and rain. In colder regions, protect plants after the ground has frozen with a layer of mulch, straw or evergreen boughs.

There's an aster for every type of garden. Tall New England and heath asters are suited for both cottage gardens and prairie plantings. The shorter New York and bushy asters colorfully edge garden borders and walkways to add end-of-the-season color to even the smallest flower beds.

Pairing asters with other fall-blooming plants, including boltonia, sedum, turtlehead (*Chelone glabra*), obedient plant (*Physostegia virginiana*), goldenrod and helianthus, allows gardeners to fashion a fabulous farewell to the growing season. It's a lavish "last hurrah" that will repeat for many autumns to come.

Plant Profile

'Alma Potschke'

Common Name: Aster.
Botanical Name: *Aster*.
Bloom Time: Late summer through fall.
Hardiness: Zones 3 to 9, depending on type.
Height: 8 inches to 5 feet.
Spread: 1 foot to 3 feet.
Flower Colors: Purple, white, red, blue and pink.
Flower Shape: Yellow-centered, daisy-like blooms.
Light Needs: Full sun or partial shade.
Soil Type: Moist and well-drained.
Planting: Plant bare-root and less-hardy cultivars in spring after danger of frost has passed; container-grown plants can be planted anytime during the growing season.
Prize Picks: 'Purple Dome,' 'Alma Potschke,' 'Professor Anton Kippenberg,' 'Apple Blossom,' 'Blue Star,' Wood's series and 'Snowdrift.'

Oriental Poppies

Flowers provide a spectacular show from beginning to end.

By Ann Wilson, Geneva, Illinois

R. Todd Davis

With a distinctive bowl-like shape and ruffled, crepe-papery petals, Oriental poppies are garden standouts in late spring and early summer. Valued for their ornamental forms since 5,000 B.C., the Oriental poppy continues to be a favorite in formal plantings, wildflower beds, cottage-style borders and naturalized settings.

But for me, the magic starts well before my poppies burst into bloom. It begins in early spring when snowmelt reveals tiny tufts of hairy, gray-green foliage that have endured since fall beneath the snow.

My no-name poppies grow along the edge of my patio, so I enjoy an up-close view of the plant's fascinating stem-to-flower progression.

I watch as the leaves spread into bushy clumps, and bristled stems rise and put forth nodding buds that are almost as attractive as the showy blossoms yet to come.

Bud to Bloom

Slowly, the oval buds shade to orange and, seemingly overnight, the nodding stems straighten and brilliant-orange cups appear. They create a kaleidoscopic effect amid my neighboring blue flax and pink and white larkspur.

Each stem bears a single flower, with petals marked by black blotches at their base and purplish-black central stamens. Poppies make a statement no matter where they're grown. They are equally beautiful when planted en masse along a south-facing foundation or growing wild in the midst of a grassy meadow.

It's easy to understand why hybridizing horticulturists have developed more than 150 cultivars from the original bright-orange Papaver orientale. Today, poppies are available in compact to tall forms that bloom in white, salmon, deep purple, lavender, orange, red and pink. They are indeed magical. When in bloom, they're worthy of standing ovations from appreciative gardeners.

Ancient civilizations also applauded the Oriental poppy. Thought to have originated in Armenia and the Turkish mountains, poppies were introduced to Europeans in the early 18th century. But long before these beauties arrived on European shores, Greek and Egyptian cultures already valued them.

Thought to assure eternal life, poppies were integral elements in Egyptian burial ceremonies; dried poppy petals have been discovered in tombs dating back 3,000 years. The Greeks believed poppies promoted fertility and offered poppy garlands to Demeter, the goddess of fertility. Early Romans eased the pains of unrequited love with sips of poppy juice.

Throughout the ages, poppies have symbolized rest and repose (picture Dorothy, Toto and their fellow travelers snoozing amid the poppy field on their journey to Oz).

During medieval times, folks steeped dried poppy petals to brew medicinal teas designed to calm colic and whooping cough. Elizabethan Brits boiled up poppy syrups as pain relievers and sedatives. In fact, its Latin name, *papaver*, may come from the word pap, used to describe the baby food that was flavored with poppy juice to encourage peaceful slumber.

Contrary to their calming imagery and tranquilizing medicinal uses, poppies are anything but sedate when in full flower. The long-lived perennial produces dozens of colorful blooms when grown in sunny, well-drained planting sites with average to fertile soil.

Nancy Rotenberg; opposite page, Mark E. Gibson/The Image Finders

Donna and Tom Krischan

POP GOES THE COLOR. The rich hue of scarlet-orange still is Oriental poppy's signature color (like the beauty at left). However, other hues are becoming more common, like pinks, salmon and lavender. Above, take a close look at these amazing details. Poppy buds are just as captivating as the blooms.

Plant Profile

Common Name: Oriental poppy.
Botanical Name: *Papaver orientale.*
Bloom Time: Late spring to mid summer.
Hardiness: Zones 4 to 9.
Flower Colors: Red, orange, salmon, lavender, white and pink.
Flower Shape: A shallow cup.
Height: 18 to 36 inches.
Spread: 24 to 36 inches.
Light Needs: Full sun.
Soil Type: Average to fertile well-drained soil.
Planting: Sow seeds and plant container plants in spring. Closely follow spacing recommendations to allow for proper air circulations.
Backyard Benefits: Dried seedpods are attractive in fall wreaths or arrangements.
Prize Picks: 'Watermelon' has watermelon-pink flowers. 'Allegro' is a shorter variety with bold, orange-red blooms. For white flowers, try the 'Perry's White' cultivar, or plant 'Degas' for salmon-pink blooms with dark veins.

Faith Bemiss

BETTER TOGETHER. The intermingling of buds and blooms on the same plant makes an interesting display for poppies. Above, a double-bloomed variety shares the light with its buds.

Planting Poppies

It's important to plant poppies in spots that drain well during the winter. Standing water will cause crown rot and may kill the plant. The plants spread by runners and need a winter chill to produce a profusion of blooms.

Sow seeds or plant container-grown Oriental poppies in spring. Poppies don't take well to division or transplanting, so for optimal results, sow the seed where you want the plants to grow. You can divide overgrown clumps or take root cuttings once the plants have gone dormant, but success isn't guaranteed.

I discovered this for myself a few summers ago, when I dug up my patio-side poppies to move them farther back in the border. (Poppy foliage dies back after the plants stop flowering, so there were unsightly gaps along the edge of this garden.) I divided what I thought were the entire root balls and moved the divisions to various sunny spots in the garden. Unfortunately, the divisions failed, but the following spring, poppies sprouted in the original patio-side location, where they continue blooming today.

Because poppies don't like to be moved and don't hold their foliage through the summer, give some thought to their placement when you add poppies to your gardens.

Interplant them with complementary-hued flowers that bloom at the same time as the poppies and with plants that will mature to hide the poppies' yellowing leaves. Good same-time companions include Siberian iris, blue forget-me-nots, artemesia, white garden phlox and violet-hued sages. Later, selections like Russian sage, catmint, boltonia, delphinium and baby's breath will camouflage the dying foliage and fill in the voids.

In late summer, poppy foliage will reemerge as small clumps. Leave these clumps in place; they help produce energy to get the plants through winter.

So Many Choices

Plant poppies in groups of three for impact and interplant different heights and colors for a poppy extravaganza. Space the plants with good air circulation in mind—tightly packed clumps are targets for powdery mildew.

Choose lower-growing cultivars like 'Pink Pearl,' white-flowering 'Royal Wedding,' and salmon-hued 'Little Dancing Girl' to place at the edge of the border or in containers. These smaller varieties can also be planted in front of taller Oriental poppies, such as 'Patty's Plum,' 'Red Surprise' and 'Prince of Orange.' Introduce different textured poppies into your landscape. Try 'Fornsett Summer,' which boasts fringed, double blossoms that are salmon pink; 'Curlilocks,' with fringed reddish-orange blooms; or 'Double Pleasure,' which features crepe-papery double blooms in coral.

Generally, poppy blooms are solid colored, but there are a number of multicolored cultivars that bring an unexpected lift to the garden. 'Picotee' boasts petals that are white at the base and tipped with apricot; 'Carousel' has white blooms with orange margins; and 'Pinnacle' offers red and white bicolored blooms.

Once just available in scarlet-orange, Oriental poppies now appear in light pinks and corals, lavender, bold raspberries, deep purples and crisp whites. Ranging from compact to towering height and pastel to vibrant in hue, Oriental poppies offer the gardener an almost endless array of planting options.

Gladiolus

You'll be glad to know these striking flowers can perk up almost any backyard.

By Ann Wilson, Geneva, Illinois

I t's easy to see why gladiolus are the stars of garden shows, floral exhibitions and flower markets. Boasting strikingly statuesque forms, swordlike foliage and tropical blooms, "glads" (as my grandmother called them) fashion impressive displays when arranged in vases, tucked into flower borders or planted in containers.

But it's those same silhouettes that often prove problematic to the home gardener.

Where do you place such an exotic-looking plant? That's the question I asked myself when my husband, John, suggested we add glads to our cottage-style flower beds. I was skeptical, but gave them a shot since the bulb-like corms were inexpensive and simple to grow.

Finding Their Place

Over the years, I have learned glads need room to shine and plenty of support to keep from tipping over in the wind. I've discovered that if I tuck the taller varieties amid my Asiatic and Oriental lilies or behind my hybrid daylilies, they will blend nicely into my garden's more casual scheme. If you're searching for a different look, shorter and hardier cultivars are good companions for old-fashioned shrub roses.

Although they're generally not cold hardy, glads planted along our home's foundation made return appearances over the course of a few summers.

Good-looking additions to the garden, gladiolus stand out as cut flowers. Just a few stems plopped into a tall vase create a show-stopping centerpiece, while a blooming bundle presented to a friend makes a memorable gift.

Blooming Beauty

A Rich Past

Unforgettable and remarkable, gladiolus have struck a chord with countless generations. Signifying infatuation and remembrance, glads are thought to be the "lilies of the field" mentioned by Jesus during his Sermon on the Mount. Glads, which are native to South Africa, western Asia and Mediterranean areas, were likely growing wild in nearby meadows.

Roman gladiators also claimed the flower as their own—the name comes from the Latin word *gladius*, which translates to "sword."

John Tradescant, gardener to Britain's Charles I, acquainted fellow Englishmen with the gladiolus in 1620. By the early to mid-1800s, hybrid gladiolus were delighting Victorians with their lavishly ruffled blossoms.

In addition to providing beauty, gladiolus corms offered the cure for a variety of ills. People used them as poultices to remove thorns and splinters, and crushed them into a powder to treat colic.

Gladiolus flowers are edible and are beginning to appear on chef's tables. The lettuce-flavored blooms, with anthers removed, can be stuffed with tasty spreads; the petals can be sprinkled as a colorful garnish or tossed into a salad.

Thanks to hybridization efforts, there are now more than 10,000 varieties of gladiolus on the market. Ranging in height from 12 inches to 5 feet, glads flower in nearly every color of the rainbow with some varieties boasting mottled, speckled and bicolored blooms.

Some cultivars have a blousy look with flowers opening side by side, while others are airier, bearing loosely stacked buds.

The tall, large-flowering garden gladiolus favored by florists are hardy in Zones 8 to 10. They are also treated as annuals in northern climates, or they can be dug up and stored over winter for use in next year's garden.

These grandiflora types generally produce one spike per corm; each spike boasts up to 28 buds with up to 12 gorgeous buds opening at one time. Flowers bloom in an assortment of colors, including white, cream, yellow, pink, orange, salmon, red, lavender and even chartreuse.

Since these cultivars grow to 5 feet or taller, they contribute vertical interest in the back of flower borders. Their great height and weighty blooms also means they're likely to need staking.

Similar in form to the garden gladiolus, cold-tender border glads, such as butterfly glads, are slightly shorter and produce smaller, but still sensational, blossoms in a wide range of hues. They grow to about 36 inches tall with sturdy stems that stand up to gusty winds.

Batt Johnson/Unicorn Stock Photos

L. Diane Lackie

Richard Shiell

BEAT THE BLUES. The large blooms of glads are a cure for the garden blahs. They come in bold and pastel hues, as well as some stunning combinations, like the 'Red-wing Butterfly' glad (bottom left).

No More Digging!

Northern gardeners will appreciate the smaller, but more robust, winter-hardy glads that thrive in Zones 4 to 9. These dwarf glads (*Gladiolus nanus*) grow to just 2 feet tall and boast 10 to 14 loose orchid-like fluted white, orange, pink or bicolored flowers on each spike. Plant these types in the front or middle of borders, and try mixing them with Dutch iris, lilies and alliums.

Glad collections, available in pastel shades and vibrant tones, allow gardeners with a penchant for variety to cultivate sweeps of complementary spires and to create multi-colored bouquets with "wow" power.

Place glads where you can enjoy their stunning blooms. Choose a sunny area in well-drained flower beds or perennial borders. Plant corms at a depth about three times their width, and between 3 and 6 inches apart. Give them at least an inch of water a week and fertilize as needed. They don't like competition, so keep the area free of weeds.

If you don't have room for the towering beauties in an established garden, designate a sunny plot just for glads. Or plant a row or two in your vegetable garden where they can be easily tended. No matter where you plant them, make sure to support taller varieties.

"I know of one gardener who planted a group of gladi-

olus in her garden and used a white piece of lattice, placed parallel to the ground, as a grow-through stake," says *Birds & Blooms* gardening expert Melinda Myers. "The strong vertical forms of gladiolus can be difficult to blend in the garden, but the lattice balanced its strong vertical features. Try softening glads with fine-textured plants such as baby's breath, thread-leaf coreopsis and cosmos."

Melinda also suggests staggering planting dates to extend bloom and cutting times. Add new corms every 2 weeks through the end of June (or later if your first-frost date falls in late autumn).

To overwinter glads, dig up the corms in the fall after the plants' leaves have turned brown. Cut leaves back to the corm and let the corms dry. After discarding shriveled or old corms, place remaining corms in trays or flats and store them uncovered in a cool, dry and well-ventilated location where temperature stays around 40 degrees.

In early spring, replant the corms and prepare for another stunning show of these sharp-looking flowers. ✒

Plant Profile

Common Name: Gladiolus, gladiola and sword lily.
Botanical Name: *Gladiolus.*
Bloom Time: Summer in northern areas to year-round in the Deep South.
Hardiness: Zones 8 to 10; winter-hardy types, Zones 4 to 9.
Flower Colors: White, cream, red, lavender, orange, yellow, deep purple, green and pink.
Flower Shape: Spikes of open, funnel-shaped flowers.
Height: 2 to 5 feet.
Spread: 1 to 2 feet.
Light Needs: Full sun.
Soil Type: Fertile and well drained.
Planting: In early spring, plant corms 3 to 5 inches deep and 3 to 4 inches apart. For continuous blooms, plant additional corms every 10 to 14 days.
Prize Picks: Grandiflora types: 'Redwing Butterfly,' 'Dancing Doll Butterfly,' 'Confetti Mix,' 'Alfalfa,' 'Blue Sky,' 'Green Star,' 'Tout a Toi,' 'Phantom' and the 'Glamini' series. Hardy gladiolus: 'Charming Beauty,' 'Impressive,' 'Sabrina,' and 'Hardy Gladiolus Mixture.'

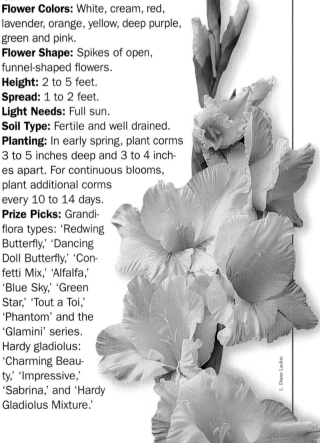

L. Diane Lackie

PENTAS

Hummingbirds love these star-shaped beauties.

By Ann Wilson, Geneva, Illinois

Once used primarily as a houseplant, pentas have made their way from hothouses and windowsills into seed catalogs, nurseries and backyard landscapes.

The versatile plant—valued for its vibrantly hued blossoms and continuous bloom time—is equally at home in flower borders, cutting gardens, hanging baskets, rock gardens and patio containers. Pentas are gotta-have-it inclusions in wildlife gardens—the plants' star-shaped flowers attract bevies of nectar-seeking hummingbirds.

The semitropical herbaceous perennial thrives year-round in sultry climates, but is a frost-tender annual in most planting zones. Four-inch domed clusters of tubular, five-petaled blooms—in red, pink, magenta, lilac, blue or white—rise from mounds of deeply veined, hairy and lance-leafed foliage.

Commonly called Egyptian star clusters, pentas originated in tropical Africa and southern Arabia. The plant's botanical name derives from the Greek word for five, penta, since each bloom has five petals, and the Latin term lanceolata, referring to the plant's lance-shaped leaves.

A Little Care Goes a Long Way

Pentas are drought tolerant once established, but do best in full sun and in fertile, well-drained soil.

Whether planted in the earth or in a pot, pentas require regular watering and thrive in evenly moist soil. Apply a layer of mulch around the plants to help soil retain moisture. Check pot-grown pentas daily—soil in containers dries out quickly, especially in the "dog days" of summer.

Propagate pentas by sowing seeds indoors at least 8 weeks before your area's last frost date or take softwood cuttings any time during the season. Place the cuttings in loose potting mix and keep moist until the cuttings develop roots sturdy enough for transplanting.

Put out nursery plants after the danger of frost has passed. Work slow-release fertilizer and organic matter into the planting bed to improve drainage and nourish plants throughout the season.

Pentas need little deadheading, but pinching back new

Plant Profile

Common Name: Pentas, Egyptian star clusters and star clusters.

Botanical Name: *Pentas lanceolata.*

Bloom Time: Summer through frost; year-round in tropical zones.

Hardiness: Zones 10 to 11; annual in other zones.

Flower Colors: Red, magenta, pink, lilac, blue and white.

Flower Shape: Tubular, five-petaled star.

Height: 8 inches to 3 feet.

Spread: 1 to 2 feet.

Light Needs: Full sun.

Soil Type: Fertile, well-drained, evenly moist soil.

Planting: Sow seeds indoors 8 to 10 weeks before the last frost date, or plant nursery plants after the danger of frost has passed. Propogate with soft root cuttings any time during the growing season.

Prize Picks: 'Stars and Stripes,' 'Pioneer Red,' 'Kermesina,' 'Avalanche' and cultivars from the New Look, Graffiti, Star and Butterfly series.

growth and removing straggling stems will prolong bloom time and help maintain the plants' mounding forms. Harvest the blooms for arrangements—cut pentas have a long vase life.

If you live in Zones 10 or 11, leave pentas in place to paint your winter landscape with tropical chromes. Pentas are marginal in Zone 9, but are likely to survive cold temperatures if protected with a layer of mulch.

Gardeners in less-temperate zones can still enjoy pentas as the snow flies. Just dig up the plants before frost hits. Bring them inside, place them in bright light, and treat them as a houseplant until the next growing season.

Array of Cultivars

Universal in their appeal, pentas have undergone a good deal of hybridization, which has resulted in cultivars ranging from 8 inches to 36 inches in height. You'll find pentas in an array of colors and sizes, and with solid green and variegated foliage.

Tall pentas cultivars worth giving a whirl include: 'Stars and Stripes,' which boasts red blooms and white and creamy-lime variegated foliage; 'Avalanche,' which has white variegated leaves and it also has white flowers; and 'Kermesina,' which bears dark-pink blooms with red throats.

Cultivars in the Star series grow 2 feet in height and are available in white and lavender. The New Look and Graffiti series offer gardeners a more compact option in an array of hues—these pentas top out at 10 inches in height. Cultivars in the Butterfly and Kaleidoscope series are midsized alternatives.

Garden Companions

Plant pentas with other perennials and annuals that have similar growing requirements and that do well in moist soil.

Place shorter cultivars at the base of cannas, elephant's ear, butterfly bush, annual vines and ornamental grasses. Pair bright-red cultivars with blue salvia to fashion eye-catching combinations that will entice butterflies and hummingbirds. If you like orange, try a partner like crossandra (pictured with the pentas on the opposite page).

Combine red and deep-pink pentas with plants favored by hummingbirds, such as milkweed, snapdragons, bee balm, zinnias and larkspur. Mix the prolific bloomers into perennial beds; they'll keep things interesting after the perennials' flowers have faded.

Use shorter varieties as ground covers or to edge pathways. Tuck loftier pentas in the middle or back of the flower border. Combine tiny and towering varieties for a mass of color in an annual bed. Or pot them up with other annuals for colorful container gardens.

Most importantly, place pentas where you can see them. Keep them in view so you can enjoy their ever-perky profiles and the winged critters that make beelines for their stellar blossoms. ✒

Steve Terrill

ZINNIA

Easy favorite earns an "A" for reliable, vibrant color

Zinnias have been enlivening flower borders for more than a century. Beloved by generations of greenhorn and green-thumb gardeners alike, zinnias have many positive points in their favor.

Zinnias offer a tremendous return on a small investment. Sow a few packs of seeds directly into the garden, and you'll be amply rewarded with a season-long show of vibrant colors and sprightly blooms. Cut a handful for a bouquet, and the plants return, happily obliging with another round of blooms.

The ever-perky blossoms also attract nectar-seeking butterflies and hummingbirds, and seed-eating birds like goldfinches.

Zinnia's timeless appeal and enduring character have also attracted the attention of horticulturists, who have taken the best traits of the old-fashioned favorite and created a range of disease-resistant cultivars, many of which have been recognized as All-America Selections winners.

Not your grandmother's zinnia, today's varieties offer an array of shapes, hues and sizes that work from the front of your flower bed to the back of the border, and in containers and window boxes.

In the Beginning

A gangly and lackluster native wildflower of the southwestern United States, Mexico and Central America, the zinnia takes its name from 18th-century botanist Dr. Johann Gottfried Zinn, who wrote the first description of the plant upon its arrival in Europe.

It wasn't until the late 19th century, when a double zinnia in vibrant hues was produced, that zinnias caught on as a garden plant. The plant's popularity increased in 1920 with the introduction of the 'Giant Dahlia' zinnia, which won a gold medal from the Royal Horticulture Society of England.

The zinnia's progress from plain Jane to picture-perfect can be seen in the evolution of its nicknames. Referred to as "everybody's flower," "old maid flower" or "poorhouse flower" by late 19th–century gardeners, zinnias later became known as "youth-and-old-age plant" because the old flowers continued to shine even as new ones blossomed. It was also known as "garden Cinderella"—a moniker that referenced the plant's ongoing transformation.

The zinnia's transformation really took off in the mid-1950s, and has picked up speed as seed growers keep developing new varieties.

Selections from A to Z

Although there are 20 different species of zinnias, only three are commonly cultivated for garden and container use. The common zinnia (*Zinnia elegans*) is the most recognizable. Today there are more than 100 different types of double, semi-double and single-flowering common zinnias available in sizes from compact to soaring, and in every color except blue. Depending on variety, they produce flowers with dahlia-like, daisy, cactus, button, pom-pom or beehive shapes.

The 'State Fair' zinnia displays 4-inch double, dahlia-like blooms in scarlet, rose, salmon, orange, yellow and white on 3-foot plants. 'Giant Cactus Mix' bears double 5-inch, cactus-type blooms on 3-foot plants. The cultivar 'Envy' boasts double, chartreuse blossoms on stems 30 inches tall. 'Benary's Giant' features dahlia-type blooms in yellow, pink, red and orange up to 6 inches across on 4-foot plants. The 'Candy Stripe' variety yields dahlia-type blooms with greenish-white petals with splashes of pink and rose.

The Mexican zinnia species (*Zinnia haageana*, formerly *Zinnia angustifolia*) boasts narrow leaves, a spreading growth habit and golden-orange, daisy-like blossoms. From this plant, hybridizers have cultivated the Crystal and Star series of plants. 'Star Gold,' 'Star Orange,' 'Star White' and 'Starbright Mixture' are heat- and disease-resistant zinnias that grow in 12-inch mounds reaching 12 to 18 inches tall. The Crystal series offers dwarf plants that grow only 8 inches tall and produce a profusion of 1-inch yellow, white or orange blossoms.

Some of the Mexican zinnias feature bi-colored flowers in shades of brown, deep yellow, russet, burgundy, red and maroon. The compact 'Aztec Sunset' is mildew resistant and produces 2-inch flowers on plants that are 6 inches high and 12 inches wide. 'Persian Carpet Mix' features double and semi-double, bicolored deep-red and yellow flowers growing on spreading plants.

Cultivation and Companions

Zinnia hybrids—often a cross between *Zinnia haageana* and *Zinnia elegans*—expand a gardener's options. These varieties have been bred to resist powdery mildew, tolerate heat and humidity, and fit into small flower beds and containers.

The Ruffles Mix is an award-winning series boasting 3-inch wide, wavy-petaled blooms in a rainbow of hues on 2-foot plants. The Profusion series offers bushy 12-inch-tall, 15-inch-wide plants smothered with 2-inch daisy-type

GREEN THUMB TIP

Zinnias are a great and inexpensive way to bring butterflies and other nectar-seeking fliers into your yard. All it takes is a few flowers to increase the traffic in your garden.

Plant Profile

'Zowie'

Richard Shiell

Common Name: Zinnia.
Botanical Name: *Zinnia species.*
Bloom Time: Early summer to frost.
Hardiness: Annual; Zinnia angustifolia hardy in Zones 9 to 11
Flower Colors: White, red, pink, chartreuse, yellow, orange, purple, coral, apricot and bicolors.
Flower Shape: Depending on variety, zinnias bear double, semi-double, or single flowers in shapes ranging from daisy-like to beehive and button types.
Height: 6 inches to 4 feet.
Spread: 6 to 18 inches.
Light Needs: Full sun.
Soil Type: Well-drained
Planting: Directly sow seeds in the garden or plant transplants after last frost date. Start seeds indoors 4 to 6 weeks before last frost date.
Prize Picks: Benary's Giants, Profusion, Star, Crystal, Dreamland, Ruffles and Thumbelina series; 'Envy,' 'State Fair,' 'Zowie,' 'Whirligig,' 'Aztec Sunset' and 'Zenith.'

blooms in an array of colors. Plants in the Dreamland series produce 4-inch, dahlia-form blooms in a wide range of hues atop sturdy, compact 12-inch plants.

The 'Zowie' cultivar (above right), a 2006 All-America Selection, catches the eye with vivid 3- to 4-inch semi-double magenta and orange flowers on sturdy 2- to 3-foot heat-resistant plants.

For the front of the border and containers, consider dwarf or miniature zinnias. Zinnias in the Peter Pan, Thumbelina, Dasher and Small World series bear vibrantly hued semi-double and double flowers on plants growing between 6 and 14 inches in height. Natives of arid desert regions, zinnias flourish in a garden's sunniest spots and perform best as summer temperatures rise.

"Zinnias are perfect plants for hot, dry locations in

Mark Turner

'State Fair'

Richard Shiell

'Zesty
Scarlet'

'Pinwheel
Golddust'

Donna and Tom Krischan

Richard Shiell

'Benary's
Giant Lime'

Richard Shiell

'Profusion Orange'

GARDEN FIREWORKS. In bright hues like yellows, reds and oranges, zinnias add spark to any flower bed. Just choose your favorite color or flower shape and start planting in your garden.

they were growing in containers.

Water plants at their base to keep water off the leaves and reduce the risk of disease. Cut flowers for bouquets and deadhead fading blooms to encourage stronger branching and continuous flowering.

Plant zinnias with companions that have similar light, soil and water requirements, Melinda advises.

"Zinnias work well with cockscomb, dusty miller and annual fountain grass," Melinda says.

Medium-height zinnias work nicely with complementary-hued cosmos, dahlias, salvia and larkspur; taller varieties mix nicely with sunflowers, coneflowers and black-eyed Susans. You might also consider pairing lower-growing Mexican zinnias with marigolds, mums and asters for a fiery and fetching fall finale.

As the growing season wanes, gather and save zinnia seeds for next spring's colorful crop (keeping in mind that hybrids won't grow true from seed). Bring fresh-cut flowering stems inside and dry them in sand or silica gel. That way, you can continue to enjoy the zesty, soul-warming blooms, no matter what bluster winter has in store.

your landscape," notes plant expert Melinda Myers. "Proper plant selection, site selection and spacing are critical to the health and appearance of zinnias. Select disease-resistant cultivars, whenever possible."

Melinda recommends planting zinnias in full sun in well-drained soil. Space small cultivars 6 to 8 inches apart and larger cultivars at least 12 inches apart. Start zinnia seeds inside about 6 weeks before the last frost date or directly sow seeds into well-worked soil after the danger of frost has passed. Plant bedding plants at the same depth as

Chapter 5

Spice up your garden with this one-of-a-kind plant.

By Kirsten Sweet, Editorial Assistant

YUCCA

With a striking resemblance to something directly out of the desert, yucca brings Southwestern ambiance to any backyard garden. But despite its appearance, the yucca is native to the southwestern *and* southeastern United States, and will grow in many zones across the continent.

This evergreen shrub truly is a blooming beauty. Its white, bell-shaped blooms typically erupt on stems that rise high above its swordlike leaves. These tough leaves can be up to 3 feet long, and like the daggers they resemble, are best kept away from areas that see a lot of walking traffic.

Yucca is a member of the Agavaceae family, along with plants like agaves and mother-in-law's tongue. It requires full sun and well-drained soil to thrive.

Some varieties stretch to 6 feet across and up to 8 feet tall, so when this plant is in bloom, it's a real conversation piece.

A Success Story

Edie Chmiel of Lawtons, New York decided to try planting a yucca a few years ago. She had been admiring her neighbor's plant for a while and finally decided to get one of her own.

"I wasn't sure where to plant it, and I really didn't think it was going to bloom," she says.

As it turns out, Edie picked the perfect spot because when her yucca bloomed, it unfurled three stalks of flowers! She

Blooming Beauty

Above, William H. Johnson, top right, Jim Baron/The Image Finders

admits she doesn't give her yucca any special attention and says it requires little maintenance.

"Patience is key because it takes a while for the yucca to bloom. Don't give up on it too early because when it does bloom, the beauty is so worth it," she says.

"Every year when it blooms, I have to go out and take another picture!"

Picking the right spot for yucca can be a challenge because of its bold features. *Birds & Blooms* gardening expert Melinda Myers suggests placing it with other low-maintenance plants that will help soften it, like the airy silhouette of threadleaf coreopsis.

Given its southern roots, it's not surprising that yucca is tolerant of heat and drought. Young yuccas can even survive as container plants in the typically dry conditions indoors. Adam's needle (*Yucca filamentosa*), Spanish dagger (*Yucca gloriosa*) and curve-leaf yucca (*Yucca recurvifolia*) are three varieties well suited to indoor planting, as long as they're placed near a sunny window.

New outdoor plantings, however, should be watered on a regular basis, but once established, yucca flourishes in dry, hot temperatures and can grow in many soil conditions as long as the location isn't too wet.

Growth Spurts

Just as Edie found out, the yucca might take a while to bloom, and once it does, there's no guarantee it'll bloom every year.

Jeanne Christensen, garden center manager at Shady Acres Perennial Nursery in New Berlin, Wisconsin, said the lack of flowers could be the result of a plant that's too immature to bloom. Another reason could be that the yucca basically is out of energy.

"One year it could put all its energy into blooming, then

Mark Turner   Kathy Adams Clark/KAC Productions

CAN'T MISS 'EM. The giant dagger yuccas in Texas' Big Bend National Park (above left) always attract attention. Above right, yucca's creamy flowers steal the show before finally forming unique seedpods. Above left is a close look at the foliage.

the next it may need to save energy," Jeanne says. "But that doesn't mean it's going to be every other year."

She said it all depends on the specific plant. Jeanne tells first-time yucca owners not to overwater it. Too many people think they need to give new perennials a lot of attention, but that is not the case with a yucca, she says.

"The yucca isn't used to that. It actually is better suited to an infertile, dry soil," Jeanne says.

The various species and cultivars of yucca have distinct looks and are grown in different places all over the country.

Some are classified as "stemless," which means the leaves emerge close to the ground, while others are the size of a small tree and may have multiple trunks with leaves.

A Flood of Varieties

The most common species is Adam's needle, which grows in Zones 4 and higher. This variety is stemless with

Plant Profile

Ben Phillips/Positive Images

Common Names: Yucca, Adam's needle, dagger plant.
Botanical Name: *Yucca species.*
Bloom Time: Mid- to late summer.
Hardiness: Zones 4 to 11, varies by species.
Height: 2 to 8 feet, varies by species.
Spread: 4 to 6 feet, varies by species.
Flower Color: White; some types tinged with green.
Flower Shape: Bell-shaped.
Light Needs: Full sun.
Soil Type: Well-drained.
Planting: To give the plants time to establish before winter, plant both bare-root and container-grown yuccas in spring or early summer.
Backyard Benefits: The flowers attract hummingbirds in summer and the dried seed- heads provide interest in the winter landscape.
Prize Picks: Yucca filamentosa is the most widely grown species, and its cultivars offer variegated leaves. Check your local nursery to find out what types grow best in your area.

tropical desert areas, as well as in southern Florida and much of coastal California. It certainly earns the name giant yucca. It can grow up to 30 feet tall and spread 15 to 25 feet wide!

There aren't many plants that surpass the yucca when it comes to providing backyard drama. This plant's strong vertical and horizontal features are hard to come by in other perennials.

It's just like Edie said, the wait for this beauty to bloom is well worth it. And even when it's not in flower, the yucca still is pretty striking!

Faith Bemis

rigid, dark-green leaves and white blooms that may be tinged with green or cream. The flowers are sometimes 2 to 3 inches wide and are lightly fragrant, especially in the evenings.

Several cultivars of Adam's needle offer slightly different leaf appearances and color patterns. 'Bright Edge' has leaves with broad yellow edges, 'Golden Sword' has yellow-centered leaves, and 'Variegata' has cream-edged leaves that are tinted pink in winter or colder weather.

Another common species that grows in much of the U.S. is the weakleaf yucca (*Yucca flaccida*). It grows everywhere but the high desert areas of the Southwest. The lance-shaped leaves are slightly less rigid than those of the Adam's needle and are dark blue-green. The flower clusters are shorter and creamy white. The 'Ivory Tower' variety has green-tinged blooms.

One impressive species, though not very common, is the giant yucca (*Yucca elephantipes*). This species grows only in the intermediate desert of Arizona and other low or sub-

FROM DESERT TO DECK. Yucca is an eye-catching choice for any garden. With its strappy leaves and beautiful, delicate blooms, you won't be disappointed in the show it provides. For unique pinkish blooms, try the *Yucca glauca* variety (right).

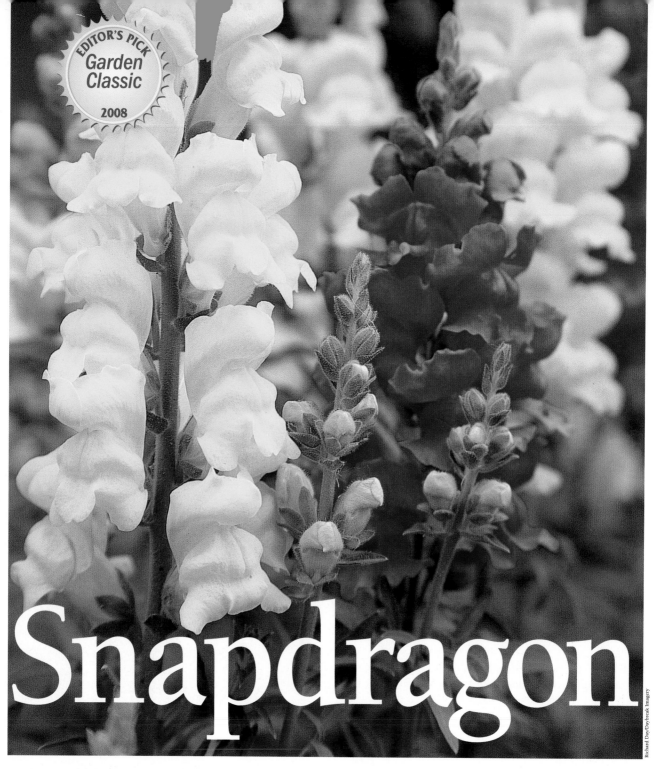

Snapdragon

This old-time favorite will add sizzle to your garden.

By Kathleen Zimmer-Anderson
Waukesha, Wisconsin

D id you know that snapdragons "roar"? When I was a girl, a neighbor showed me how to pinch the eye-catching tubular flower to make its "mouth" open and close.

After that, I spent the better part of a summer afternoon plucking individual snapdragon blossoms from my mother's flower garden. I would gently squeeze the sides of the top and bottom petal clusters as I made up quiet tales of brave knights battling these vividly colored "dragons."

Of course, I did hear loud cries when my mom caught me with a mountain of snapdragon blooms on my lap and a bunch of denuded snapdragon stems in the nearby flower bed!

To this day, I find snapdragons enchanting. And occa-

Plant Profile

Common Name:
Snapdragon.
Botanical Name:
Antirrhinum majus.
Bloom Time: Summer to fall; in areas with mild winters and hot summers, snapdragons will bloom in winter and spring.
Hardiness: Annual.
Flower Colors:
White, pink, purple, red, orange and yellow; some hybrid blooms are bicolored.
Flower Shape: Ruffled, tubular blooms that resemble jaws.
Height: 6 inches to 4 feet.
Spread: 6 inches to 2 feet.
Light Needs: Partial to full sun.
Soil Type: Moist, well-draining soil.
Planting: Seeds can be planted directly in flower beds as soon as the soil is workable. Or purchase nursery-grown hardened off snapdragons for spring planting.
Prize Picks: The 'Rocket' series produces heat-tolerant, tall snapdragons with flowers in a variety of colors that look great in the garden and in bouquets. 'Liberty' cultivars are intermediate in size and don't need staking. The 'Bells' cultivar is a dwarf variety that blooms early, turning out long-lasting, hyacinth-like flowers.

sionally, I still like to pull a blossom off of the plants I grow in my own backyard and make it snarl.

Legendary Looks

Snapdragons are easy to identify, thanks to the spikes of unusual, five-petaled flowers in a range of solid and bicolored hues. The blossoms are so distinctive that they have inspired other nicknames besides snapdragon, including toad's mouth, lion's mouth and dog's mouth.

The seedpods that appear after the flowers have a faded look like snouts and are responsible for snapdragon's botanical designation, *Antirrhinum*. The name comes from two Greek words—*anti*, which means "like," and *rhinos*, which means "snout."

A native of southern Europe, the snapdragon has long held a place in gardens from Greece and Italy to Great Britain, the U.S. and Canada. It was once cultivated in the Mediterranean for its seeds because they contain a lot of oil. The vibrant blooms, which come in pink, red, purple, white, orange and yellow, also helped dye fabric.

Today, there are some 30 to 40 species in the Antirrhinum family, the most popular of which is the common snapdragon (*Antirrhimun majus*). Common snapdragons come in a variety of shapes and sizes and fit in almost any kind of garden. Well-liked cultivars include the low-growing 'Floral Showers' series that reach 6 to 8 inches tall, and 'Bells,' another dwarf variety that provides long-lasting blooms in solid and bicolored shades.

The 'Sonnet' and 'Liberty' series are two prime medium-height selections. Both produce enduring blossoms that make nice cut flowers for bouquets.

As a rule, snapdragons don't favor hot conditions, although the 48-inch-tall 'Rocket' cultivars can handle heat. And if you want a different look, try the 'Madame Butterfly' variety. It grows to 36 inches and features rich, double blooms that resemble azaleas.

Easy to Grow

Snapdragons are treated as annuals, but these plants will often self sow, even in colder climates. When they do, the plants tend to bloom late in the season and fade quickly as summer heats up. This is why most gardeners consider them annuals and plant them yearly, instead of waiting around on blooms.

Once plants are established, water regularly and add a layer of mulch to keep roots cool. Fertilize early in the season if you like, but stop when the plants bloom, if the weather turns hot or dry, or if your snapdragons drop leaves and look stressed.

Tall varieties tend to topple. To avoid this, try staking or plant something sturdy next to them for support. Deadheading regularly before seedpods form will encourage any size snapdragon to keep on blooming.

Hot weather might temporarily halt blooming, but that doesn't mean the show is over. Simply prune any plants that have become overgrown or leggy and be patient. Come fall, when temperatures drop, you'll have another lavish display of color.

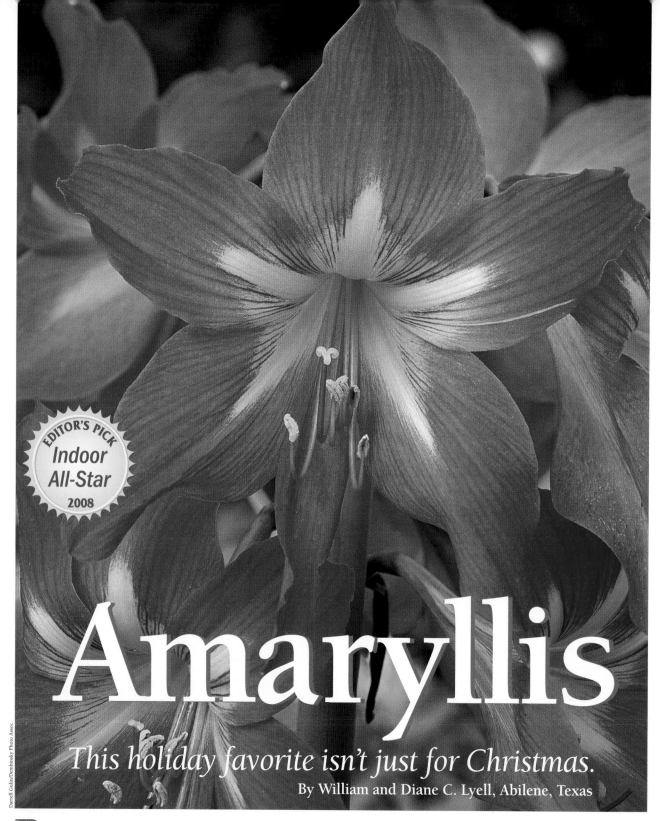

EDITOR'S PICK
Indoor
All-Star
2008

Darrell Gulin/Dembinsky Photo Assoc.

Amaryllis

This holiday favorite isn't just for Christmas.

By William and Diane C. Lyell, Abilene, Texas

Bold and bright...big and sassy...that's amaryllis! Few can resist these large, trumpet-shaped beauties during the drab days of winter. That's why millions become Christmas plants to add a burst of festive color during the holiday season.

But amaryllis aren't merely for Christmas. Here in Texas, we're able to enjoy ours year-round, and with a little effort, so can you.

This native of Central and South America derives its name from Greek and means "to shine." And, though it comes from a tropical environment, its popularity means it's easy to find just about anywhere plants are sold.

An Early Gift

The best selection is available on-line. A quick search will turn up fancy, large-blooming plants, miniature varieties, double bloomers, the unreal Cybister hybrids (with fantastic, spiderlike blooms) and the newest hybrids on the market.

Plant Profile

Common Name: Amaryllis.

Botanical Name: *Hippeastrum.*

Bloom Time: January through April.

Hardiness: Generally grown as a houseplant.

Flower Colors: White, pink, salmon, red, orange, green and yellow; some hybrids have bicolor blooms.

Flower Shape: Funnel or trumpet-shaped blossoms; both single and double flowering varieties.

Height: 1 to 3 feet.

Light Needs: Full sun or bright, filtered light.

Soil Type: A well-draining potting mix.

Planting: Plant from November to February in a container that is 1 to 2 inches wider than the bulb. Use a rich potting mix and make sure the bulb's shoulders are just above the soil surface. Water plants sparingly until rapid growth begins.

Special Care and Propagation: After flowering is complete, remove flower stalks. Apply a dilute solution of flowering-plant fertilizer every other week or as needed while foliage grows, usually for 3 to 5 months. By midsummer, reduce watering or stop completely to allow the bulb to become dormant.

Prize Picks: 'Star of Holland' has large red blooms with white star shapes in the center. 'Picotee' produces showy white flowers with red margins, and 'Lady Jane' offers double rosy apricot flowers with white stripes.

Warning: All parts of the amaryllis are poisonous.

Diane C. Lyell.

NATURAL DECORATIONS. Bold hues make amaryllis a perfect holiday accent, and they are very popular container-grown plant. Above are the Red Lion, Lady Jane and Aphrodite varieties.

Once you've selected a variety, buy the biggest bulbs possible. Why? The larger the bulb, the more blooms you get! Large, mature bulbs can produce as many as four outstanding flowers per scape, or flower stalk.

Because amaryllis traditionally are associated with Christmas, fall is the best time to buy bulbs. We pick up new varieties in October and November and plant them in clay pots that allow 1 to 1-1/2 inches of space around the bulb. Amaryllis prefer to be pot-bound, with only the top portions, or shoulders, of the bulbs above the soil.

About 6 to 8 weeks after planting new bulbs, we have colorful blooming plants all over the house for Christmas and New Year's celebrations. When spring comes, we move the plants to the backyard, where they serve as container plants. Their tall, broad leaves provide an architectural profusion of green.

Because we live in Texas, we don't need to bring all our amaryllis inside for winter. Instead, we stop watering them as our freeze date approaches, and move them to the south side of the house where we cover the pots with 4 to 6 inches of straw. When spring arrives, we remove the straw, and the plants produce blossoms about 2 months later.

In colder climates, however, amaryllis must be brought inside to keep them alive once the temperature starts to drop. Straw won't protect them from severe winter cold.

Cold-Weather Success

In these regions, store your amaryllis in a place that maintains a constant 55° temperature. Make sure to keep them away from light and don't water them—the plants need this dormant period to recharge and bloom again.

If you'd like to coax them to rebloom at Christmas, you'll need to keep them in this cool, dim place for 6 to 8 weeks. Then move the pots to a bright window that receives at least 4 hours of direct sun each day. Water them thoroughly when the soil starts to dry. In another 6 to 8 weeks, you'll have an armful of gorgeous blooms.

Forcing amaryllis to rebloom isn't easy, but if you're up for a challenge, the bright colors of a success make it worth your efforts.

Amaryllis come in a varied array of shapes, sizes and hues that are sure to please the pickiest plant lover. Best of all, you can influence when your bulbs bloom—whether you want blooms amid the snow and cold of winter, or on a balmy spring day. You can even do both if you like!

179

176

182

170

180

CHAPTER 6

ALL ABOUT HUMMINGBIRDS

Hummingbirds Quiz   172

Feed Hummingbirds
by Hand   174

Rufous Hummingbird   176

Did You Know?   179

A Hobby That Took Over   180

Hummer Happenings   182

Photos this page: left, Jim Sloanaker; below, Anthony Mercieca; opposite page, clockwise from top left: ruby-throated, Maslowski Productions; rufous, Charles W. Melton; long-tailed sylph, Allen Chartier; ruby-throated, Michelle Earle

174

172

1

Name That Hummingbird

How well do you know these migrating marvels?

Story by George Harrison, Contributing Editor—Photos by Anthony Mercieca

Hummingbirds are one of the most sought-after feeder birds in the world. They're unlike any other backyard visitor—they look like flying jewels, act like insects, hover like helicopters, entertain like circus performers, eat with a "needle" and fight like bullies.

In fall, North American hummingbirds are on the move, migrating from their summer breeding grounds in the North to their winter retreats in the tropics. This means that hummingbirds of all types may be passing through backyards to sip a little sugar water here and there.

The adults are the first to leave in late summer. Then, at the end of September, the juvenile hummers follow, even though most have never flown farther than the backyard next door.

So, during migration, how do the young birds know where to fly? This question has boggled humans for ages.

We know that it is the amount of light, or really the lack of it, that signals their departure. But how do they know what direction to go? And how do they know when they've arrived to their winter homes?

The scientific answer is that they are genetically programmed, but this seems too simple to me. I prefer to let the

feat remain one of the most amazing mysteries in nature.

While there are at least 319 hummingbird species in the world, there's only 18 that enter the United States and Canada. And of those, only eight travel to regions well north of Mexico.

For most of the country, the ruby-throated hummingbird is most common, since it's the only one that regularly nests in the eastern half of the United States. Don't give up hope on seeing others, though. Migration season occasionally brings a rare visitor to the backyard.

If you did have an unusual hummingbird species stop at your sugar-water feeder, would you know what it was? We're putting you to the test in this month's quiz. Match the photos on these pages to the species listed below left.

2

ALLEN'S	CALLIOPE
ANNA'S	COSTA'S
BLACK-CHINNED	MAGNIFICENT
BROAD-BILLED	RUBY-THROATED
BROAD-TAILED	RUFOUS

Want to FEED HUMMINGBIRDS by HAND?

You're three steps away from making it happen.

By Dave Sapienza, McArthur, Ohio

Hear at Lake Hope State Park, we like to think that we've started a phenomenon.

It all began more than 10 years ago when I was outside, replenishing the sugar water in one of our hummingbird feeders. As the park naturalist, attracting birds to our area is one of my favorite parts of the job.

I reached up to hang the feeder when a ruby-throated hummingbird zoomed in for a drink. I stood frozen, watching in awe as the bird sipped from the feeder in my hand. At that moment, I knew I was onto something.

We started hand-feeding hummingbirds around the nature center where I work, and in 2002, it became an official program in the park. Now, we have hundreds of visitors each year, eager to join in during feeding time. We estimate that during any given program, roughly half the participants will attract a hummingbird to their hand-held feeder.

Some people try different tricks to lure hummingbirds to their feeder—brightly colored shirts, red hats and floral bracelets. You name it, and someone has tried it. From my experience, though, I don't know what kind of impact the different techniques have. Many times, our visiting

174

hummingbirds don't seem to have any rhyme or reason for which feeder they choose to stop at.

Do you want to hand-feed hummingbirds? We'd love to have you visit us the next time you're in Ohio. Until then, here's our three-step program that you can try at home to increase your chance of success.

1 Choose the Right Feeder. We've tested many sugar-water feeders over the years, and we finally found a winner from the company First Nature. Even if you don't buy from this company, they provide good criteria for what you should look for in a sugar-water feeder.

One of the features we like about our feeders is that they are all plastic with red parts that don't fade in the sunlight. They also come apart in three pieces, which exposes all part for easy cleaning. Plus, the feeder itself has a wide mouth, which helps with cleaning, too.

Perhaps one of the best features of it is that there are no yellow parts that may attract bees. Finally, the feeders have comfortable perches 360 degrees around, so there's always plenty of room.

2 Get the Right Mix. We use a mixture of four parts water to one part sugar, and we do not add red food coloring. The red on the feeders is enough to attract the hummingbirds, so why use another product that isn't necessary?

We know it's simple, but our method seems to be working. We go through more than 50 pounds of sugar each year!

3 Have a Little Patience. There is no magic involved when it comes to attracting hummingbirds to feed from your hand, though it does require patience.

First, get the hummingbirds in your area used to your feeders that are already hanging. Once they are comfortable, begin taking your feeders down for 10 minutes at a time. Put them out of sight, and then begin offering nectar with a floral hand-feeding tube. Try to hold it close to where your regular feeder usually hangs.

Don't give up if they don't come right away. They'll be curious at first, and it might take them a few times to build up the courage to drink from your hand-held feeder.

Now you should have everything you need to feed hummingbirds by hand. The first two steps are easy. It's the final requirement—patience—that will make you most successful.

Jim Slonaker

Readers' Hand-Feeding Tips

When we don the hat, we get a real bird's-eye view of the hungry hummers.
—*Tommy Crawford*
Yorktown, Indiana

Perfect Perch
My children and I learned that if we rest our fingers on the perches of our hummingbird feeders, the birds will readily perch on them as they drink the sugar water (below). The experience is amazing! —*Debbie Eberting*
Clinton, Missouri

Make-Your-Own Feeder
I found a way to make a handheld hummingbird feeder from household items. Glue a red piece of fabric or a plastic flower to the top of a film canister and pierce a hole through both the flower and lid. Fill the canister with sugar water, cap it up and remove your active hummingbird feeder. Then stand still and wait for the hummingbirds to discover the treat.
—*Betty Pierce*
Slaterville Springs, New York

An Old Hat Trick
My wife, Linda, and I have developed a fun way to view hummingbirds up close. We took a wire coat hanger, bent it into a "cup holder" and attached it to an old red baseball hat (that's Linda above). Then we secured a red plastic bottle top upside down at the far end of the holder and filled it with sugar water.

These golden fliers know no boundaries.

By George Harrison
Contributing Editor

RUFOUS HUMMINGBIRD

Mary Plimpton will never forget the day a rufous hummingbird visited her Springfield, Virginia backyard.

"You can imagine my surprise when I looked out my window and saw this odd-looking hummingbird hovering over my pineapple sage," she says. "It wasn't the typical ruby-throat that I'm accustomed to seeing."

Mary looked up the bird's range and found that while it mostly stays in the West, it's not rare for the birds to migrate through the East, especially along the coasts.

This is just one of the things that makes the rufous special. These golden-throated jewels are the most abundant of all western hummingbirds. They are in virtually every backyard and garden from the Rocky Mountains west to the Pacific Coast.

They are also the most northern nesting hummingbird in the world, making it all the way to southern Alaska in summer.

Power in Numbers

Years ago, I was producing a PBS special in the Northwest about bird gardens, when I got to witness the abundance of rufous hummingbirds firsthand. We were working in several yards where rufous were common. I'll never forget how those tiny jewels kept the gardens bustling with visits to flowers and sugar-water feeders. They buzzed here and there, chasing, courting, building nests and feeding young, from sunup to sundown.

The spectacular coloring of the rufous is another reason this bird is unique. It is the only North American hummingbird with a solid rufous back. In fact, these brownish-red birds are often mistaken for Allen's hummingbirds, but the rufous backs on the males give them away.

The females of these two species are a little trickier to distinguish. They look nearly identical. The way to tell them apart is the tail. Rufous hummingbirds have broader tail feathers with notched tips.

On its breeding grounds in the Northwest, the male rufous has a temper to match his fiery appearance. He is pugnacious and seems to delight in fighting with other birds, not only in the vicinity of the nest, but also while feeding, flying or just perching.

His emotions are no less dramatic when it comes to mating, including his dazzling courtship. I like to think of him as the Evil Knievel of the bird world. I've watched a male rufous rocket from high in the sky to the ground, checking his flight just a few inches from a perching female. He's a daredevil all right—and puts on quite a show at the same time.

A Feathered "Friend"

Many of us who feed hummingbirds have stories about how the birds return to the exact same spot where the feeders hung the year before. Hummingbird expert and author Alexander Skutch tells one of my favorite stories about the friendship between an ill artist and a male rufous hummingbird.

"During the year that the artist Arthur Fitzpatrick lay sick in a California sanatorium, he had a feeder hung outside his bedroom window where he could watch the feathered visitors. After the usual skirmishing, a male rufous hummingbird won firm possession of it as his 'feeding territory' and spent much of his time there, sipping syrup and chasing away intruders."

Skutch goes on to write how the hummingbird's presence helped speed up Fitzpatrick's recovery. When he was

---

A FLASH OF ORANGE. Warm-brown feathers and a bright-orange throat make the rufous stand out from fellow hummingbirds, many of which are green. The males (at left and below) exhibit the most distinct and brilliant coloring, while the juveniles (above right) and the females have the rufous hue only on their sides.

Backyard Birding Bio

Common Name: Rufous hummingbird.
Scientific Name: *Selasphorus rufus.*
Length: 3-3/4 inches.
Wingspan: 4-1/2 inches.
Distinctive Markings: Male has a brownish-red back, burnished-gold throat patch, white bib and green shoulders. Female has a green back and lacks the golden throat, though she may have some gold throat spots.
Voice: The call note is a soft chip; in flight, the male's wings make a distinct trilling buzz or whistle.
Nesting: Nest site may be the low-drooping branches of conifers, vines or the roots of upturned trees. The nest is a tiny cup of plant fibers, mosses, lichens and spider silk.

Two white, bean-sized eggs comprise a set, which the female alone incubates for 12 days. The young, often too large for the nest, leave in about 20 days.

Diet: Red flowers are especially attractive to rufous hummingbirds for both nectar and insects. Columbines, penstemons, tiger lilies and paintbrushes on alpine meadows are their favorites.
Backyard Favorite: Hummingbird feeders containing sugar water.

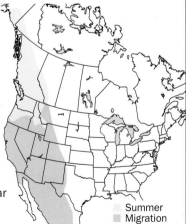

■ Summer
■ Migration

GREEN THUMB TIP

Like all hummingbirds, the rufous is attracted to red blooms. Some good flowers to plant include columbines, penstemons, tiger lilies, paintbrushes, bee balm, honeysuckle, cannas, geraniums, cardinal flower, primrose and phlox.

outside, the hummingbird even flew around his head and hovered in front of his eyes.

As the story goes, on the day Fitzpatrick returned home, the same rufous that had visited his feeder followed him to his house 8 miles away. The artist and hummingbird continued their visits. Every day, Fitzpatrick took a walk, and his rufous friend was never far away. He enjoyed the company and always had something to look forward to.

Though Skutch admits the whole thing sounds like a fairy tale, he says it somehow rings true. "It's about the best hummingbird story I know," he says.

In the Backyard

Like many hummingbirds, the rufous is attracted to red blooms. Good flowers to plant include columbines, penstemons, tiger lilies and paintbrushes.

Rufous nests are usually on drooping branches of conifers, 5 to 50 feet above the ground. Don't expect to find them easily, though. At less than 2 inches in diameter and decorated with lichens and spider silk, they blend into the surroundings.

If you look at the range map, you'll see that in summer, the best place to spot a rufous is in the far Northwest. However, don't let that stop you from looking for these hummingbirds in your garden. You never know when they'll be passing through.

Remember that lone rufous in Mary Plimpton's yard? It ended up staying through the winter...she kept a heat light over the feeder so it wouldn't freeze. The experience made Mary a hummingbird fan for life, and now she always keeps her eye out for them, hoping for another rufous sighting.

"The experience certainly cemented my interest in hummingbirds," Mary writes. "I even decided to change my license plate to RUFOUS."

GATHER 'ROUND. Above right, a male rufous hummingbird lands on a sugar-water feeder while a female tends to her nestlings. Below, juvenile and female hummingbirds eat their fill.

Sid and Shirley Rucker

Sid and Shirley Rucker

Alan G. Nelson/Dembinsky Photo Assoc.

Did You Know?

You won't believe the things hummingbirds can do!

Remarkable. Amazing. Extraordinary. Magnificent. With words like these commonly used to describe hummingbirds, it's no wonder *Birds & Blooms* readers are so captivated by these jewels of the sky.

So what makes the birds so impressive? We thought you'd never ask! Take a look at some of these fascinating facts. This is one impressive resume.

Donna Ikenberry

While resting, a hummingbird takes 250 breaths per minute.

Hummingbirds can't fly until their body temperature reaches 86°.

Hummingbirds have large flight muscles, about 25% of their body weight.

Hummingbirds are named for the sound their wings make while they fly.

To survive, hummingbirds must drink almost twice their weight in nectar every day.

Hummingbird eggs are about the size of jelly beans.

Rolf Nussbaumer

The average hummingbird nest is about 2 inches in diameter.

Hummingbirds' wings move in a figure-eight pattern. This allows the birds to hover and fly in all directions—even upside down!

Maslowski Productions

Providing a light mist of water is a great way to attract hummingbirds to your backyard.

Even at rest, a hummingbird's heart rate is eight times faster than that of a human.

The Cuban bee hummingbird is the smallest warm-blooded animal in the world. The male weighs less than a dime.

Hummingbirds show they are "on guard" by ruffling their crown feathers.

The oldest hummingbird recorded was 14 years old.

Male hummingbirds don't help raise their young.

It would take 150 average-sized male hummingbirds to equal 1 pound.

Hummingbirds have 40 to 60 taste buds. Humans possess about 10,000.

Hummingbirds do not migrate in flocks. They fly alone.

Hummingbirds beat their wings about 50 times a second, so they appear as a blur.

A hummingbird's tongue has grooves on the sides to help it catch insects.

Maslowski Productions

Hummingbirds have about 1,500 feathers.

Hummingbirds have weak feet and legs. They use them only for perching and preening.

Thanks to excellent memories, hummingbirds often return to the same flowers or feeders year after year.

Ben Clewis

Photo: Marvin Catoor/The Image Finders

All About Hummingbirds

A HOBBY THAT TOOK OVER

This Michigan birder has been all over the world in search of "flying jewels."

By Stacy Tornio, Managing Editor

When Allen Chartier was 8 years old, he made a life-changing decision: Dinosaurs and outer space were out...it was time to shift his interest to birds.

"My uncle had a big influence on me growing up," Allen says. "He was a bird-watcher and used to tell me about all the interesting birds he saw during his service in World War II. It was so intriguing to hear those stories."

Interest Takes Flight

At 11, Allen had his own set of binoculars and a bird book. With those, he could name most of the birds in his neighborhood.

Over the years, Allen's love for birds grew, and he began developing a fascination for hummingbirds.

"I'm into pretty colors," Allen said. "I marvel at the shiny, iridescent greens and red throats of ruby-throated hummingbirds."

It's not just ruby-throats (like the one above) that Allen loves, even though it is the only hummingbird that regu-

larly frequents his Inkster, Michigan backyard. He and his wife, Nancy, have traveled to 28 countries and have seen nearly half of the world's 339 hummingbird species.

One of their favorites is the Ecuadorian hillstar, a hummingbird in Ecuador known for hanging upside down on flowers. The wedge-tailed saber wing is another interesting hummingbird that they came across in Mexico. Allen describes this bird as having a unique song with a long, gurgling twitter.

"It was one of the most unbelievable sounds I've ever heard from a bird," he says.

The more Allen learned about hummingbirds, the more captivated he became. As he looked around for research on hummingbirds in his area, there was a lot miss-

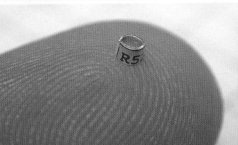

THE RIGHT TOOLS. When banding, Allen (opposite page) uses a tiny band (center left) that fits around a hummingbird's leg. While he mostly handles ruby-throats (like the one he's holding between his fingers at far left), he has traveled around the world to see other hummingbirds. Some of his favorites include the Ecuadorian hillstar (immediate left), the chestnut-breasted coronet (top left) and long-tailed sylph (above).

ing. Allen couldn't find the kind of information he was after, so he took matters into his own hands.

"That's when I started the Great Lakes Hummer Net, and I became a licensed hummingbird bander," Allen said. "Since 2000, I've banded hundreds of hummingbirds."

Allen travels all over Michigan, Indiana and Ohio to band hummingbirds at parks, nature centers and even private backyards.

He catches them in special traps, then bands them in less than 2 minutes. *Birds & Blooms* reader Carl Pascoe hosted Allen at his house to band more than 50 hummingbirds on his balcony in West Bloomfield, Michigan.

Where Have You Been?

"Our hope is that one day a bird banded on our balcony will be recaptured by another bander somewhere along its migration route," Carl says. "This will add an-

other piece to the puzzle of where these amazing little creatures travel in their remarkable journeys."

Banding isn't all the Great Lakes Hummer Net does. Allen says his organization serves as a resource for all hummingbird fans in the area.

"I want people to send me their observations related to nesting, arrival time, migration, etc. of hummingbirds," Allen says. "This will help me learn more about all of the hummingbirds in the region."

While Allen mostly sees ruby-throats in his area, he always keeps his eye out for the rare appearances of others. He's banded a handful of rufous hummingbirds, and has also heard of sightings of an Anna's in Ohio and a black-chinned in Indiana.

"I get to see some pretty amazing things," Allen says. "This is just a hobby, but it's also the kind of hobby that takes over."

All About Hummingbirds

HUMMER HAPPENINGS

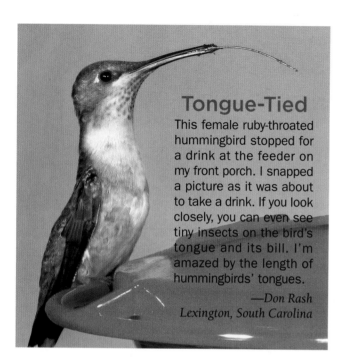

Tongue-Tied

This female ruby-throated hummingbird stopped for a drink at the feeder on my front porch. I snapped a picture as it was about to take a drink. If you look closely, you can even see tiny insects on the bird's tongue and its bill. I'm amazed by the length of hummingbirds' tongues.

—*Don Rash*
Lexington, South Carolina

Back to Basics

At our home in the mountains of northwestern Arizona, we've been blessed to have seen five of the 14 hummingbird species known to visit the state.

We regularly see hummingbirds like Anna's, black-chinned, broad-tailed and rufous. Last fall, a single blue-throated hummingbird stopped by for a few days on its way south for winter. We quickly flipped through our bird guide and recognized the hummingbird right away.

As we spent time confirming its individual physical characteristics, we later realized we didn't take a moment to simply appreciate the bird's beauty. It's easy to fixate on details and forget about the rest.

After that encounter, I took this photo of a hummingbird at dusk (above right). The silhouette of its proud form and long bill reminds me of the beauty all hummingbirds share. I don't even know what species this is, but it doesn't matter.

—*Susan Mather, Kingman, Arizona*

Crazy About Redheads

I've always loved to work outside where I can see nature up close and personal. I remember how the hummingbirds flocked to our backyard when we lived in North Carolina.

My hair was auburn, with just enough red to interest the hummingbirds. On several occasions, my feathered friends would buzz around my head, as if they were searching for nectar in my hair.

Those sweeties would happily play in my hair as I hung laundry out on the clothesline. Now, as the weather is turning colder, I like to think of those hummingbirds flitting around my yard. It always gives me warm memories!

—*Georgia K. Lawson*
St. Paul, Virginia

He Had Birds and Brooms

We put a hummingbird feeder by our front porch one year and attracted two hummingbirds. The next year we added three more feeders and saw six hummingbirds. We spend a lot of time sitting on the front porch watching them feed. The hummer wars get very interesting and funny.

One afternoon we discovered that one of them found her way into the garage and couldn't get out. My 8-year-old son, Cody, wanted desperately to help our little friend. He got out a soft-bristle broom and held it in the air. Eventually, the hummingbird landed on it (above left). He was so excited. He proudly carried the hummingbird outside to release it. The bird flew away and then came back and landed on his broom again, as if to say "thank you."

—*Charity Hutnnick, Dillsburg, Pennsylvania*

A Rare Opportunity

Long ago at our cabin in Colorado, we learned how to get hummingbirds to sit on our fingers as they fed. We taught our children and grandchildren the trick, too.

No one was as surprised as we were when our granddaughter Lydia (left) not only had a hummingbird sit on her finger, but was able to pet it as well!

—*Nancy Smith, Marysville, Kansas*

Beak-to-Beak

While bird-watching in Stokes State Forest, a hummingbird suddenly appeared at eye level, hovering about 3 feet away and looking directly at me. As I stood motionless, it gradually moved to within 1 foot of my face and then moved around my head, carefully examining me.

It then flew up to the top of my head for about 15 seconds. After a rest, it continued its inspection. We were literally "beak-to-beak," and I could feel the air from its beating wings. The bird then inserted its bill into my left nostril, paused for a couple seconds, moved back, then examined my right nostril before abruptly departing.

In my 40 years of observing birds, this ranks as one of the most unusual experiences that I have encountered.

—*Charles Pozzi, Denville, New Jersey*

Smile and Say, "Sugar Water"

My husband, Dean, and I are avid hummingbird watchers. Recently, we replaced our French doors with a sliding glass door to make a larger area in which to watch the birds.

We never thought this would cause the reflection to be different, but it did. While sitting in our living room, we would hear a thump every now and then, not really sure what it was. We finally discovered that the birds were flying into the new door!

After hearing a thump one day, we went out to find a hummingbird lying in the dog food dish. I wasn't sure what to do, so I reached down and picked up the little bird.

The bird seemed to pose for us, and it sat in my hand (above) until I placed it in a flower. I'm not sure who had the best time during this experience—my husband taking the pictures, me holding the hummer, or the hummer posing for its photo shoot!

—*Linda Russell Ruffin, North Carolina*

Late Start

My daughter and I were getting ready for work when we heard a thud on our door. I went outside to find a ruby-throated hummingbird dazed from hitting the door.

I picked it up to see if it was still alive, and it attempted to fly, landing on the tire of my car. I needed to get going to work, so I tried to approach it. When I did, the bird flew off and landed on my window ledge with its bill open, as if it wasn't getting enough air.

I ran inside and got a small bowl and filled it with water for the bird, and it jumped onto the back of my hand (below). The hummingbird then took a few drinks of the water before launching off my hand, circling my head three times and flying off. —*Linda Dykstra*
Camden, Tennessee

Reader Tip: To keep birds from flying into windows and doors, there are a number of ways to break up the reflection. You can hang items in front of the window (string or plastic streamers work well), use window decals, or rub soap on the outside of the glass.

LOYAL HARRY

By Lee Strickland
Columbus, Mississippi

A day in early March proved to be a very emotional day in my life. I had just learned that my father had been diagnosed with terminal cancer. On that sad day, I also met a new friend.

Gazing out my kitchen window, I thought about Dad and all of the great years we spent together. As I reminisced, a little ruby-throated hummingbird (like the one above) appeared at my window and pecked at the screen. There weren't any insects on the window, so I figured he was trying to get my attention to bring him some food.

I dug out a plastic feeder and started to get it ready for him. As I gathered the feeder and food, "Harry," as I named him, followed me around the house from window to window.

I put the feeder in a tree and Harry drank for a while. The whole day, he stayed by my side. As I weeded, he followed me—especially enjoying my honeysuckle vine and foxgloves.

While I was sipping my coffee the next morning on the patio, Harry returned and boldly landed on the arm of my chair. That summer, I spent many days being entertained by my new friend. During Harry's stay, I purchased six hummingbird feeders and used about 75 pounds of sugar. Every year since, Harry has been the first of the hummingbirds to arrive, and the last to leave. He always brings many friends. The year my father passed away, I had more hummingbirds than I could ever imagine. I estimated over 100 birds were in my yard at one time.

One year, March rolled around again, and as usual, Harry appeared at my kitchen window. I put out the feeders, but I think Harry sensed that something was wrong as he flew erratically around me. My mother had recently passed away, and I guess Harry could tell I was sad. Once again, he stuck close to me all day and throughout the summer.

Harry would bring more friends each year. Whenever I would exchange an empty feeder for a full one, all of them would fly away to nearby trees or shrubs—except Harry, who perched on my hat or shoulder.

When I'm out on the patio, Harry hops on the rim of my coffee cup, the table or the arm of my chair. At times I wonder if he's trying to talk to me. He always makes the first move, and I respond by telling him how happy he has made me.

Because of Harry, we have dozens of hummingbirds. Many of them will only stay for several days and then leave—but Harry stays for the whole summer.

I imagine Harry is now an aged bird. It will be a sad year when his friends return without him.

Can't Trick a Hummer

One day, I was trying to get a natural-looking photograph of the hummingbirds that feed in my backyard. I exchanged the feeder with a hanging ivy geranium, hoping to catch them feeding there instead.

The change completely confused the hummingbirds. They flitted around the patio, looking for the feeder and ignoring the flowers.

It turns out, I didn't move the feeder far enough away… because they found it! One hummer flew circles around it (perhaps wondering how the feeder got there). Then it flew up to me, chattered and flew away. It seemed like I'd just been chastised.

I learned my lesson that day. I'll never replace their feeders with flowers again!

—*Virginia Allen*
Batesville, Indiana

Five-Star Restaurant

EDITOR'S PICK — Creative Dining 2008

My son, John, has been legally blind since he was a small child, but he loves taking pictures. This photo (right) is one of my favorites.

He always feeds hummingbirds using small goblets filled with sugar water on the rail of his deck.

And the birds let John know how much they like the attention and star treatment by seemingly posing for photos!

—*Lela Relaford*
Olalla, Washington

'THIS IS OUR FEEDER'

By Regina Hitchcock, St. Johns, Arizona

Bertha Bridge

I love hummingbirds.

There's just no two ways about it. Whether they are fighting each other off, flying in circles over my head as I fill a feeder, or just peacefully sipping at my petunias, I love their antics.

Last summer, a bright-orange rufous hummingbird (like the one at left) ruled the roost. His shimmery, copper-colored throat glistened in the sun as he sipped nectar from a sugar-water feeder and flew off to chase rival birds.

When he wasn't chasing other hummingbirds, "Big Red" (my name for him) would sit on the wire above my pole bean tower or on top of my bench. Many days I would sit and watch him for hours at a time.

As summer went by, the birds visited my feeders less as native wildflowers grew more plentifully. I actually had to empty nectar from feeders every few days because they simply weren't drinking it fast enough.

One of those times, I reached up to pull a half-empty feeder from the hanger, and seven birds suddenly decided I was invading their space. Birds flew at me and over me. One even circled so menacingly that I thought twice about reaching for the second feeder.

When I did reach for it, two birds began sipping from it as it was dangling from my fingers. I waited until they were finished, then walked away. I came back later to clean and refill that one.

After I was done with both feeders, and the hummingbirds had fresh nectar, they finally seemed to realize that I meant no harm and let me pass in peace.

But I'll never forget the day I was "under attack."

Welcome Wagon

When we moved to our new home a few years ago, I put up a sugar-water feeder (right), hoping hummingbirds would find it. By the end of that summer, two hummingbirds visited it regularly. And to my excitement, the number has increased each year. I am now up to three feeders and grow a lot of brightly colored flowers to meet the demand. Some of the hummers are very attentive and let us know when we aren't keeping the feeders filled.

And if we wear bright clothing, they will sometimes buzz close to us to see if we're flowers. It gives us quite a start, but we're so happy to share our home with them.
—Brandi Tellin, Blairstown, Missouri

The More, the Merrier

One day in early summer, while my husband and I were sitting in our living room, we noticed the hummingbirds swarming around the feeders like bees.

This behavior is more typical in late August before the birds migrate from our Colorado mountains for warmer climates. But here they were, as many as 12 hummers sharing the feeder at one time or hovering as they waited their turn!

Every few minutes, a squabble would erupt and they would disappear for a minute, then return and start all over again.
—Julia Francis
Evergreen, Colorado

Early Bird

It was still pretty early for the hummingbirds to arrive, but in March, I noticed one scoping out my backyard, looking for food. I rushed to set up one of my feeders with sugar water.

The next weekend, it snowed, but this little guy had plenty to eat (below). Luckily, spring weather followed soon after.
—Michelle Showalter
Prescott, Arizona

Not quite...

Closer...

Kathy Dewine

UNINVITED GUESTS

T he red hummingbird feeder appeared innocent enough as I lifted it from its Christmas wrappings. No pretending was necessary as I expressed my gratitude to the student who had given me the gift. In fact, I could hardly wait to try my luck at hosting hummingbirds.

When spring came, I mixed up the powdered nectar that came with the feeder. Within a week, several hummingbirds began daily visits to sip the sugar water.

Then the problems began to arise.

Winged Party Crashers

First, yellow jackets (top left) discovered my tasty nectar. Our hummers shied away when the wasps were drinking. Sometimes, I found our neighborhood woodpecker sitting on the barbeque grill, guzzling sugar water from the feeder. To solve both problems, I purchased a new feeder with bee guards over each opening and a wire for hanging.

When the supply of powdered nectar was gone, I borrowed a friend's recipe for sugar water and started making my own.

I believed my worries were over until I saw wood ants traipsing down the wire that supported the feeder.

Those rascals like sugar water, too? I gasped.

The ants could crawl right through the bee guards, causing our hummers to back away.

Something had to be done.

Then I thought of greasing the wire at the top of the hummingbird feeder with petroleum jelly. Slathering on every smidgen of sticky jelly the wire could hold, I created a barrier no ant could cross.

Finally!

Steve Gardner

Finally, all of my feeder problems were solved! Or so I thought.

That red-bellied woodpecker (above) soon discovered it could cling to the perches at the bottom and suck the feeder half dry at a single "clinging."

How can one feeder attract so many problems? I fumed.

Marching out to battle, I played my final card. I unscrewed the perches.

That did it!

No wasps, ants or woodpeckers have been able to steal our hummingbird nectar for the past few years.

Worth the Wait

Every April, as soon as we see the first tiny visitor (like the ruby-throated, above) hovering near the kitchen window, we fill the feeder and hang it in the exact same location as the year before.

And if we happen to forget, the anxious hummers fly over to the window as if to say, "We're here...and we're thirsty!"

—*Juanita Rayburn Blanton*
Beeville, Texas

Downtime Entertainment

I work at a fire station that's surrounded by pine trees. One of the guys at the station put up hummingbird feeders in the trees to entertain the firefighters on slow afternoons.

Before long, our little friends arrived, and one of them built a nest in a pine tree. After watching the nest for about 30 minutes, I was able to get this great picture (left).

—*Ken Winfield, Millington, Tennessee*

EDITOR'S PICK
Magic Moment
2008

FLIGHT SCHOOL

Leaving the nest must be a scary but thrilling time for hummingbirds. For 4 hours, I observed as two juvenile black-chinned hummers attempted to take flight.

I realized that although the two appeared almost identical (above), they were perfect opposites. One of them was a lot more audacious than the other. As I watched, the daring bird launched out in a fluttering fall into a wall.

The young bird seemed all right as it bounced and skipped along the ground. But I was afraid that the neighbor's cat might interfere, so I picked the bird up and placed it back in the nest.

That first crash must have had no ill effects, because the bird flew in short trips from fence to trees and back again, until it settled halfway up a eucalyptus tree.

The cautious one watched, looking a bit uneasy. The mother jetted back and forth from the hummingbird feeder to the nest, feeding the cautious juvenile. Whenever she could locate the bold one, she fed it, too. Finally, the cautious fledgling fluttered down to a trellis wire 3 feet below. It hung on with a tight grip, righted itself and began preening. The mother buzzed in to feed it, then went back to the feeder to tank up to feed the bold one in the eucalyptus tree. Between feedings over the next 2 hours, the cautious one preened and practiced flapping (above). Its awkwardness was hilarious.

Whether from loneliness or desperation, the cautious one let go and lifted off, landing with a plop on a nearby palm frond. After a short rest, the bird joined its nest mate in the tree. They both graduated from flight school.

—*Mark Weinrich, Mesquite, Nevada*

CHAPTER 7

PLAN A GREAT GARDEN

Life of a Plant Hunter	190
Secrets to Grow on	194
Santa's Garden	196
Country Retreat	199
Best Garden Ideas	202

THE LIFE OF A Plant Hunter

You don't have to be an expert to find the "mutants" in your garden.

By Stacy Tornio, Managing Editor

For years, Mike Arnold encouraged his students to go out into the plant world and "hunt" for new varieties of wildflowers.

As a professor in the horticulture department at Texas A&M University, Mike knew that researchers are always developing and improving plants to appeal to backyard gardeners. And he wanted his students to get a taste of what the process takes.

Pretty soon, Mike's students turned his own advice back on him. "Why don't you try to develop new varieties, too?" they asked.

Mike didn't have a good answer, so he took them up on the challenge. Along with some help from graduate students, Mike began collecting seeds from wildflowers

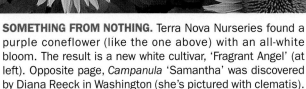

growing along the side of the road. Today, he receives credit for discovering *Helenium amarum* 'Dakota Gold' (pictured below left), a type of sneezeweed that is compact and heat tolerant—perfect for everyday gardeners.

"We wanted it to be a low-maintenance bedding plant for the garden," Mike says. "It just needed a little work from its current form in the wild."

It took a few years, but Mike and his team finally got the flower into a fairly uniform plant. They weren't able to complete the genetics required for developing a new plant, so they turned 'Dakota Gold' over to the Ball Discoveries program. Ball Horticultural Company runs it in an effort to encourage new discoveries in gardening.

"We licensed our current research with Ball, and then they made our vision come to life," Mike says. "And to think—it all started with some students who were trying to make me eat my own words."

Encouraging Discoveries

Brian Corr is the new crops development manager for Ball in Chicago, Illinois. The company offers one of the biggest "plant discovery" programs to home gardeners with its Ball Discoveries program.

Over the years, some of the program's successes have included wave petunias, *Plectranthus* 'Mona Lavender,' *Alternanthera* 'Purple Knights' and *Argyranthemum* 'Madeira.'

While horticulture researchers and professionals have developed many of these plants, Corr says their program is open to ordinary gardeners, too.

"It just takes sharp eyes, a love of plants and a little determination to find a new variety," Brian says.

One of Ball's most popular discoveries is 'Purple Majesty' millet. It came from a professor at the University of Nebraska-Lincoln, who had no intention of growing an ornamental plant.

Dave Andrews was breeding millet for agricultural purposes when he discovered a purplish plant in his crop from India. Dave had no use for the unique-looking millet—it did not help him in his goal of developing a good grain-producing plant—but he knew there was

something special about it.

The millet went to the university's genetics nursery where students could study its unusual characteristics. It stayed there for years, without Dave thinking anything of it. Then, in 1996, the millet caught the eyes of a nursery owner who was visiting the school. He suggested Dave enter it in the All-America Selections, a contest designed to promote new garden seed varieties. In 2003, 'Purple Majesty' won the rare Gold Medal award from the AAS, which is reserved for extremely exceptional new plants.

" 'Purple Majesty' millet is all over the world now," Brian says. "It's doing well as a great landscape plant."

In Search of "Mutants"

Terra Nova Nurseries in Oregon is another company that offers a plant discovery program to everyday gardeners. Owner Dan Heims started the nursery with a discovery of his own. In the 1990s, he was traveling overseas when he noticed an interesting coral bell plant. Within a few years, he introduced coral bells 'Snowstorm' to the United States.

"It was a strong plant, and I got it into tissue culture so we could reproduce it here," Dan says. "That provided the seed money for Terra Nova, and then I started my breeding program."

Since then, Terra Nova has introduced a number of new plants to the United States, through their own findings and those of other gardeners.

For example, *Echinacea* 'Fragrant Angel' is a coneflower that Terra Nova developed through their nursery. It's unique because of its pure-white, scented flowers. They cultivated it from a single purple coneflower plant that had one of its branches come up white (above photos).

"This happened in our nursery, but it can happen in any garden, too," Dave says. "Approximately one in every 10,000 plants has a mutation. You just have to keep your eyes open."

That's exactly what Diana Reeck did in her Washington garden. She found a campanula plant that was beautiful and unusually fragrant, so she worked with Terra Nova to develop it into something they could mass pro-

FROM FARM FIELD TO GARDEN. Dave Andrews is credited with bringing 'Purple Majesty' millet (pictured above) to the garden. Dave is pictured with his wife (above right) in front of the plant, which can grow more than an impressive 5 feet tall.

duce. The result is *Campanula* 'Samantha.'

Pioneers in Horticulture

Some of the best plant discoveries have come from people known as "plant hunters." Bobby Ward, author and gardener, profiles a number of these well-known plant enthusiasts in his book, *The Plant Hunter's Garden*.

"Many of these people aren't necessarily trained botanists. They've come to this just for their love of plants," Bobby says. "Their passion and drive led them to look for new plants that might be available for them to grow."

Many of the plant hunters featured in Bobby's book travel overseas to look for plants that are new to North America. It's not as simple as just finding interesting plants, though. The people who are successful have to find the plants, get permission to gather the seed and then test the growing conditions, which can take several years.

It's not always a happy ending. Many "discoveries" often end in defeat, and it can take years before a plant is ready for production. Even then, some plants are never good candidates for mass distribution, and are better suited for specialty nurseries and growers.

One of the people featured in Bobby's plant hunter book was Bob McCartney. He is one of the owners of Woodlanders, a nursery specializing in rare and exotic plants. They only have a handful of staff, which is different than a large company like Ball Horticulture, but they've been around for nearly 30 years and receive business from all over the world.

"We have a category that we refer to as 'plant nuts,' and we love them because they love our plants," Bob says. "These plant nut people don't just buy something because it's pretty. They want something specific."

GARDEN FAVORITES. Wave petunias (above) are probably the best-known introduction from Ball Discoveries. At left, *Heuchera* 'Midnight Rose' came from Terra Nova's new plants program.

One of the most popular plants at Woodlanders is the pure-white Kentucky wisteria 'Clara Mack' that a local helped them find.

Step Outside the Box

While Ball and Terra Nova both have good plant discovery programs, they aren't always the perfect solution for gardeners. These companies have specific criteria as to what qualifies a plant for their program.

If a plant doesn't fit with them, it doesn't mean all is lost. Many times, specialty nurseries like Woodlanders will be more interested in special varieties than a large company. Other outlets to try include native plant societies and local botanical gardens.

For gardeners who might be interested in discovering new plants themselves, Bobby encourages them to step outside the boundaries.

"We've been too restrictive in the past about what textbooks say will grow where," he said. "This is a new renaissance in gardening. Be creative and energetic about trying to grow new plants in your area. Even if the books say it won't grow there, sometimes it's worth a shot."

Plant hunter may sound like an exotic term, but Bobby says it can define anyone interested in gardening.

"A plant hunter isn't necessarily just someone who goes on horseback or rides on a yacht in China looking for plants," Bobby says. "There are many plants in your backyard. If you have an interest and an eye for it, then it might have merit."

NOW WHAT?

If you find a plant with unusual characteristics growing in your garden, try one of these resources first. Web information for Ball and Terra Nova is available through the Links section of the *Birds & Blooms* Web site.

Ball Discoveries. Chicago, Illinois. Submit your plant information via their Web site.

Terra Nova Nurseries. Canby, Oregon. Submit your plant to Terra Nova by following the "New Plants Wanted" directions on their Web site.

Native plant societies. There are native plant societies all over the country. Check with your county Extension office for recommendations.

Botanical gardens and nurseries. These horticulturalists really know the plants in your area best and are often happy to look at your local "discoveries."

Secrets to Grow On

The "best of the best" home-tested gardening secrets.

Perennial Party

For a few years now, gardeners in my area have been holding perennial parties. Each spring and fall, a different gardener hosts the gathering in their backyard.

It's a great time to exchange tips, advice and plants with fellow gardeners. We have roughly 150 gardeners who are involved.

We organize the plants into light needs, herbs, daylilies and hostas. We have thousands of different plants!

A few of the ladies involved are Master Gardeners. They answer questions before the round of trading begins. We take turns picking plants until they are all gone.

I've filled entire flower beds with these free plants (like the bed at right). I look forward to the event every autumn. I hope others can use this idea to create a perennial party in their area.   —*Connie Baumann, Lino Lakes, Minnesota*

Flowering Pumpkins

Here's a pretty and practical fall decorating tip. A hollowed-out pumpkin makes a spectacular container for an autumn floral bouquet of colorful marigolds, mums and zinnias.

If you're using a large pumpkin with a variety of tall flowers, tuck in a small scarecrow or other decorative elements.

Another good use for a hollowed-out pumpkin is to lay it on its side, and have miniature gourds and pumpkins spilling out of it. Add a few nuts and some clusters of colorful dried leaves for the final festive flair.

—*Karen Ann Bland, Gove, Kansas*

Lighten the Load

If you put your annuals in large clay pots, then you know how heavy they can get. I have a simple solution.

Try putting empty milk jugs in the bottom of the pot before you fill it up with potting mix. The lids need to be on the jugs so they don't collapse. You can also use 2-liter soda bottles.

This will help fill some unnecessary space in those large containers. You just add your potting soil on top of the jugs, and then plant as usual. With this method, your containers will be lighter, and you'll even save on potting mix.

—*Lynn Surber, Scottsburg, Indiana*

Perfect Planter

When I had to cut down an old evergreen tree in my backyard, I knew I still wanted to use the leftover trunk. For a while, the log just sat in my yard, and the woodpeckers loved tapping on it in spring.

Now, the log is perfect for planting impatiens (left) with its multiple woodpecker holes. Each spring, I fill nearly every hole with a plant. It's a great planter and quite a conversation piece. Thanks to the woodpeckers for the idea!

—*Linda Sampson, Rye, New Hampshire*

High and Dry

I suspended this flower basket (above) on my porch with a metal spring, which lets me know when it's time to water.

When the basket is lighter, it sits higher. So, when it's high, it's dry...and when it's low, it's wet!
—*Dan Waters, Sr. Birmingham, Alabama*

Broken Art in the Garden

Have you ever broken one of your favorite pots? I have, and I know exactly what that sinking feeling in the pit of your stomach feels like. Well, stop worrying. You don't have to feel bad anymore. Just turn your broken pots into garden art!

I use my broken pots in the garden to give the appearance that my plants are growing out of pieces of pottery. Just plant your flowers as usual, then find an appropriate piece of broken flowerpot and place it in the ground next to the flowers. You can use your pot pieces in any way. I even like to add critters to liven up the scene in my garden.

So don't grieve over those favorite broken pots any longer. They can still be part of your garden for a long time.
—*LaVerne Otis*
Bellflower, California

Egg on Your Seedlings

Here's an easy way to start seedlings. Fill a cardboard egg carton with potting soil. Use a pencil to make two depressions in each cup—1/4 inch deep for small seeds and 1/2 inch for large ones. (A good rule of thumb is to plant at a depth twice the diameter of the seed.) Plant two seeds per cup, cover with soil and water lightly.

When each plant has four leaves, cut the egg cups apart, remove the cardboard and plant them right in your garden.
—*Mrs. V. Prince, Houston, Texas*

Have Some Peppermint

One year, the critters in my backyard really challenged me. The chipmunks and deer wouldn't leave my plants alone!

During the first part of the growing season, I reacted to their destructive behavior calmly. But later in the season, I decided it had to stop. None of my deterrents were working. I was desperate for a solution.

That's when I discovered peppermint oil. A man repairing my sidewalk suggested I try putting it on my plants. He said the chipmunks didn't like it. When I went to the health food store to buy the oil, the salesperson said it would keep rabbits away as well.

What a find! Not only did the peppermint oil work, but my entire yard also smelled great. The only problem, as I discovered, is you have to reapply the peppermint oil after each rain. It's still my favorite thing to use to keep critters out, though.
—*Doris Miller, Libertyville, Illinois*

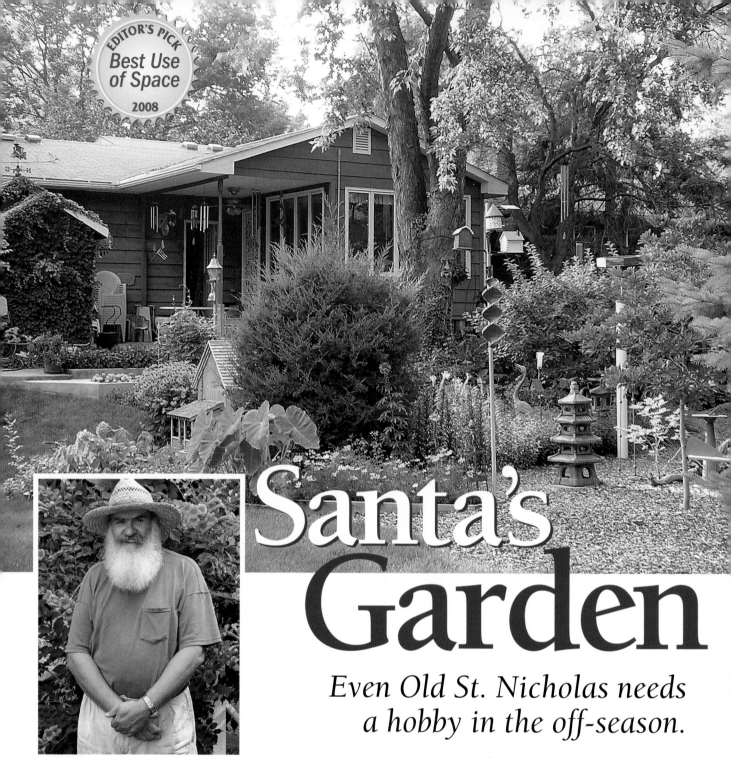

Santa's Garden

*Even Old St. Nicholas needs
a hobby in the off-season.*

By Bud "Santa" Lutz, Eagan, Minnesota

Whenever children visit my backyard, I start to hear the whispers. "Is it really him?"…"Look at his beard!"…"Where do you think he keeps the reindeer?"

I simply smile. "It's really me," I say. "This is my summer home away from the North Pole."

I like to think I'm showing my visitors a different side of Old St. Nicholas. He's not all about reindeer and toys—although there are toys. Here in Minnesota, Santa spends his summers gardening and playing with trains! I call my backyard the Lutz Railroad Garden, and it's considered a tourist site here in Eagan, just outside of the Twin Cities. Every year, hundreds of people stop by to see my plants and

watch the trains. I love sharing it with everyone.

I've been gardening most of my life, but I didn't incorporate the trains in the backyard until 2000. The local newspaper was at my house, doing a feature on my water gardens when I mentioned how I wanted to build a railroad between the waterfalls and blooms.

At that point, it was just an idea. But after they left, I figured I'd better go ahead and get started on it. I already had two waterfalls and a river in place, which I built more than 20 years ago. I did all of the work myself, though I admit, I do have a cement mixer, which helped a lot.

To me, cement is the perfect choice if you're looking for

FUN AND COLORFUL. Bud Lutz fills his garden with colorful blooms like clematis (above right) and pink cosmos (left). When Bud isn't tending to his flowers, he's working on the miniature railroad and train (above left) that winds its way through his yard.

durability. It gets a crack here and there, but that just means the plants around it get an extra drink.

The water features in my backyard were the perfect setting for my railroad, so I started building right away. By the time I finished, the track made its way through a tunnel, under one of the waterfalls and around the river.

Another interesting water feature in my backyard is a contraption my daughter Mitsy picked up for me in Thailand. It's called a bamboo deer chaser and works like a fountain. The water starts at the top and then runs down the bamboo shoots, little by little, while making a clacking sound.

Mitsy saw it in a hotel while she was on a business trip there. She knew I would like it, so she contacted the person who made it and got them to create another one just for me. So now I can say that I have a one-of-a-kind fountain in my backyard.

If there's one thing I try to do in my garden, it's to make it unique. One of the ways I do this is by planting interesting trees. My motto is that if it's different and weird, then I'll try it.

When I first built my house, we didn't have a single tree in the entire lot. Now, trees and shrubs fill the area. I

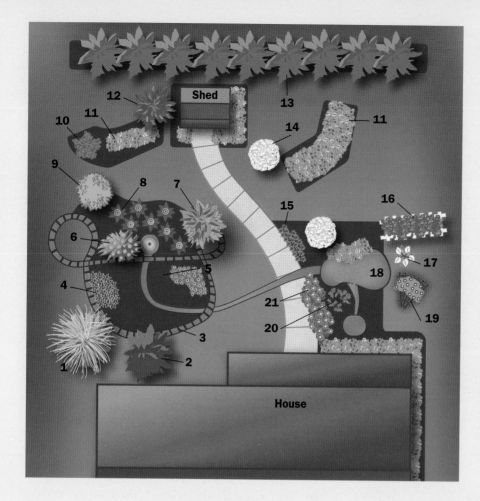

Plant List

1. Corkscrew willow
2. Redwood
3. Train track
4. Coleus
5. Black-eyed Susan
6. Tree peony
7. Japanese maple
8. Canna
9. Ohio buckeye
10. Contorted filbert
11. Flower bed
12. Larch
13. Spruce
14. Magnolia
15. Poppy
16. Trumpet vine
17. Calla lily
18. Pond
19. Clematis
20. Double-flowering almond
21. Cosmos

have a wide variety, including a contorted filbert, a corkscrew willow and a double-flowering almond.

I love to experiment with trees. Sometimes they work, sometimes they don't. But it's fun to try new things. The same goes for flowers. From my bright-red poppies to pure-white calla lilies, everything developed over time.

One of my favorite flower features in my yard is the trumpet vine that grows over the arbor near my pond. I started it with a single cutting, and now it seems to have endless blooms every year. The hummingbirds love it!

I can't stand to see plants go to waste and love sharing with others. I've given away dozens of cuttings from my trumpet vine, and whenever I find a sapling from my Ohio buckeye trees, I dig it up, pot it and give it away.

For the Kids

I've had people from all over the world in my garden, but some of my favorite visitors are the kids. They love watching the trains go around the village. They also stare at me with

their big eyes, wondering if it's okay to tell me what they want for Christmas.

I always take the time to sit and visit with them. After all, Santa is always listening and watching, even when he's gardening.

GREEN THUMB TIP

Have fun when you garden. Whether you add a railroad, like I did, or other accessories, it really brings life to your garden.
—*Bud Lutz, Eagan, Minnesota*

Country Retreat

Over 12 years, they created a lush landscape among the fields.

By Dave and Lynn Ewert, Watertown, Wisconsin

During the winter, we can't help but daydream about spring. Sorting through yard photographs taken this past summer makes our minds swim with ideas for the upcoming growing season.

Those same photos also remind us of what we've accomplished over the past 12 years. We literally started from scratch.

Dual career changes a dozen years ago meant that we had to sell our first rural house. Agreeing that we wanted to remain in the country, we were thrilled to purchase a 12-acre parcel of land. But when our children saw the bare cornfield that spring, they were less than enthusiastic.

To convince them, we pointed out the property's highlights, like the solid limbs on a large, 60-foot ash that would support rope swings, and a big oak that was the perfect spot for a tree house. Then the kids pronounced that several long swathes of land would be great for go-carts. We also discovered abandoned trolley tracks that gave us access to remote areas to explore by bike or horse.

Soon, we started planning the layout of our new property, keeping in mind that we wanted a sizeable landscaped yard as soon as possible. By fall, we had seeded the lawn, and our home was complete the following Christmas.

CULTIVATE COLOR. Annuals, started from seed, provide bright hues (above and at left) throughout the Ewert's yard. Plants like barberry, clematis and gold-tipped juniper line a walk (below). Opposite page, masses of wildflowers grow in a nearby field.

scaping around the house. One, dubbed our "rock garden," consists of a half-moon shaped, fieldstone-lined planting area anchored by small flowering shrubs and filled with mass plantings of colorful annuals. It serves as a focal point near the garage.

We also constructed two 50-foot-long gardens along the split-rail fences that line the driveway. One spot contains perennial plantings, and the other overflows with annuals each summer.

Rolling Along

We were still steaming ahead when fall arrived. That season saw us building a small cedar deck off our dining room that leads into the backyard.

> **GREEN THUMB TIP**
> We grow our own annuals from seed because it's cheaper. That means we have more money to spend on other areas of our garden.   *—Dave and Lynn Ewert*

Spring into Action

After moving in, we created a landscape design so that we'd be ready to go as soon as the weather warmed up. First, we put in evergreens, planting 50-plus Austrian pines as a northern windbreak, and 16 blue spruces in several group plantings.

When that was done, we installed numerous shade trees, including maple, pin oak, honey locust, Japanese birch and ginkgo.

Ornamentals were also part of the plan, ranging from French lilac, pagoda dogwood, weeping mulberry and flowering crabapple trees. We also planted various dwarf fruit trees, plus raspberry and blackberry bushes.

Finally, we transplanted about 80 12-inch-tall Fraser firs we'd started as seedlings and brought with us from our first home. And we were just getting warmed up!

Our next major task involved landscaping around the house. Keeping in mind all the seasons, we chose plants that would provide color or interesting foliage...or both. The varieties we planted included spirea, globe blue spruce, shrub roses, hydrangea, ornamental grasses, sedum and ferns.

We started several raised flower beds shortly after land-

Plant List
1. Juniper
2. Wave petunia
3. Sedum
4. Coleus
5. Flower bed
6. Impatiens
7. 'Goldmound' spirea
8. Blue spruce
9. Wagon flower bed
10. Silvervine fleeceflower
11. Rose garden
12. 'Anthony Waterer' spirea
13. Pond
14. 'Goldflame' spirea
15. Wildflowers
16. Iris
17. Daylily
18. Cleome
19. 'Karl Foerster' feather reed grass

Winter forced us to take a break from our outdoor efforts, but we continued to plan new landscape additions for the next year—and beyond. As soon as spring returned, we built a walkway to our front entrance, and a sidewalk and patio off the deck using a do-it-yourself form and dyed concrete. That was a once-in-a-lifetime project!

Since then, we've added about 4 acres of wildflower plantings (below), and a small pond with a patio and cedar arbor. This has become the most relaxing spot in the yard. To welcome spring, we planted hundreds of tulips, daffodils and other bulbs throughout the yard.

Compared to the initial flurry of activity, we slowed our landscaping efforts once our children became more involved with sports and school activities—but we enjoyed every minute we spent outside.

Now that they've both graduated from high school, we have the extra time we need, and we're busy focusing on our country sanctuary. Recently, we put in a rose bed within sight of the living room and added a pair of mass planting areas between the blue spruces.

The biggest projects to date have been the big pond we dug at the rear of our property, surrounded by native plantings, and a permanent greenhouse that replaced our temporary cold frame.

Starting from Seed

In the past, we grew some plants from seeds in that cold frame, but with the additional mass planting areas we've added, we realized that we had to start almost all of our annuals from seed—and that meant we needed a greenhouse. Once we had that structure in place, we were in business.

The process begins in our basement, where we can easily maintain consistent temperature and humidity levels. After transplanting the seedlings, we move them out to the greenhouse, which has running water, electricity, an LP gas heat source and fans.

Each year, we order too many seeds to compensate for those that don't germinate—and we don't want to be short on annuals for the yard! Of course, we've never had either problem and always end up at capacity in the greenhouse, with enough extra flowers to donate to our church.

What's on the horizon? We want to work on attracting wildlife, especially birds, and we're always open to new ideas. As our yard matures, we enjoy it more and more...almost as much as we love coming up with a new plan to work on in the future.

BEST GARDEN IDEAS OF THE YEAR

Cool Crop

Spring is the perfect time to plant lettuce. It thrives in cool weather, and leaf varieties will mature in 40 to 50 days, so you can harvest it much earlier than most other garden edibles.

To create our own green blend, just mix different leaf lettuce seeds in a bowl, then scatter them over the soil. Thin when plants are a few inches tall. Save the thinnings to make a delectable salad of baby greens.

Homemade Greenhouse

My husband, Jim, is very creative, and he's made many unusual things. He constructed this small greenhouse (below) from sections of an old patio door. He lined the inside with shelving he bought on sale at a bargain store and covered the top with chicken wire.

In early spring, he covered the roof and door opening with plastic to get the desired greenhouse effect. He started lettuce, green and lima beans, gourds and flowers in this greenhouse.

Friends and neighbors visited often throughout the spring and summer to check the progress of Jim's garden and to share in its bounty.

—*Mary Lou Millard, Bear Lake, Michigan*

A Visual Treat

A couple of years ago, I tried a new flower in my condo garden. I couldn't resist the name— 'Chocolate' morning glory.

I was pleased with the results (right). It had a velvety appearance and blooms the color of cappuccino with a touch of pink. I saved the seeds to share with the other gardeners in my family!

—*Grace Greene*
Louisville, Kentucky

Pinch to Grow an Inch

Pinch the shoot tips of mums, impatiens, petunias and coleus. It'll delay flowering a bit, but the result is bushier growth. Stop pinching by July.

The Right Way to Water

When watering your lawn, it's best to apply a good soaking of 1 to 1-1/2 inches in a single application each week. Divide the applications in half for sandy and quick-drying soils, and adjust for rainfall accordingly. This promotes deep roots so the grass will be less susceptible to drought.

A Touch of Garden Magic

With a little creativity—and some savvy recycling—it's easy to create a low-cost focal point for your garden.

Bruce Reagan's artist daughter transformed an eyesore in his backyard into a whimsical attraction (top right).

"These two large tree stumps were a real problem until my daughter turned them into a fairy house," Bruce writes from North Syracuse, New York. "She painted a door and some windows, then added rooftop gardens, driftwood and a ceramic chimney."

They also added a stone pathway and a garden gnome that lights up at night. "The grandkids were overjoyed," Bruce says.

An old baker's rack (near right) serves as a graceful trellis for morning glories and moonflowers at Lisa Reichley's home in Perkiomenville, Pennsylvania.

"My husband picked up the rack, minus the shelves, from someone's trash," Lisa relates. "I knew right away it could be a lovely trellis somewhere in our yard. I guess one person's trash is another person's trellis!"

Lisa Scherer put her creativity to work by changing the view under her lilac tree (far right).

"I painted an old window frame with outdoor craft paint and sealed it with an exterior polyurethane spray," says Lisa of Marianna, Pennsylvania. "I used stencils and glass paint for the words, then applied a glass sealer."

She left the window glass intact, but notes that replacing it with Plexiglas would be the safest option.

A Gem of an Idea

I'm a rock hound and for a decade taught about lapidary (the art of cutting gemstones) as a volunteer at the Soldiers Home in Orting, Washington. Over the years, many good-hearted, generous people had donated lapidary equipment, rocks and uncut semiprecious gemstones for the lapidary shop.

On a visit to the home a while back, I noticed benches outside the infirmary, but there was nothing pretty to look at. So I decided to plant azaleas in a small weed-covered patch between the two wings of the infirmary. When I started to dig, I discovered a 6-inch-deep concrete water basin. I soon found out there had been a fountain in that location many years ago.

I proposed to the administration that a new fountain be created in that old water basin. The Puyallup Gem and Mineral Club, of which I'm a member, would do the work using the equipment and rocks in the lapidary shop. I would donate the pump.

It took a while, but the project was finally approved. The fountain sparkles with gemstones from all over the world—banded agate from India, tiger eye from Africa, lapis from Pakistan, jade from Canada and many, many others (left). The squirrel is perched on an amethyst crystal-lined lava tube from Brazil. Even the waterwheel is made from gemstones!

But, most importantly, the patients at the home can now enjoy some beauty while sitting on the benches.

—Foley B. Abbott, Orting, Washington

203

Homegrown Pineapples

I started this plant from the top of a pineapple I bought at a grocery store," writes Dorothy Butman of Bunnell, Florida. "It took 18 months to get two pineapples, but they were the best I had ever eaten. Now, my daughter and I are growing 25 pineapples in containers."

Streamlined Seed Storage

My wife is an avid birder, but keeping all the birdseed in the garage made a huge mess. This photo (below) shows my solution.

We store safflower, nyjer, peanuts, cracked corn and black-oil sunflower seeds in 12-gallon, clear Sterlite containers with lockable lids. The first three come in bags that we empty right into the new containers. The other two require overflow bins, which sit beneath the smaller ones.

By keeping the seed types separate, instead of mixing them as we used to, we attract a greater variety of birds and waste less seed. The birds don't have to pick through the seed to get what they want—they just go to their favorite feeder.

They're happy, and so are we! And with no bags on the floor, our mice problem is zero.
— *Richard Slesar*
Franksville, Wisconsin

Trees Shed?

If your fruit tree drops fruit in June, don't be alarmed, says B. Rosie Lerner, the Extension consumer horticulture specialist st Purdue University in West Lafayette, Indiana.

It is part of the natural thinning process for most trees to prevent excessive loads and avoid breakage of the branches. This process is often called the June drop.

Don't Push It

Sometimes it's best to just let nature take its course. Perennial plants need to finish their summer growth cycle on their own. Don't encourage late-season growth with heavy fertilizer applications or excessive pruning near the end of the summer growing season.

In fall, don't cut down black-eyed Susans, coreopsis, cosmos, sunflowers and purple coneflowers. Their dried seed heads make natural bird feeders.

Thrifty Planter Idea

When I found this old fertilizer spreader (below) at a thrift shop, I immediately visualized it as a flower planter for my yard. A neighbor painted the two beautiful birds on the front, and I filled it with petunias. When the weather turned cooler, I put winter pansies in the planter for folks to enjoy as they strolled by.
—*Hillard Newsome, Louisville, Kentucky*

Stump Takes on New Life

Some people are never stumped for ideas. When a storm damaged their dogwood tree several years ago, this couple cut off the tree a few feet from the ground. Then the fun began.

"That fall, my wife, Polly, painted a face on the stump," writes P.H. White Jr. of Dyersburg, Tennessee. "And for Halloween, she decorated it as a witch."

Since then, they've decorated it as many characters, and for different seasons and holidays, like a fall scarecrow or a Thanksgiving display. The local newspapers printed photos of it, and it's on the route to a school, so word spread about their stump.

"Every time we talk about removing it, we hear, 'Please don't cut down the stump!'

"We've had a lot of fun, but Polly and I are about to run out of ideas. We've offered it for adoption...but no takers as yet!"

Trash Becomes Treasures

These readers have really taken the recycling message to heart. They transformed broken household items into unique flower planters to create a "homey" atmosphere in their gardens.

"After many uses, my Crock-Pot sprang a leak," writes Regie Powell of Powell, Ohio. "Rather than throw it out, I cut off the cord, added some dirt and I had a new planter (below left) for my front porch."

Kelly Mitchell of Port Moody, British Columbia created a unique planter, and then got a surprise plant as well.

"My teapot had the slightest crack in the bottom, so I turned it into a flowerpot (below center)," she says. "I planted some hens and chicks in the opening, but a few weeks later, these impatiens appeared—growing not only out the lid, but out the spout, too! It was quite a surprise, since I don't normally plant annuals."

Outside her home in Elkton, Kentucky, Debbie Turner transformed an antique item into the perfect spot for cascading annuals.

"I found my mother-in-law's old wringer washer in her garage," Debbie says. "I have it sitting on my front porch (below) and am using it as a plant stand."

216

218

208

212

214

GLAD YOU ASKED!

Critter Combat	208
Moths vs. Butterflies	210
Problem Soils	212
America's Most Wanted	214
Butterfly Gardening on a Budget	216
Beauty and the Bugs	218
Best of Glad You Asked!	220

Photos: at left, Rob Curtis/The Image Finders; opposite page from top left: monarch on zinnia, Tom Edwards/Unicorn Stock Photos; nasturtiums, Donna and Tom Krischan; garden, Mark Turner; oriole, Tom Uhlman/The Image Finders; bear, Rebekah Sandeen

Keep four-legged pests out of your bird feeders with these easy tips.

By George Harrison, Contributing Editor

CRITTER COMBAT

Imagine looking out your kitchen window and seeing a black bear on your bird feeder! It happens, especially in the spring when bears come out of hibernation and are very hungry.

Most backyard birders will never have to contend with bears at their feeders, but all have to deal with some form of four-legged critter. You don't have to let them take over, though. Here are some of the most common four-legged feeder pests, along with tips to keep them out of your yard.

Clever Little Foes

Squirrels—Almost everyone has gray squirrels, red squirrels and chipmunks trying to steal birdseed from feeders. To keep your feeders free of these pests, consider my rule of 5-7-9.

Squirrels cannot jump from the ground higher than 5 feet, from a nearby tree more than 7 feet, or drop from above more than 9 feet. So, if you place a feeder 5 feet from the ground, 7 feet from trees and buildings, and 9 feet from any overhang, you're off to a good start, but you're still not quite finished.

To ensure squirrel-free feeders, use baffles. If your feeder is on a pole, put a baffle underneath; if it's hanging from a wire, place a baffle on top. The combination of baffles and the 5-7-9 rule should deter squirrel raiders.

Raccoons—These night raiders are more clever and destructive than squirrels. Therefore, they require stronger baffles and tighter seed storage containers. If you use garbage cans to store seed, secure the lids with bungee cords, or put heavy bricks or stones on top.

They like suet, too. I either bring my suet in at night or

use bungees to secure the feeder to a tree.

If you don't use strong deterrents, beware. Your seed— or even the whole feeder—could be missing the next day!

Beating the "Big Guys"

Deer—If you place bird feeders higher than deer can reach, there should be no problem. They will stand on their hind legs to eat seed from a feeder, but if it's 7 or 8 feet off the ground, they can't reach it. Use a pulley to raise and lower high feeders. This makes cleaning and filling a lot easier.

Bears—As with deer, if you can place the bird feeders beyond the reach of bears, which may mean 8 to 10 feet high, the bears will have to look elsewhere for food.

Not the Cat's Meow

Cats—Though they won't eat your birdseed, felines in the backyard may try to raid the visitors at your feeders. If you have cats, the best solution is to keep them indoors.

Don't worry about your cat getting bored inside. In my book *Bird Watching for Cats*, I show how cats watch birds through windows…just like people do. Plus, an indoor cat is healthier and lives longer than an outdoor cat.

If the culprit is a neighbor's cat, then you have more of a social problem. While it's not an easy thing to resolve, try talking to your neighbors to work out a solution.

The bottom line is that any backyard that attracts birds will also attract other wildlife, some of which is unwelcome. The challenge is to keep the unwelcome animals from eating or destroying the bird food and feeders.

I hope these tips will help you attract more feathered friends, and fewer four-legged pests.

BACK OFF! Don't let furry pests invade your backyard bird feeders. Squirrels (above right), raccoons (left) and bears (below) are all common culprits. You can stop them in their tracks with a few easy feeder adjustments. Try using baffles or simply raising the height of your feeders to deter them.

Maslowski Productions

Rebekah Sandeen

MOTHS VS. BUTTERFLIES

Learn how to tell these two groups apart with a few simple tricks.

By Tom Allen, Contributing Editor

Moths and butterflies look like similar creatures, but don't let them fool you. Moths outnumber butterflies by more than 10 to one, and the two groups can really be confusing. However, you can learn a few simple tricks to help tell them apart.

The simplest way has to do with timing. Butterflies are active during the day, and most moths are active at night. Butterflies depend on sunlight to find food and seek out mates. So if you see a flying flower during daylight hours, chances are you're seeing a butterfly.

Unfortunately, that's not always the case. There are a number of moths that fly during the day.

Color is the next thing to look for when distinguishing butterflies from moths. Most butterflies, but not all, have bright colors that help with the mating process and ward off predators. Brightly colored butterflies attract mates from quite a distance, and colors can be very important in butterfly courtship displays.

Though a few day-flying moths are also brightly colored, most are a dull gray, brown, white or a combination of the three. Their coloring tends to be duller because they rest on trees, the ground and on rocks during the day to avoid predators.

In general, butterflies are thinner bodied that moths—with the exception of skippers. Skippers tend to be dull in color and have large heads and robust bodies. Unlike butterflies, most moths are not strong fliers.

If you're still not sure if you're seeing a moth or butterfly, there's one distinguishing feature that never fails. Look at the antennae. Butterflies have enlarged clubs at the tips of their antennae. The clubs may be slightly curved,

Rob Curtis/The Image Finders

round or oblong.

Moths, on the other hand, have either tapered or feathered antennae, and do not have clubs on the ends. However, the hummingbird moth's antennae tend to get larger toward the tips.

When it comes to caterpillars, it's even more difficult to tell the difference between butterflies and moths, unless you are familiar with their host plants. There is one big difference, though. Butterflies form a chrysalis, and moths spin cocoons.

A chrysalis is a hard outer shell that is attached to the host plant, either upright or upside down, depending on the behavior of each species. Moths have a different approach altogether. They pupate in soft cocoons that they spin from silk.

One other difference between moths and butterflies is how they keep warm. This isn't something that is easy to see, but it is interesting.

Both creatures are cold-blooded, so they need to warm their bodies on chilly days in order to be active.

Glad You Asked!

During the day, butterflies find a perch and bask in the sun, often with their wings outstretched to absorb more heat.

Moths have to use a different method, since they are nocturnal. They vibrate their wings rapidly for periods of time while perched. This creates friction and warms their bodies.

So the next time you see a flying flower in your yard, take a close look at it, especially at the antennae. You'll know how to distinguish moths from butterflies in no time!

LOOKS CAN BE DECEIVING. This cecropia moth (above) proves that butterflies aren't the only ones with bright colors. Another difference between moths and butterflies is their antennae. Butterflies have distinct clubs on their antennae tips, like the bronze copper (opposite page) and buckeye (below).

Skip Moody/Dembinsky Photo Assoc.

All photos: Mark Turner

Problem Soils

Our resident plant expert explains how to make the best of bad situations in the garden.

By Melinda Myers, Contributing Editor

A beautiful garden starts with the soil. Unfortunately, most landscapes don't come with great soil. Ask any gardener, and they'll often complain that theirs is too rocky, sandy or filled with clay.

If this sounds familiar, then don't fret. I have some quick fixes and long-term solutions for all your less-than-perfect garden soils.

Think Organic

The best solution for any soil type is organic matter. Rotten manure, compost or peat moss can help sandy soils retain water and help clay soils drain more quickly. In addition, this amazing amendment adds nutrients and creates a better environment for microorganisms, worms and other soil dwellers that help promote a healthy root environment.

To apply the organic matter to your soil, work 2 to 4 inches into the top 6 to 12 inches of soil. Repeat the process every year or so as needed.

Afterward, it's a good idea to mulch the surface of your soil. This is an especially good quick fix for sandy soils that often dry out quickly. For mulching, use evergreen needles, shredded leaves, herbicide-free grass clippings and other organic materials.

Organic mulches help suppress weeds, moderate soil temperatures and conserve moisture. As the mulch breaks down, it adds nutrients and organic matter, thus improving the soil.

Keep in mind that it takes nature 100 years to make 1 inch of great topsoil, and it takes just a few minutes to destroy it. Improving your soil might be an involved process, but the results are worth it.

Chapter 8

NOT A PROBLEM. If you have sandy or rocky soil, try drought-tolerant plants like ornamental grasses (right) and asters (left). Asters also make a good choice for clay soil, as does nodding pink onion (pictured above).

Fast Track to Success

If you're looking to speed things up, you might consider bringing new soil into your landscape. You can either dig out and replace the bad soil, or create a raised bed or berm on top of the area of poor soil.

Just be sure the topsoil you purchase is better than what you already have. Ask friends and neighbors for quality topsoil suppliers in your area. Then ask the company about blended mixes made for planting beds. This should help you get started in the right direction.

Creating raised beds or berms with your existing soils is also an option. Oftentimes, soil just needs better drainage, and the good news is it can be as simple as raking the edges of the bed to the center to elevate the planting surface. You will be surprised at the difference even a few inches can make.

Timing is also critical in soil preparation. It should be moist—not wet or overly dry—when you work with it.

GREEN THUMB TIP

An easy way to improve the soil in your yard is to add more topsoil. If you go this route, make sure that the soil you are buying is better than the soil already in your garden. To find a quality distributor, ask around. Garden club organizations, neighbors and friends are often the best resources.

Glad You Asked!

Cultivating wet soil results in compaction and clods that last all season. Overly dry soil loses its structure, which can cause the surface to blow or erode away.

To test if yours has the right moisture for planting, grab a handful of soil and gently tap it. If it breaks into smaller pieces, it's time to dig into it. If it's nothing but a mud ball, then go back inside and check out the catalogs while waiting until it's okay to plant.

Flowers That Matter

Last, and perhaps most important, is to match the plants you grow to the soil and growing environment already in your backyard. Even if you don't have perfect soil, you can still choose plants that will succeed in your specific garden conditions. Ask fellow gardeners and nurseries for suggestions on good plants for your area.

With sandy or rocky soils, try drought-tolerant plants like sedum, yarrow, prairie smoke, poppy mallow and ornamental grasses. Good clay-tolerant plants include swamp milkweed, nodding pink onion, wild senna, baptisia and New England asters.

And this is only the beginning. If you succeed in improving your soil, you'll be able to grow more plants than you ever imagined. So dig in and start creating the soil you've always wanted.

Learn how to attract some of the most colorful birds in North America.

By George Harrison
Contributing Editor

America's Most Wanted

Some of the most colorful birds in North America will never come to your backyard for seed. This doesn't mean you can't attract brightly colored feathered friends like warblers, orioles and tanagers, though. You just have to know how.

Many birds that visit backyards are predominately insect-eaters, which makes them a little bit harder to see up close and personal. During spring and summer, even the traditional seed-eaters such as northern cardinals, American goldfinches and black-capped chickadees eat more insects. Many will feed only insects to their nestlings as

well. So the challenge in warm months is to bait the insect-eating birds into our yards as we do the seed-eaters.

Let Them Eat Fruit

The easiest way to lure a few of the spring and summer residents is with feeders containing sugar water, fruit or jelly.

Hummingbirds and orioles are famous for their interest in sugar water. Placed at eye-level and near natural cover, sugar-water feeders are busy as hummingbirds buzz in and out for sips of the sweet nectar. Orioles, too, will use hummingbird feeders, but a slightly different configured oriole feeder, containing the same liquid, will be more attractive to them.

Orioles and even grosbeaks will often start coming to backyards in spring if you offer orange halves. They eventually lose interest in the oranges though. As you see this start to happen, try switching to sugar water to keep their attention. In my yard, I start orioles out on sugar water and continue offering it to them through mid-September, when they fly south.

Fruit is also a popular treat among many other interesting birds. Tanagers, gray catbirds and northern mockingbirds may become frequent visitors to feeders offering fruits and jellies. From grape jelly (which is also popular among orioles) to apples, oranges and raisins, birds love these sweets. You might even attract some red-bellied woodpeckers.

Suet cakes are another way to attract insect-eaters. Though woodpeckers dine primarily on insects found in the bark of trees and rotted wood, suet cakes will often catch their attention, too.

Of course, if you want bluebirds, the best bait is a container full of wiggling mealworms, available from pet stores or on the Internet. I even have my mealworm feeder next to my bluebird house to make the search for food easier on the busy parents.

Water Is Just Right

Even if we attract a few birds with the sugar water, fruit and mealworms, the vast majority of summer birds in our backyards are purely insect-eaters. They will not be inter-

Richard Day/Daybreak Imagery

BIRD BANQUET. Think beyond birdseed when it comes to feathered friends, and there's no limit to the bird species you can attract, including red-bellied woodpeckers (above), Baltimore orioles (opposite page) or northern mockingbirds (below left).

ested in any kind of bird feeder.

The secret to snagging these beauties is water. Warblers, flycatchers, vireos, American robins and other thrushes, cedar waxwings and owls can't resist the call of running water.

I use a simple setup in my own yard. Two circulating birdbaths—one with three levels, and one that cascades from a top pool—make splashing sounds that bring in some of the most beautiful insect-eaters you can imagine. I always seem to have a new visitor every year. These water features are also very attractive to spring and fall migrants that stop for a quick drink or a bath before pushing onward to their southern destinations.

Though a circulating bath, powered by a small pump, is the best water feature to catch a bird's attention, a still water birdbath on a pedestal will also work. Either way, remember to clean both types periodically to assure pure, fresh water for the birds. Soon, you'll be hosting the beautiful birds you've always dreamed of!

Maslowski Productions

Glad You Asked!

Butterfly Gardening
on a budget

Attract flying flowers to your yard without spending a lot of money on plants.

By Tom Allen, Contributing Editor

Fall is the perfect time of year to start a butterfly garden in your backyard. You don't have to spend a lot of money on plants, though. There are many budget-friendly options that will attract your favorite flying flowers.

Magic of Milkweed

Monarchs are one of the most popular butterflies. Luckily, it doesn't take much to lure these beauties into your garden. Just plant milkweed—this is the monarch's host plant, and you can find them easily and inexpensively at most local nurseries.

Keep in mind that there are several milkweed species, and some will be more suited to your area than others. But

overall, milkweed serves as an excellent nectar source for monarchs and many other butterflies as well.

Another excellent source for many butterfly species is butterfly bush (*Buddleja*). These plants are budget-friendly, and do well in most climates. When picking varieties, the best colors for butterflies are deep purple and lavender. Beware, however, that they are considered invasive in some regions.

Other good nectar plants include phlox, an excellent border plant, and lilacs for spring blooms. Good summer options include mint, blazing stars, thistle and purple coneflower (right). If you want blooms that will continue through fall, try asters, zinnias and yarrow.

If you're looking to get lots of flowers for not a lot of money, then annuals like violets, pansies and nasturtiums are perfect for your garden. They easily grow from seed or are inexpensive choices at garden centers. Plus, they attract a wide range of butterflies.

Violets are the host plant for most fritillaries. Pansies (and also Johnny-jump-ups) are good for attracting variegated fritillaries.

Make a Long-Term Impact

Small trees and shrubs are essential for any butterfly garden, and if you watch, you can find good end-of-season sales. In my own flower beds in Florida, one of my favorite shrubs is I leadwort or blue plumbago. It has beautiful blue flowers on which the cassius blue caterpillar feeds. I also have the white-flowered native species of this, but I've noticed the butterflies prefer the blue flowers to the white ones.

Bahama cassia and privet cassia shrubs offer nice clusters of yellow flowers and attract the cloudless sulphur, a species that will invade northern states in favorable years.

One of my favorite butterflies is the orange-barred sulphur, which comes to my dwarf species of tree senna. I also love swallowtails, and for these beauties, I have three different pipevine species along my fence to attract the polydamus or gold-rim swallowtails.

BUFFET OF BEAUTY. Try budget-friendly zinnias (opposite page) to attract fliers like monarchs. Plant butterfly weed for fritillaries (top left). Violets (top right with a swallowtail) attract fritillaries, while purple coneflowers (above) are good nectar sources.

Success Without Flowers

If you have a vegetable garden, then you already have a good start for attracting black swallowtails. When planting your garden this spring, add dill, fennel, carrots and parsley because swallowtails will use them as host plants.

If you are able, it helps to plant your butterfly garden near a wooded area. Many butterflies like to stay close to woods, so this would allow you to attract even more species.

You don't always have to have blooms to attract butterflies. Some common lawn grasses and even weeds are important butterfly host plants.

Take clovers for example. They are host plants for the eastern tailed-blue, various sulphurs and cloudywing skippers. Lawn grasses are host plants to various skippers. Wood nymphs will also use the grasses if you let them grow tall in small patches at the edges of your yard.

There is no secret formula for attracting butterflies. If you're willing to spend a little extra time in the garden experimenting with plants, you're likely to be successful.

Some of your most desired butterflies may not appear in the first year. But you should never have to spend a fortune. Hopefully, this is just the start of hosting butterflies in your backyard.

BUTTERFLY BIT

You can find great end-of-season deals if you're willing to do a little searching. Both local and on-line nurseries sell plants, shrubs and trees at deep discounts in fall.

Keep your garden pest-free without using chemicals.

By Melinda Myers, Contributing Editor

Beauty and the Bugs

Stop. Don't reach for that can of pesticide without reading the label and thinking about alternatives. Many people use pesticides to kill unwanted insects and plants, but they aren't always helpful. In fact, less than 3% of insects in the world are actual problems. All the others play an important role in our backyard.

The Real Pests

For example, insects like lady beetles, lace wings, praying mantis and other predacious insects actually eat the real pests in our gardens. When we spray for bad insects, we often kill the good guys that help keep the pest population under control.

Fortunately, there are many nontoxic solutions to getting rid of pests, from new products on the market to tried-and-true techniques that gardeners have used for years.

It all starts with proper identification. As a "plant doctor," I see lots of interesting lumps, bumps, creepy crawlies and slimy, rotting masses. Gardeners often tell me that they sprayed, but it did no good. That's because pesticides aren't always the solution. You must know the enemy to know how to best manage it.

The Internet is a great resource to start with when you're trying to diagnose a plant problem. Make sure you're using a reputable source like a university Web site that contains research-based information.

Pluck, Drop and Stomp

Once you know the problem, you can finally look for a solution. One of my favorite techniques for insect management is the "pluck, drop and stomp" method. The young

Alan and Linda Detrick

ter, though. For these plant huggers, the pluck and stomp method is the best way to go.

If you're trying to get rid of unwanted plants in your garden, good old-fashioned weeding is probably best. It may not be your first choice, but remember, it's good exercise!

You can also try barriers to manage weeds and other pests. Mulch barriers cover the soil surface and reduce the number of weed seeds sprouting. This means fewer weeds for you to pull. Plus, it's good for your soil.

Barriers also work for insects, though the method is slightly different. Try lightweight floating row covers like ReeMay and Grass Fast. They allow air, light and water to reach the plants, but prevent pesky insects like maggots and cabbage worms from laying their eggs on your garden plants. They also keep out bees, so you'll need a different strategy when growing plants that need bees for pollination.

Old Garden Remedies

There are plenty of other nonchemical methods for controlling specific pests. Use a yellow bowl filled with soapy water to attract and trap aphids. Also try setting out beer in a shallow can to trap snails and slugs.

If these don't match your gardening style, there are many natural products to try, such as insecticidal soap and lightweight horticulture oils. These products are hard on pests but easy on the environment. Be sure to read and follow directions because they can be harmful if not used properly.

So try putting your pesticides aside and consider other pest-management strategies this gardening season. You might be surprised to find out what works! ✦

gardeners at the Royal Botanical Gardens in Hamilton, Ontario shared this with me, and it works great.

Simply pluck the unwanted pest, such as beetles off potatoes, slugs off hostas and plant bugs off of phlox. Then drop the pest to the ground and stomp them out. If you're a bit squeamish, you might find a strong blast of water is a good way to knock off some of these insects, too.

Don't expect to get slugs off plants with just with water.

KEEP THE BEAUTY. Nasturtiums (below) commonly fall victim to aphids, while hostas (opposite page) often have slug problems. Nonchemical pest control helps control bugs, and it's environmentally friendly. Above left, take a close look and you'll see small aphids covering this plant's stem and blooms.

Donna and Tom Krischan

GLAD YOU ASKED!

Best Butterfly Questions 2008

Tom Allen shares his butterfly know-how.

Criss-Cross

This white flier (below) has black markings that seem to form a cross on its wings. Are these unusual, or is this just a species that I'm not familiar with?
—*Laurie LaFond, South Glens Falls, New York*

Tom: This is a clymene moth (*Haploa clymene*), which is active at night. Its markings are very interesting, but also quite common.

You probably don't recognize this flier because it's mostly out at night. Unfortunately, we miss out on a lot of beautiful moths like this one because of their nocturnal behavior. As a caterpillar, it feeds on eupatoriums, but it also uses oaks, peaches and willows. To increase your chances of seeing this flier again, look near these plants.

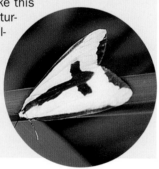

Leave My Tomatoes Alone

What are those huge green worms that can devour tomato plants? Is there anything I can do to stop them from ruining my crop? —*Joan Lancioni, Sterling, Massachusetts*

Tom: The large caterpillars you find devouring your tomatoes belong to the sphinx or hawkmoth group. There are two species that feed on tomatoes, the tobacco hawkmoth (also known as the Carolina sphinx) and the tomato hawkmoth (also known as the five-spotted hawkmoth).

Both are large moths with long, narrow wings that are brown in color with several striations.

The caterpillars (also known as hornworms) can be nuisances if several begin to gather in one area. One or two won't affect the production of your plants, but a group will. Check your tomatoes regularly. If you see several caterpillars gathering on one plant, simply remove them.

Often with these caterpillars, you'll see several tiny, white cocoons attached to their bodies. These are the pupae of wasp parasites that feed on the caterpillar. They find the cater-

pillars on the tomatoes and lay several eggs inside it by piercing its body, eventually killing it.

If you notice this, then leave the worm alone! These insects actually help gardeners in the long run. Let nature take its course, and, hopefully, you'll have beautiful tomatoes to show for it.

Details on Doris

What can you tell me about the Doris longwing butterfly?
—*Doris Okhtokiyuk, Vancouver, Washington*

Tom: The Doris longwing is a tropical butterfly found from Central America south to Peru, Venezuela, Guyana, Brazil and Trinidad. As with other tropical Heliconian butterflies, there are many color forms of this flier. They usually have large yellow spots on their forewings and rays of blue to green in the hind wings. The background color is black.

The host plant for these butterflies includes various species of passion vines, which are common in the tropics. Because of their slow, lazy flights, they are beautiful to watch. You'll find them in butterfly houses around the country.

Interesting Insect

This pretty insect (right) is a frequent visitor in my garden. Can you tell me more about it?
—*Lucille Taggart Glen Mills, Pennsylvania*

Tom: This insect is a widow skimmer dragonfly. It is common in gardens across the country.

This flier catches its prey with its wings. It will eat just about anything it catches, including mosquitoes, so the widow skimmer is a welcome addition in many backyards.

Dragonflies are pretty amazing insects. They can fly in any direction or hover in midair. The larvae of dragonflies, called nymphs, live in warm waters of ponds, lakes or marshes.

This is a good insect to have in your garden.

Prickly Caterpillars

My boyfriend and I were kayaking in Harford Country, Maryland. When we stopped to rest along the shore, we spotted these caterpillars (below). Can you tell me more about them? —Patricia Erickson, Street, Maryland

Tom: The caterpillars you saw belong to a beautiful moth that is often referred to as the hickory horned devil. It is the royal walnut moth, a member of the Saturniidae family. The luna and the cecropia, both common moths, also belong to this group.

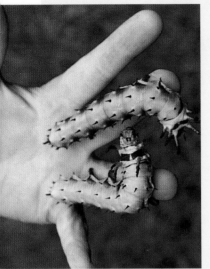

Hickory horned devil caterpillars pupate in the ground under leaf litter and often crawl on the ground in search of a place to pupate.

The royal walnut moth is a large red and gray moth with pale yellow spots on the wings. People rarely get to see it up close, except near lights where it will stop and rest during its nocturnal flights.

The host plants for this moth include ash, hickory, black walnut and others. An interesting note about these beautiful moths is that as adults they have no mouthparts for feeding. Therefore, they only live for a few days on stored energy they use to reproduce and lay eggs.

Large and in Charge

This is one of the largest caterpillars I've ever seen (below). This crawler was munching on dandelion leaves. It looked prickly and was almost 2 inches long! What is it?
—Donna Kronen, Newton, New Jersey

Tom: The caterpillar you photographed actually belongs to a moth—the giant leopard moth. This is a fairly common species in your area as it ranges from southern Canada to Florida and Texas.

The moth itself is white with black spots and rings on its

hairy wings. Since these fliers are nocturnal, you'll usually find them near lights in the evening. In the morning, people often spot them clinging to a plant or vegetation on a wall.

These moths usually have two broods over the course of a season. Their caterpillars will eat a wide variety of plants, including, as you discovered, dandelions.

Beneficial Bee?

Is this green and yellow bee (right) harmful or beneficial? They burrow in the sand here in Florida.
—Susan Fox
New Port Richey, Florida

Tom: The bee in your photo appears to be a mining bee. These bees live in the ground in burrows. Often, several bees will construct their burrows close to each other, so if you see a large number in one area, this is probably why.

These bees are quite common throughout the United States and are very good pollinators, so they are beneficial. These green and yellow bees are the same ones that sometimes land on a person's arm looking for perspiration.

Confused Swallowtails?

I was surprised to find these two swallowtails (below) of different species trying to court one another. Can you explain their behavior? —Kenneth Hugel
Rockford, Illinois

Tom: You saw a pair of black swallowtail butterflies going through a courtship display. The male has a lot more yellow on his wings compared to the female. The male looks like a different species, but it's really not.

In many species of butterflies, males and females differ in their appearance. This particular species is quite interesting when it comes to color differences between the sexes. The female closely mimics the poisonous pipevine swallowtail and has blue on its hind wings.

Male butterflies are attracted to females that send out pheromones shortly after they emerge from the chrysalis. Suitors soon arrive and engage in courtship flights with the female. Mating takes place after that.

GLAD YOU ASKED!

Best Gardening Questions 2008

Melinda Myers offers remedies for some of the most common garden problems.

Out of Nowhere

These beautiful flowers (below) popped up in my backyard. I would love to have more of them. Do you know what they are?
　　　　　　　　　　　　　　　　—*Mary Tate*
　　　　　　　　　　　　　　Goochland, Virginia

Melinda: These spring bloomers are star-of-Bethlehem (*Ornithogalum umbellatum*) flowers. You shouldn't have any trouble getting these flowers to come back in your garden. If you wait a few years, you'll probably have enough to share with others, too.

　These flowers multiply rapidly. They even reproduce by seed, which is probably how they mysteriously appeared in your yard. The are a bit too assertive in the garden, so plant with care. If you're able to manage them, though, you'll enjoy the show they put on late spring or early summer. They also are tough plants, tolerating full sun to partial shade and even drought conditions.

Looking for "Seymour"

I would love to grow carnivorous plants like Venus flytraps and sundews. I've studied how to grow these plants, but I can't seem to succeed. Any advice?　　　　—*Jeffrey Winter, Aurora, Colorado*

Melinda: As you discovered, this is a difficult group of plants to grow. They are native to bogs, so you have to work a little harder to get them to grow in other locations.

　The Venus flytrap is hardy in Zones 8 through 10 and grows as a houseplant in other regions. The sundews are hardy over a wider region, including Zones 3 through 9, depending on the species. Hardy types can be grown outdoors in bog gardens; less hardy ones indoors as houseplants.

　Both plants benefit from the moist, humid conditions of a terrarium. Use an aquarium or purchase a terrarium for this purpose. Keep it out of direct sun to avoid cooking the plants.

　Grow the plants in an organic soil and keep it moist. Cover the terrarium opening to increase the humidity around the plants. You will need to vent the top if condensation collects on the sidewalls. Keep trying. The reward of success will far outweigh the battle.

Browning Ginger

I've had several beds of wild ginger around our shady yard for more than 30 years. It's been a great ground cover. A couple of years ago, I noticed some leaves were turning brown. When I looked further, I found tiny, white insects like white flies on the leaves. What's going on with my plants?
　　　　　　　　　　　—*Dorothy Allen, Midland, Michigan*

One of Every Color

Not only was I surprised to see last year's petunia survive winter, but it also bloomed in seven different colors (right)! I'm sure I only planted one petunia color. Can you tell me why this happened?　　—*Terri Robbins, Tigerton, Wisconsin*

Melinda: What a beautiful surprise! My guess is that this year's beautiful bloom is the offspring of seeds from your hybrid petunia from last year. Hybrids combine the characteristics of one or more plants. As a result, the offspring don't always look like the parent plant they came from.

　The offspring of hybrids can vary quite a bit. The flowers may look like one of the parent plants or even a combination of their traits.

　This cluster of petunias shows how offspring can pick up a variety of colors from their hybrid parents.

Melinda: Canadian ginger is relatively pest free, so the insects you found might not be causing the symptoms.

White flies are pests on a wide variety of plants. Fortunately for northern gardeners, these pests do not survive harsh winters. They come into the landscape on bedding plants or white-fly-infested houseplants that move outside for the summer.

You may want to check your watering practices and soil drainage. Summers of drought can cause browning on ginger. It usually survives, but will look a bit stressed.

Another possibility is root rot, which can cause the plants to brown. This can result from excess rains, too much watering and poor drainage.

Though we can't control the weather, we can add organic matter to soil to improve drainage. We can also mulch to conserve moisture, and when we do need to water, do so thoroughly but less frequently.

A Solution for Sharon?

I have a pink rose of Sharon bush that is 4 years old. It buds fully, but then the blooms fail to open. My white rose of Sharon plants do fine. What could the problem be?
—*Elizabeth Folsom, Newbury, New Hampshire*

Melinda: Some plants, like people, are more susceptible to stress. For example, too much or not enough water or fertilizer can cause buds to drop before opening.

Start by evaluating the current growing conditions. Though both plants receive the same care, the soil or light may vary, causing problems for the pink flowering variety, and not your white one.

For the best results, keep the soil moist, avoiding extremes on either end. Mulch the surrounding soil with shredded leaves, bark or other material to help conserve water, and keep the soil consistently moist.

Avoid excess fertilization. Most gardeners kill their plants with kindness rather than neglect. Have a soil test to find out if any changes need to be made to your feeding schedule.

Cracking the Case

This "egg" plant (right) was a lot of fun for my mother and me last summer. We saved the seeds to pass on to others next spring. What is this plant and how should we preserve the seeds?　　—*Laura Welu, Davenport, Iowa*

Melinda: Your mystery plant is a white-fruited eggplant. Often sold as an ornamental, it is also edible. People love eggplant for its colorful and unusually shaped fruit.

You can save the seeds (as long as it is not a patented variety) to replant, though there is no guarantee a new plant will produce the same size and color of fruit as the parent. For the best results, allow several fruits to dry on the plant. The fruit will eventually drop off so you know the seeds are ripe. Cut the fruit, removing the flesh and section that held the seeds. Put the rest in a bowl, working it with your fingers as you add water. The seeds will separate and sink to the bottom.

Once clean, spread the seeds on a paper towel to dry. Then store them in an opaque, airtight container in a cool place over the winter until planting time arrives.

Ashes in the Garden

Is it okay to put ashes in a garden? I have a wood-burning stove and always dump my ashes there. But then someone told me it was bad for the soil. What do you think?
—*Kim Malkasian, Brookfield, Wisconsin*

Melinda: Wood ash is not the best soil amendment for your garden. It does very little to actually improve the soil. In addition, it also tends to be alkaline, or sweet, which can increase the soil pH. Those with alkaline or high pH soils, like you have in your area, should not use this in the garden.

Pretty in Pink

These pink flowers (left) come up in summer and bloom twice in the season. Can you tell me what they are and more about them?
—*Stacy Hendrickson Bessemer, Michigan*

Melinda: A close look at the flowers will give away the common name—cup and saucer. This flower is a type of Canterbury bells (*Campanula medium* 'Calycanthema'). They are European natives and biennial in nature.

The first year, the plant produces leaves. Then in the second year, you will have beautiful flowers. The plants often reseed themselves, creating the illusion of a perennial.

You can sow these seeds in spring. The plants prefer full to partial sun and moist, well-drained soil.

Wild Thing

This 'Easy Wave' petunia (below) grew in a greenhouse where I work. Can you explain its unusual growth? The widest stem is about 2-1/2 inches.　　—*Colleen O'Neal Muskegon, Michigan*

Melinda: This physiological disorder is called fasciation. The flattening of stems and proliferation of buds can be seen on a wide variety of plants including lilies, celosia, willows and succulents.

This bizarre growth is often induced by exposure to a broadleaf herbicide, certain environmental conditions, pests, or for no apparent reason. Breeders have taken advantage of this to propagate fantail willow, crested celosia and several different succulents. Enjoy the surprise, and be sure to share it with your gardening friends.

Glad You Asked!

GLAD YOU ASKED!

Best Birding Questions 2008

George Harrison answers some of your toughest birding questions.

Pelican Facts

I used to live in Florida, where pelicans are common. What can you tell me about these fascinating birds? For instance, where do they nest, and how do the parents feed the young?

—Norma Crider
Morristown, Tennessee

George: The most common pelican in Florida is the brown pelican (like the one at left). However, white pelicans may also winter there.

These birds often travel in colonies along the bays and inlets. They nest 8 to 20 feet high among mangrove thickets and usually lay three eggs per nest. Both parents incubate the eggs.

The young remain in and around the nest for 9 to 12 weeks after hatching. Both parents feed them by allowing the young to stick their heads into their bill pouches to get food.

Susan Killion

Welcome Back

When should I hang my hummingbird feeders for the return of my feathered friends?
—Frank Haley
Haddonfield, New Jersey

George: Early May is a good time to hang up your hummingbird feeders. In the South, migratory hummingbirds begin tapping sugar-water feeders in backyards in early April.

If you don't get them up early enough, the hummingbirds will often remind you. They will return to the spot where the feeders were last summer and hover there looking for them.

Added Insulation

Are there advantages to adding wood shavings or cedar sawdust to the bottom of nest boxes during winter?
—Dick Muesing, St. Peter, Minnesota

George: It is a good idea to add wood chips to a birdhouse in winter. Many birds use houses for roosting, so it helps to add some insulation for them. In turn, doing this might help attract more cavity-roosting birds at night.

Bluebirds, for instance, are one type you're likely to attract. In fact, you could even attract several bluebirds to a single birdhouse. Birds often seek warmth and insulation from each other during cold weather. I've seen pictures of as many as 13 eastern bluebirds in the same house on a winter night.

So if you can, give the birds a little extra insulation this winter. You might attract a new feathered friend.

Out of Nowhere

This large bird (below) appeared at my daughter's backyard feeder in Lake Elmo, Minnesota. She's lived at that house for 39 years but has never seen a bird like this. What is it?   *—Irene Beatty, Shellsburg, Iowa*

George: The mystery bird is a juvenile green heron, a common water bird in most of Minnesota. There's a good reason your daughter hasn't seen this in her yard before. It eats small fish, and spends nearly all of its time stalking its prey along lakes and streams.

These birds aren't backyard feeder birds, since they don't venture too far from the water. This is one of the smaller herons at 18 inches long.

Reach for the Sky

This buff-bellied hummingbird (left) was in our backyard one day. It looks like it's stretching. Can you explain its unique pose? —Kim Slonaker, Mathis, Texas

George: This is a great photo of a buff-bellied hummingbird in a very interesting position. You have a pretty good guess. This bird could have been stretching.

Another possibility is that it might have been displaying its feathers, trying to attract a mate. If the hummingbird was in this pose for long, it was probably sunning itself, as most birds do when given the opportunity. Whatever it was doing, it's a fun photo.

Doing the Laundry

Is it okay to offer the lint from my laundry dryer to the birds during nesting season? —Judie Schmidt, Newport, Oregon

George: I believe it is probably okay to offer the lint from your laundry dryer, though many people might disagree on this. Some argue that the birds could get tangled in it because it's often tightly woven.

If you are worried about the birds' safety, just offer an alternative. Very short pieces of string or yarn are more acceptable nesting material, and the birds will definitely use it!

A Taste for Salt

Is it harmful to feed birds salted nuts? —Heather Sanders, South Point, Ohio

George: Salted nuts are not harmful to birds, but the great question is will they eat them?

All birds require a certain amount of salt in their diet, and many satisfy that need by eating salt along northern roadways in winter.

I have tried feeding birds salted seed, but they never seem to want to eat it. Perhaps it contains more salt than they require.

Disappearing Chickens

More than 75 greater prairie-chickens roamed our farm back in the 1990s. Now, only two remain (below). Can you tell me what's happening to them?
—Robert Byczynski, Stevens Point, Wisconsin

George: There is an ongoing study of greater prairie-chickens in central Wisconsin by the biologists at the University of Wisconsin-Stevens Point.

While the population isn't booming, there still is a viable population in your area. In fact, it's one of the few areas in the United States where you can find this bird.

The birds are still in your area, but they might be shifting away from the location that you know.

Other places where you can find greater prairie-chickens include Oklahoma, Kansas, Nebraska, Texas, North Dakota and South Dakota.

Buena Vista Grassland is a unique spot in Wisconsin where you can make reservations to sit in a blind to see the prairie-chickens. (To make a reservation, call 1-715/346-3259.)

Can't Make Heads or Tails

The last couple of summers, a hummingbird without a tail has been coming to our feeder. The bird has a long, distinct flight pattern. Do you know what we're seeing?
—Lowell and Valina Ford, Kerby, Oregon

George: There are a couple of possibilities to explain what you're seeing.

First of all, many juvenile hummingbirds have shorter tails than their parents because they haven't fully developed. This photo (above) shows a juvenile hummingbird in Gary Meredith's yard in Laguna Beach, California. At first glance, it appears to have no tail.

There are also some hummingbirds that just have shorter tails by nature. In your area in particular, the calliope hummingbird has a very short tail. This would be my best guess as to what you are seeing.

225

232

234

240

244

230

236

228

235

BONUS

242

Easy Oriole Feeder	228
Pint-Sized Pond	230
Cozy Abode	232
A Bright Idea for Birds	234
Make a Splash with a Birdbath	235
No Deadheading Zone	236
Do-It-Yourself Containers	239
Dive Right In	240
Winter Wonderland	242
Spice Up Your Windowsill	244
Gardeners on the Go	246
Plant a Hummingbird Haven	248
Birdhouse Guidelines	250
What's Your Zone?	251

Photo this page: Maslowski Productions; opposite page, bird
in birdbath, Richard Day/Daybreak Imagery; Baltimore oriole,
Gail Varney; wave petunias, Ball Horticultural Company

EASY ORIOLE FEEDER

Add a little orange to your backyard with this handy project.

No need to break the budget when it comes to feeding orioles. With this simple orange feeder, you're sure to bring these beautiful birds to your backyard—after all, they can't resist citrus in the spring.

The best part is this project may not even cost a dime, because there's a good chance you probably already have enough scrap lumber and hardware around the house to build several of these surefire feeders.

This feeder was inspired by one designed by Daniel Medbury of Plymouth, Michigan. We've simplified it a bit so anyone can build it—even a child with a little adult supervision. In less than an hour, you'll be hanging your own exclusive oriole feeding station.

Here's What You'll Need...

✓ One scrap 2 x 4, at least 13 inches long

✓ One 1-inch x 8-inch board, about 12 inches long

✓ One 1/4-inch dowel, at least 18 inches long

✓ Four 2-1/2-inch galvanized finishing nails

✓ Four common nails

✓ Waterproof carpenter's glue

✓ One screw eye for hanging the feeder

Recommended Tools...

✓ Table saw

✓ Power drill

✓ Combination square

BALTIMORE ORIOLES can't resist citrus during springtime.

EASY AS ORANGE PIE

1. Cut a scrap 2 x 4 at least 13 inches long.

2. Cut two 45° angles to form a centered peak on one end (this will become the top). Use a combination square or tri-square to help draw the cutting angles.

3. "Dog-ear" the corners at the bottom end of the 2 x 4 by sawing about 3/4 inch off each corner at a 45° angle.

4. Drill two 1/4-inch holes through the 2 x 4. Center one hole 1-1/4 inches from bottom of the board and the other 6-1/2 inches from bottom. Make sure you drill the holes perpendicular to the 2 x 4. This will ensure that your perches will be straight. (See the box at bottom right for a helpful hint.)

5. Cut two roof pieces from the 1-inch x 8-inch board. One section should measure approximately 6 inches x 7-1/4 inches and the other 5-1/4 inches x 7-1/4 inches. If you'd like, dog-ear the outside corners of the roof pieces by cutting off about 1 inch from each corner at a 45° angle.

6. Nail the roof pieces to the 2 x 4 peak with two common nails. The longer piece overlaps the shorter.

7. The oranges are held onto the feeder by spearing them onto 2-1/2-inch finishing nails. Center these nails on each side of the 2 x 4 about 3 inches above each perch hole. Drive the nails about 1 inch into the 2 x 4 at a downward angle so they hold the oranges better.

8. Cut the 18-inch dowel in half for perches. Insert the dowels into the holes and center them. A little waterproof carpenter's glue in the holes will hold the perches firmly in place.

9. File or cut a flat spot in the center of the roof peak for a screw eye, which is used to hang the feeder. Drill a pilot hole first—this will prevent the wood from splitting.

A coat of deck stain is optional, but it'll help protect the wood from weather. Be sure the stain is dry before using the feeder.

Then cut two oranges in half, spear them onto the nails and wait for the orioles to show up while you enjoy a glass of iced tea.

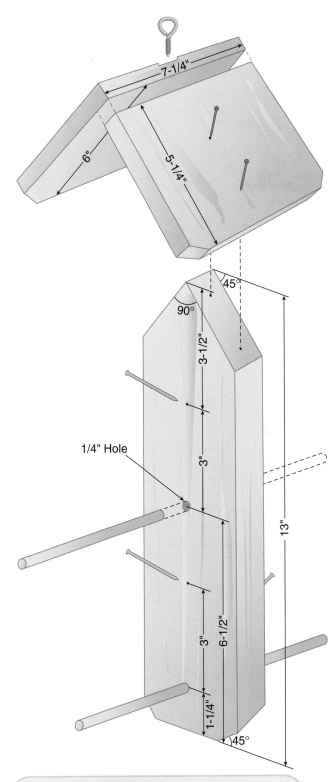

DRILLING A PERPENDICULAR HOLE

If you don't have a drill press to make perpendicular holes, ask a helper to stand to the side and guide you while drilling. As you line up the drill, your helper can "eye it up" from several sides to make sure you're holding the drill bit perpendicular to the board. This method won't replace a drill press, but it's better than going it alone.

PINT-SIZED POND

All you need is a barrel to create to a tiny pool of serenity.

Most of us would love having a soothing pond right outside the back door. Unfortunately, ponds can be expensive as well as a lot of work to install. And many yards simply don't have the space for them.

"Don't let that stop you though," says Christine Davis of Platte City, Missouri. "Do what I did—make a small garden pond from an old wooden barrel.

"It doesn't cost much and fits just about anywhere. Mine's even small enough for our deck," she says. "Plus, the experience may give you the confidence to eventually try your hand at building a larger pond."

Christine's design is remarkably simple, requiring only a half wooden barrel and a sheet of heavy-duty plastic to complete. If you don't mind spending a little more money, you can simplify the project even further by substituting a rigid preformed plastic insert in place of the plastic liner.

Submerged and floating leaved plants are the best choices for a pond this size. The leaves of submerged plants sit at least partially below the water level. These plants act as filters, keeping the water clear and oxygenated. Floating leaved plants, like water lilies, do their part by shading the water, which discourages algae growth.

So go find an old barrel. They're available at most garden centers, nurseries as well as hardware stores. In just a few short hours, you could be enjoying a refreshing tropical paradise in your own backyard.

EDITOR'S PICK
Small Idea,
Big Impact
2008

Here's What You'll Need...

✓ **Half wooden barrel**

✓ **1/2-inch staples**

✓ **One 10-foot x 25-foot roll of heavy-duty plastic**

✓ **Cinder blocks, bricks or plastic pots**

Recommended Tools...

✓ **Scissors**

✓ **Staple gun**

LET'S MAKE A SPLASH

1. Cut a 10-foot length from the roll of heavy-duty plastic. Thoroughly check the inside of the barrel for anything sharp that may puncture the plastic.

   Fold the plastic in half to create a double thickness and center it inside the half wooden barrel. Have someone help smooth and press the liner along the bottom and sides of the barrel. Cut off the excess liner at the top of the barrel, leaving about 12 inches overlapping the rim.

2. Select a location for the barrel. Once it's filled with water, it'll weigh over 200 pounds, making it too heavy to move, so it's best to spend a few extra minutes finding a suitable location.

   Most pond plants prefer full sun, so choose a spot that receives at least 5 to 6 hours of sunlight a day. Try to keep the pond away from trees that will drop a lot of debris.

3. Begin filling the barrel with water, smoothing the plastic as the water rises. The pressure will force the liner against the inside of the barrel. When it's about half full, turn off the water and trim the plastic around the rim again, leaving only 1 or 2 inches overlapping the top.

Step 1: Smooth liner into barrel and cut off excess plastic.

Step 4: Fold excess plastic toward inside wall and attach it to the inside rim with a staple gun.

Step 3: Fill barrel half full, smoothing the plastic as you go.

Step 7: Use cinder blocks, bricks or plastic pots to give your plants a boost. Be careful not to damage the plastic liner.

4. Fold the excess plastic toward the inside wall and attach it to the inside of the rim with a staple gun and 1/2-inch staples. Place the staples about 4 inches apart. Make sure they go through all the layers of plastic.

5. Finish filling the barrel until the water is just below the staples.

6. Let the water warm up before adding your plants. If you have treated water, add a water conditioner to remove the chlorine, or just wait a few days for it to evaporate.

7. Begin placing the plants in the pond. To position plants at the proper levels, you may need a few cinder blocks, bricks or plastic pots (black ones blend in well) for them to rest on. Add these items carefully so you don't damage the liner.

A couple of goldfish will also create additional interest, or you may want to try installing a small fountain. But keep in mind that water lilies and many other floating plants do best in calm water.

All that's left is finding a comfortable chair nearby to enjoy your tiny tropical paradise.

The Best of Birds & Blooms Bonus

COZY ABODE

Sturdy nest box will give your feathered friends a refuge for years to come.

You don't find many birdhouse patterns like this. We were charmed by its sturdy simplicity as well as its classic good looks. Coincidentally, the man who designed and built it—Bill Dunn of Greendale, Wisconsin—is a "neighbor" who lives near our offices.

Bill started building birdhouses some years back as a high school freshman in a woodworking class. Several years later, while serving with the military in Korea, he built houses for the local birds.

Now he's retired and still building birdhouses. Over the years, Bill estimates that he's constructed about 300 abodes for his feathered friends. "Whenever I want a new one, I go downstairs, find out what kind of wood I have and start building," he says.

This particular house is designed for smaller birds such as chickadees, bluebirds or wrens. The pieces (except for the optional chimney and perch) can all be cut from a 6-foot piece of 1-inch x 8-inch pine board. So what are you waiting for? Grab a board and start building!

ONE OF MANY. Bill Dunn (right) has built hundreds of birdhouses in his basement workshop. He shares one of his favorite plans for a house that will attract a variety of backyard birds.

TIME TO TALK SHOP

1. Cut the pieces for the birdhouse from a 6-foot 1-inch x 8-inch board by following the board layout on the next page.

2. Cut a 45° peak on the front and back pieces. These angles are easy to cut on a table saw using the miter gauge, but they can also be cut with a hand saw. To saw these angles, first draw them by marking the center point at the top edge of the board. Then draw a guideline with a combination square.

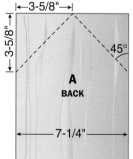

3. Cut off each corner of the floor piece at a 45° angle to provide added ventilation and drainage.

4. Bill located the entrance hole 4-3/4 inches up from a center point marked at the bottom of the front board. We recommend checking the birdhouse-building chart on page 39 first. Then use an appropriate-size spade bit to drill a hole that's the right size and in the right position for the type of bird you wish to attract. Drill until the tip of the bit starts to come through the other side, then flip the board over and continue drilling from that side. Finish the hole by smoothing with a piece of sandpaper.

5. Round the bottom of the mounting board by using a 1-quart paint can to draw a guideline at the bottom of the board, then cut along the line with a saber saw. Cut the top of the board to match the peak.

6. Assemble the house. Start by attaching the sides to the back with 1-1/2-inch finishing nails. Then attach the front to the sides.

7. Position the floor so it sits up 3/4 inch from the bottom of the house. Predrill holes through the sides, then attach the floor with 1-5/8-inch deck screws from the sides. Unscrew the floor to clean out the birdhouse after nesting season.

8. Attach the short piece of roof with 1-1/2-inch finishing nails. Allow a 3/4-inch overhang in back to cover the mounting board. Then nail the larger roof piece

Chapter 9

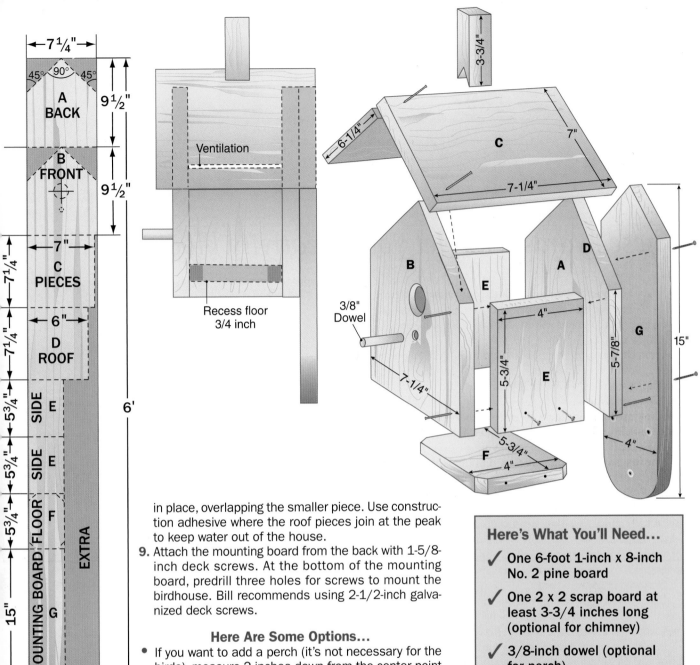

7 1/4"

45° **90°** 45°

A BACK

9 1/2"

B FRONT

9 1/2"

7 1/4"

7"

C PIECES

7 1/4"

6"

D ROOF

5 3/4"

SIDE E

5 3/4"

SIDE E

5 3/4"

FLOOR F

MOUNTING BOARD

G

15"

4"

6 1/4"

EXTRA

6'

Ventilation

Recess floor 3/4 inch

C

6-1/4"

7"

7-1/4"

B

3/8" Dowel

7-1/4"

E

5-3/4"

E

4"

E

5-3/4"

F

5-3/4"

4"

D

A

3-3/4"

G

5-7/8"

15"

4"

in place, overlapping the smaller piece. Use construction adhesive where the roof pieces join at the peak to keep water out of the house.

9. Attach the mounting board from the back with 1-5/8-inch deck screws. At the bottom of the mounting board, predrill three holes for screws to mount the birdhouse. Bill recommends using 2-1/2-inch galvanized deck screws.

Here Are Some Options...

- If you want to add a perch (it's not necessary for the birds), measure 2 inches down from the center point of the entrance hole. Drill a 3/8-inch hole through the board for the perch, which is made from a 3-inch-long piece of 3/8-inch diameter dowel. Squeeze glue into the hole and tap in the dowel.

- Bill gave the birdhouse a "cozy" feel by adding a decorative "chimney" as the finishing touch. He used a leftover piece of handrail, but since flat wood is much easier to work with, we suggest using a scrap piece of 2 x 2 as shown in the plan above.

  Cut a 90° notch in the center of a 2 x 2 for the chimney by making a 45° cut on each side. It's safer to cut the notch in a longer 2 x 2, then cut the piece to length. Glue it to the peak. When it dries, predrill holes on both sides of the chimney and fasten with four 1-1/4-inch wire brads.

- For a more finished appearance, round the front edges of the roof with sandpaper or a router with a roundover bit (this needs to be done before assembling). You may want to protect the wood with a coat of paint stain or polyurethane before mounting.

Here's What You'll Need...

✓ One 6-foot 1-inch x 8-inch No. 2 pine board

✓ One 2 x 2 scrap board at least 3-3/4 inches long (optional for chimney)

✓ 3/8-inch dowel (optional for perch)

✓ 2-inch and 1-1/2-inch finishing nails

✓ 1-5/8-inch galvanized deck screws

✓ 1-1/4-inch wire brads (optional for chimney)

✓ Waterproof construction adhesive

Recommended Tools...

✓ Table saw

✓ Saber saw

✓ Power drill

✓ Combination square

A Bright Idea for Birds

These "yardsticks" let your creativity bloom.

Want to add a splash of color to your yard and attract birds at the same time? These clever and easy-to-make garden decorations will do just that! Your young artists will enjoy making their own, too.

Elma DiMona and Sue Ebbitt (below), both of Pawleys Island, South Carolina, came up with the idea for these creative "yardsticks" and wanted to share it with other *Birds & Blooms* readers.

The yardsticks are simple to put together—use a ready-made spindle, a steel rod and the dishes of your choice... and best of all, the painting is up to you!

The first step is to add a metal rod in the bottom of the spindle. This is the part that sticks in the ground so moisture doesn't ruin the paint job.

Use a 1/4-inch threaded steel rod and cut off a 12-inch piece with a hacksaw. Drill a 1/4-inch hole in the bottom of the spindle to the full depth of the drill bit. Add a dab of construction adhesive in the hole and tap the rod in with a hammer.

Now you're ready to paint.

Just remember, have fun with it—the sky's the limit! We asked one of our local talents, Sally Chadwick of Greendale, Wisconsin, to create these colorful designs for us (right).

Before painting, she added an undercoat of exterior primer to the spindles.

Then we visited a local thrift store to search for the appropriate dishes. The variations are endless. We picked a bright-yellow china cup, a clay pot saucer and a blue metal bowl. Eventually, the cup and saucer will hold birdseed, while the bowl provides a refreshing mini birdbath. If you use a clay item like we did, paint the inside to keep moisture out.

After the paint is thoroughly dry, attach the cups or bowls to the spindles with waterproof construction adhesive. Construction adhesive is now available at most hardware stores in small tubes, so a caulking gun is not needed.

Allow the yardsticks to dry overnight, then "plant" the brightly colored decorations in your backyard.

MEASURING UP. Elma DiMona (on the left) and Sue Ebbitt created these clever "yardsticks" (above) to attract more backyard birds to visit. They are a fun, colorful and unique way to offer your feathered friends food and water.

Here's What You'll Need...

- ✓ A ready-made spindle
- ✓ A steel rod
- ✓ Dishes, cups and bowls of your choice
- ✓ Construction adhesive
- ✓ Exterior primer
- ✓ Paints

Recommended Tool

- ✓ Hacksaw

Make a Splash with a Birdbath

A sure-fire way to attract a variety of birds to your yard.

What's the trick to attracting more colorful birds to your backyard? Just add water! A birdbath is inexpensive and almost guarantees more winged activity.

Like humans, birds need water to survive. It's not only essential for quenching their thirst, but bathing is vital to keeping feathers in tip-top condition.

Water also invites more species to a backyard. Birds that eat only insects never visit seed feeders, but they'll make regular appearances at a birdbath.

Birdbaths come in many shapes and sizes, from copper to ceramic and ponds to pedestals. The possibilities are endless. No matter what kind you choose, keep these pointers in mind:

1. **Imitate nature.** Birds aren't picky about style and are most inclined to visit a bath that resembles a natural puddle. That's why placing one on or near the ground is a good idea.

2. **Location, location.** Place your birdbath near trees and shrubs. This gives the birds a quick escape from predators. Songbirds will avoid birdbaths that are out in the open.

3. **Shallow is safer.** Make sure the basin has gently sloping sides and water no deeper than 1 to 3 inches. If your birdbath is deeper, place a flat stone in the bottom to give birds a place to stand.

4. **Color does matter.** Avoid birdbaths with white basins because birds may have a hard time seeing the water. Earth tones are a better choice.

5. **Now hear this.** The sound of running or dripping water attracts birds from quite a distance. For the most action, add a submersible pump, mister or dripper to your birdbath to make water move.

Easy-Care Birdbaths

There's little bother when it comes to maintaining a birdbath. All you need to do regularly is scrub the inside of the basin and change the water every couple of days. Here are more tips:

- Place your bath close to a water source for easy filling and cleaning.

- Prevent algae buildup by occasionally soaking the basin with a solution of equal parts vinegar and water. (Cover it with a clean garbage can lid to keep the birds out). Rinse several times before adding fresh water.

- Since free-flowing water may be hard to come by in winter, install a birdbath heater. This are readily available at hardware stores and garden centers.

No Deadheading Zone

With these seven no-maintenance annuals, you'll have lots of time to kick back and enjoy.

By Cheryl Richter, Lincoln, Nebraska

Annuals are an instant hit with busy gardeners. That's because a few flats of colorful annuals can make any yard look like a million bucks in no time at all.

Like other garden plants, however, some annuals require more care than time-challenged green thumbs can afford to give. On top of basic watering, fertilizing and weeding chores, geraniums, petunias and salvia, for example, need deadheading (removing flowers as they begin to fade) to keep them blooming rather than going to seed.

For the gardener who wants less work and more enjoyment, there's still hope. You can have an easy-to-maintain kaleidoscope of color with these seven annuals that keep giving, yet ask little to nothing in return.

MAINTENANCE-FREE ANNUALS

1 Impatiens. If you have a shady area that needs color, impatiens are a no-brainer. They've made me look like a Master Gardener without me even trying, and can do the same for you.

Native to Africa, these popular plants were stowaways on trading ships and became naturalized in Central and South America. Today, breeders have developed impatiens that bloom in almost every color imaginable.

Their leaves are green to bronze, and the single or double flowers create continuous color in shady beds, borders, hanging baskets and containers. You'll get the most from your plants with sufficient water and fertilizer.

2 Wax Begonia. These brightly colored plants have small flowers in shades of pink, red, salmon and white with bright yellow "eyes." Their thick glossy foliage also comes in a range of colors, from dark green to a more sun-tolerant bronze.

Wax begonia, also commonly called fibrous and everblooming begonia, is at the top of my no-fuss list—the only thing I need to give them is water. Even then, I can let the soil dry between waterings in shade.

They grow well in partial to full shade and flourish in borders, mixed plantings and containers. They also are a nice plant to combine with other cool-colored flowers,

such as purple, green and blue.

3 Melampodium. This vigorous drought-tolerant plant caught my eye because it produces masses of small daisy-like blooms. The beauty is that it flowers continuously right into fall.

Melampodium is a native to Mexico and Central America, making it an ideal choice for gardens like mine that have lots of humidity and heat during the summer months. Its dark-green leaves and abundant yellow flowers brighten beds, borders and containers. All the plant requires is plenty of sunshine and well-draining soil.

4 Flowering Tobacco. This relative of the tobacco plant is also known as nicotiana. The stems rise from a rosette of leaves and are covered with star-shaped flowers in shades of pink, red, maroon, lavender, white, yellow and green.

Many varieties produce fragrant blooms all season long on tall stems that sway in the breeze. They're also a nice backdrop when planted in clusters beyond border plants.

Flowering tobacco is an excellent plant to attract hummingbirds and butterflies, livening up your no-fuss garden.

Common Name: Wax begonia.
Scientific Name: *Begonia semperflorens.*
Size: 6 to 12 inches tall and wide.
Flowers: White, red, pink and salmon.
Bloom period: Summer to first frost.
Light: Partial to full shade.
Soil: Moist and well-draining.
Additional benefits: Attracts hummingbirds.

2 Wax begonia

Cheryl Richter

Cheryl Richter

Impatiens 1

Common Name: Impatiens.
Scientific Name: *Impatiens walleriana.*
Size: 6 to 18 inches tall; 12 to 24 inches wide.
Flowers: A broad variety of colors, including white, orange, red, pink, lavender, coral and yellow.
Bloom period: Summer to first frost.
Light: Partial to full shade.
Soil: Moist and well-draining.
Additional benefits: Attracts butterflies and hummingbirds.
Common Name: Wax begonia.
Scientific Name: *Begonia semperflorens.*
Size: 6 to 12 inches tall and wide.
Flowers: White, red, pink and salmon.
Bloom period: Summer to first frost.
Light: Partial to full shade.
Soil: Moist and well-draining.
Additional benefits: Attracts hummingbirds.

SEE MORE
MAINTENANCE-FREE
PLANTS AND PROFILES ➡

5 Annual Vinca. If you experience lots of heat in summer, annual vinca, also known as Madagascar periwinkle, is the perfect plant. It flourishes in full sun and doesn't need excessive watering or deadheading.

An upright plant that spreads with age, it's perfect in the garden or as a container planting. Its heat tolerance and appearance make annual vinca a perfect substitute for impatiens in hot dry locations.

The glossy green foliage makes a nice backdrop for the solid or bicolor flowers. Bring the plants or cuttings indoors over winter for a windowsill of blossoms.

6 Sweet Alyssum. Believe it or not, this beautiful low-growing border plant covered with clusters of delicate little flowers is a member of the mustard family. Its tiny blooms are fragrant and come in white, pink and lavender hues.

I love this annual because it blooms for months in full sun to partial shade. It does best in cool weather. After the heat of summer, cut it back to encourage new growth and blooms. It also works nicely in rock gardens and containers.

7 Wave Petunias. I take back what I said earlier about petunias. While most need extensive deadheading, Wave petunias and many other newer introductions seem to defy the laws of nature. They produce continuous blooms without removing the spent flowers.

These petunias make a great ground cover. They have a low-spreading habit, fanning out up to 3 feet and bringing lots of good color into an area.

Wave petunias are also perfect for hanging baskets, window boxes and large containers. They'll spill over the edges with a cascade of purple, blue or lavender flowers.

Cheryl Richter

Common Name: Melampodium

Scientific Name: *Melampodium paludosum.*

Size: 18 inches tall.
Flowers: Deep yellow.
Bloom period: Summer into fall.

Light: Full sun.
Soil: Well-draining.
Additional benefits: Drought tolerant.

Melampodiun **3**

Cheryl Richter

4 Flowering tobacco

Common Name: Flowering tobacco.
Scientific Name: *Nicotiana alata.*
Size: 10 inches to 5 feet tall; 6 to 24 inches wide.
Flowers: White, red, pink, lavender, green and yellow.
Bloom period: Summer to first frost.
Light: Partial shade to full sun.
Soil: Rich, moist and well-draining.
Additional benefits: Attracts butterflies and hummingbirds.

Cheryl Richter

Annual vinca **5**

Common Name: Annual vinca
Scientific Name: *Catharanthus roseus*
Size: 6 to 24 inches tall and wide.
Flowers: White, pink, rose-pink, red, lilac and some with a contrasting eye.
Bloom period: Early summer.
Light: Full sun.
Soil: Well-draining.
Additional benefits: Drought tolerant.

Cheryl Richter

6 Sweet alyssum

Common Name: Sweet alyssum
Scientific Name: *Lobularia maritima*
Size: 4 to 8 inches tall; 10 to 15 inches wide.
Flowers: White, pink, lavender and apricot.
Bloom period: Spring through frost.
Light: Full sun to partial shade.
Soil: Well-draining.
Additional benefits: Attracts butterflies.

Ball Horticultural Company

Wave petunias **7**

Common Name: Wave petunias
Scientific Name: *Petunia x hybrida 'Wave*
Size: 4 to 6 inches tall; spreads 3 to 4 feet wide.
Flowers: Purple, blue, lavender, lilac, pink and rose.
Bloom period: Spring through frost.
Light: Full sun.
Soil: Well-draining.
Additional benefits: Fills in large areas.

Chapter 9

Do-It-Yourself CONTAINERS

Extend the season with these glorious displays

Green with Ivy

This two-season window box planted by Kim Albright in Winston-Salem, North Carolina stays green throughout fall and winter.

"My husband does the landscaping for a shopping center, and I pitch in with the planting," she says. "People often go for a lot of color in the fall, but that doesn't keep through the winter. So I rely on greenery in my autumn arrangements."

To add color, Kim planted a few yellow violas that tolerate cooler temperatures. She suggests planting these flowers last so you can space them throughout the foliage.

Why it works: Kim creates a symmetrical design using lots of pairs, complemented by a single autumn fern that draws attention to the center of the window box. The tall sedge and dangling ivy provide balance.

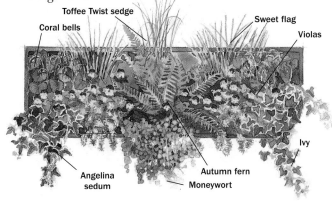

Toffee Twist sedge
Coral bells
Sweet flag
Violas
Ivy
Angelina sedum
Autumn fern
Moneywort

Planter size: 42 inches long.
Growing conditions: Partial shade.
Shopping List:
1 Autumn fern	2 Coral bells
1 Toffee Twist sedge	2 Golden variegated
1 Moneywort	sweet flag
6 Violas	2 Ivy
2 Coral bells	2 Angelina sedum

Power of Threes

"Putting together this pot of beautiful foliage was almost like doing a puzzle," says Nancy Shelton of Plymouth, Minnesota.

"I found plants that fit together well and considered the shape of each one," she says. "I tried different textures and colors."

To assemble this arrangement that will last until the first fall frost, Nancy started with the tall fountain grass in the center. She potted the rest of the plants three at a time, putting each variety in a triangular pattern.

Why it works: Nancy uses a striking contrast of leaf shapes and colors. Coleus accents the arrangement especially well. She also leaves very little space between each plant, giving the pot a full look.

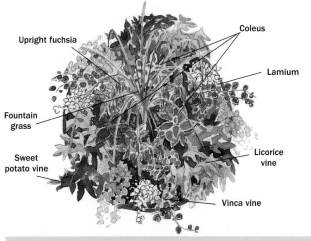

Upright fuchsia
Coleus
Lamium
Fountain grass
Sweet potato vine
Licorice vine
Vinca vine

Illustrations: Larry Mikec

Planter size: 18-inch diameter.
Growing conditions: Morning and evening sun; midday shade.
Shopping List:
1 Fountain grass	3 Vinca vine
3 Upright fuchsia	3 Licorice vine
3 Coleus (3 different colors)	6 Sweet potato vine
3 Lamium	(3 black, 3 lime)

Dive Right In

This mosaic birdbath is both attractive and easy to make.

By Barbara Matthiessen
Port Orchard, Washington

RP Photo

Your backyard birds will be splashing in style with this unique birdbath that's simple to make. Piecing together the bright basin is easier than you might think, requiring just a few basic materials and half an afternoon.

For the top of the birdbath, I covered an ordinary clay flowerpot saucer with precut glass tiles and grout. It took only 2 hours to do, plus drying time.

When I finished it, I set my creation on a plant stand in our herb garden. The finished birdbath, excluding the stand, measures 12 inches across and 1-3/4 inches high.

Note: The following directions allow you to duplicate Barbara's design— you'll need 45 blue tiles, 45 green and 34 white—then follow the design in the assembly diagram at right. However, it's easy to change the look of this birdbath. Experiment with the tiles to form any pattern you prefer, or attach them randomly for a different look.

For materials, Barbara used Plaid Make-It Mosaics tiles, tile adhesive, tile nippers, grout and topcoat tile sealer.

Here's What You'll Need...

- ✓ **12-inch terra-cotta saucer**
- ✓ **Plant stand to hold 12-inch sauc**
- ✓ **Newspaper**
- ✓ **Ruler**
- ✓ **Pencil**
- ✓ **Small disposable plastic contain**
- ✓ **Jumbo craft stick (for stirring)**
- ✓ **124 3/4-inch square glass tiles**
-   **Toothpicks**
- ✓ **Tile adhesive**
- ✓ **Safety glasses**
- ✓ **Work gloves**
- ✓ **Tile nippers**
- ✓ **1-pound package white sanded grout**
- ✓ **1-quart disposable container**
- ✓ **Latex or vinyl gloves**
- ✓ **Household sponge**
- ✓ **Soft cloth**
- ✓ **Tile sealer**
- ✓ **1-inch foam brush**

START AT SQUARE ONE

1. Make sure the saucer fits onto the top of the plant stand and is clean and dry.

   Measure saucer to find the center and mark this point with a pencil. Using your ruler and pencil, draw a horizontal and vertical line through the center point, dividing the inside bottom of the saucer into four equal sections.

2. Place newspaper over work surface. Pour about 1/2 cup of tile adhesive into the small plastic container. If desired, allow adhesive to stand for about 30 minutes to thicken. This will help the tiles adhere to the saucer more quickly.

3. Wearing safety glasses and work gloves, use the tile nippers to cut two green square tiles in half to create four rectangles. Repeat with two white square tiles.

4. Rotate saucer in front of you so the marked lines are in an "X" position. Referring to the assembly diagram at left for position, place a blue square tile (without adhesive) onto the saucer at the marked center point. In the same way, place blue square tiles along each of the marked lines around the center tile to make a large X, leaving a small space between each tile as shown in the diagram and photo.

   Referring to the diagram for position, lay out complete tile design on the bottom of saucer, filling in each of the four sections with green, blue and white square tiles and cut pieces as shown. Trim the squares to fit as needed.

5. Following tile adhesive manufacturer's instructions, apply adhesive to the tiles and adhere the pieces to your saucer as planned.

   Adhere remaining white, blue and green square tiles around inner sides of saucer, alternating colors.

   Let adhesive dry as directed by the manufacturer.

6. Wearing latex or vinyl gloves and following grout manufacturer's instructions, mix grout in the disposable 1-quart container using a jumbo craft stick. Immediately spread grout over the surface of the saucer with your hands, pushing the grout into all cracks and grooves.

   Smooth grout across all surfaces and remove excess. Allow grout to sit as directed by the manufacturer.

7. Remove excess grout with a damp sponge, rinsing out the sponge between each wipe. Continue until the tops of the tiles are clean of grout. Let grout dry as directed by the manufacturer.

8. Buff tiles with a soft cloth to remove any haze that is left over from the grout application.

   Following tile sealer manufacturer's instructions, apply three coats of sealer using the foam brush. Allow sealer to dry as directed.

9. Set your completed saucer in the plant stand and fill it with water. Then place it in your backyard and watch for winged activity! To prevent cracking, bring the birdbath indoors during freezing weather.

ASSEMBLY DIAGRAM

WINTER
WONDERLAND

Attract more songbirds to your backyard
in winter with these 7 essentials

By George Harrison, Contributing Editor

I get excited when the scenes outside my picture windows begin to look like a Christmas card. As my gardens rest, my snowy backyard springs to life with the colorful activity of winter birds.

On a typical cold day, I can look out the window and see pairs of northern cardinals gorging themselves on sunflower seeds. Black-capped chickadees and white-breasted nuthatches dart from feeder to feeder, and acrobatic woodpeckers work a suet feeder from the trunk of an ash tree.

With a little effort and common sense, you, too, can awaken to a Christmas-card backyard scene filled with colorful fascinating birds every winter morning. Read on…

Provide the Basics

The secret to attracting birds to a backyard, regardless of season, comes down to three simple things: *cover, food* and *water.* In winter, these basics are even more important to survival.

- **Cover** is the natural vegetation where birds can escape from predators, find protection from freezing rain and snow, or roost at night. Trees, shrubs and hedges are all part of this equation. Evergreens are particularly helpful in winter. Their dense needles provide shelter from wind and offer excellent protection from the elements.
- **Food**, both natural (berries, nuts and seeds) and feeder offerings (seeds, suet and fruits), provides fat that birds rely on to survive the cold.
- **Water**, in birdbaths, ponds or natural flowing streams, is vital to birds' survival, particularly in winter, when it's more difficult to find open water in colder climates.

Instant Cover

If you can't plant trees and shrubs until next spring, there's no reason you can't create "instant cover." Pile branches and twigs to form brush piles, where birds can hide and be protected from the weather.

Discarded Christmas trees also make excellent almost-natural cover when they are positioned upright near a bird feeder. Even evergreens in large pots will do the job until they can be planted when the ground thaws.

Heated Water

If temperatures dip below freezing in your area, you can still provide water for birds. Many heated birdbaths and small electrical heaters (below) for existing birdbaths are available.

And don't worry about your feathered friends. Birds know when it's too cold outside to bathe, but just like us, they always need fresh water to drink.

More Feeders, More Birds

One style bird feeder doesn't fit all, so offer a variety if you want to attract the most birds to your backyard.

- Ground feeders cover sparrows, dark-eyed juncos and doves.
- Tray-type feeders provide solid perching surfaces for cardinals, grosbeaks and jays.
- Hanging feeders attract finches.
- Tree-trunk feeders like laminated suet cages (below) are ideal for woodpeckers, nuthatches and brown creepers.

Set out feeders that cover these four feeding niches, and the birds will surely come.

Varied Menu

You need to offer a variety of foods to attract different kinds of birds.

Cardinals, chickadees, nuthatches and finches love sunflower seeds. Finches are attracted to the tiny black nyjer seed (most people call it thistle) and mourning doves, sparrows and dark-eyed juncos relish wild birdseed mixtures. Woodpeckers are particularly attracted to suet cakes or animal fat you can get at any butcher, as are titmice and black-capped chickadees.

Remove Snow and Ice

If a feeder is covered with ice and snow, the birds won't feed. Give them a hand and brush or knock off ice and snow to allow the birds to get to the food. I keep an extra brush and scraper, like the kind used to clean a car windshield, near my birdseed container.

Freshness Counts

During winter, it's not unusual for the birdseed to get wet. And once it does, it's sure to clump and clog feeders.

If an active feeder suddenly seems deserted, this is the first thing to check because they can't get to the food.

The easiest way to solve that problem is to shake up feeders before you fill them. This dislodges the clumps. If the food is soaked, dump it and replace it with fresh dry food. With fresh food, cover and water, the birds are sure to make your backyard home. ✦

Photos this page: Richard Day/Daybreak Imagery

> ### BIRD-WATCHER'S SECRET
> Peanut butter is an excellent cold-weather treat for birds because it provides lots of fat to keep them warm. It's easy to serve, too. Just tie yarn or heavy string to the end of a pinecone, spread on the peanut butter and hang it from a tree. If that's not easy enough, simply use a butter knife to spread the peanut butter into the rough bark of a tree. Contrary to popular belief, peanut butter is perfectly safe for birds—they won't choke on it.

The Best of Birds & Blooms Bonus

SPICE UP YOUR WINDOWSILL

You can hang this herb garden right outside your kitchen window.

Here's a project that is doubly satisfying. That's because this window-box herb garden will not only perk up your sill, it will also add some zest to your cooking.

It can be sized to fit any window, but it makes the most sense to hang it near the kitchen, where you can snip whatever herb best complements the meal of the day.

Growing herbs in pots is a great way to keep them under control and have a variety right at your fingertips. It also eliminates many chores of large-scale gardening.

If herbs aren't your thing, that doesn't mean you have to write off this project. The clever design is perfect for holding pots of colorful annuals, too.

In fact, you can easily extend the growing season by planting early spring bloomers, such as violas, then as they begin to fade, swap the pots with new ones filled with summer annuals. Late in the season, change the pots again, adding ones filled with chrysanthemums, which will brighten your windowsill until the first frost.

Here's What You'll Need...

- ✓ 1-inch x 8-inch rough cedar board (the length will be determined by the width of your window)
- ✓ One 2-inch x 8-inch rough cedar board, 15 inches long
- ✓ 2-1/2-inch and 2-inch galvanized deck screws
- ✓ 2-inch galvanized finishing nails
- ✓ Waterproof construction adhesive
- ✓ 6-inch clay flowerpots
- ✓ Glue stick

Recommended Tools...

- ✓ Table saw
- ✓ Power drill
- ✓ Saber or band saw
- ✓ Level
- ✓ Combination square

244

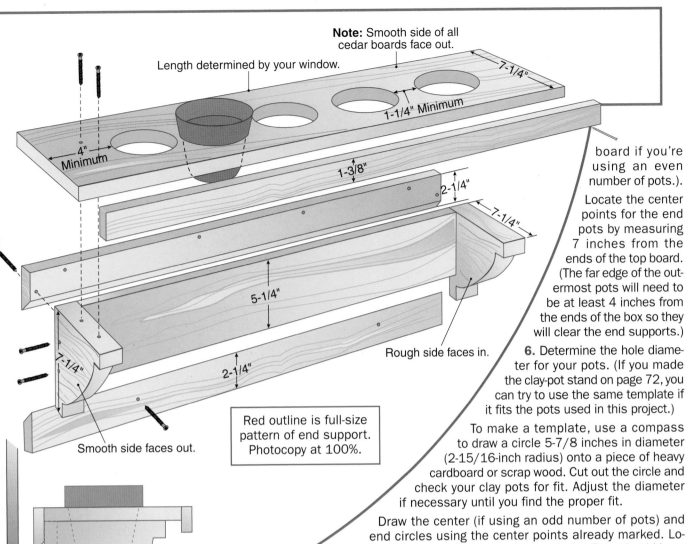

Note: Smooth side of all cedar boards face out.

Length determined by your window.

7-1/4"

1-1/4" Minimum

4" Minimum

1-3/8"

2-1/4"

7-1/4"

5-1/4"

2-1/4"

7-1/4"

Rough side faces in.

Smooth side faces out.

Red outline is full-size pattern of end support. Photocopy at 100%.

board if you're using an even number of pots.). Locate the center points for the end pots by measuring 7 inches from the ends of the top board. (The far edge of the outermost pots will need to be at least 4 inches from the ends of the box so they will clear the end supports.)

6. Determine the hole diameter for your pots. (If you made the clay-pot stand on page 72, you can try to use the same template if it fits the pots used in this project.)

To make a template, use a compass to draw a circle 5-7/8 inches in diameter (2-15/16-inch radius) onto a piece of heavy cardboard or scrap wood. Cut out the circle and check your clay pots for fit. Adjust the diameter if necessary until you find the proper fit.

Draw the center (if using an odd number of pots) and end circles using the center points already marked. Locate the remaining pots between them. (They should have a minimum of 1-1/4 inches between them.)

7. Mount the back board between the end supports so the pieces line up flush at the top and back. (**Note:** The smooth side of all cedar should face out.) Drill pilot holes through the end pieces and attach with 2-1/2-inch deck screws.

8. Attach the top board to the end supports. The top board overlaps each end support by 2 inches. Drill pilot holes and attach with 2-1/2-inch deck screws.

9. Cut the front trim board the same length as the top board from a 1-inch x 8-inch board and rip it to 1-3/8 inches wide. Attach the trim to the front edge of the top board with construction adhesive and 2-inch finishing nails.

10. To make the mounting boards, cut a 1-inch x 8-inch board to the same length as the back, including the end supports. Rip the board 4-1/2 inches wide. Then rip the board again with a 30° cut down the middle, making the two-piece mounting board. Use 2-inch deck screws to attach one mounting board flush with the top and end supports, making sure the angle points down. Attach the other mounting board to your house (above or below the windowsill), making sure it's level and the angle points up (see illustration above).

Let's Build a Window Garden

1. Measure your window to determine the overall length of your window box.

2. Make two photocopies of the end-support pattern at right (outlined in red). With a scissors, cut out the paper patterns 1/2 inch beyond the guidelines. Tack each pattern to the 2-inch x 8-inch board with a glue stick. Place the straight sides flush with the corners of the 2-inch x 8-inch board. (Notice that the grain runs horizontally.) If necessary, square the corners of the board first.

Cut out each end support with a saber saw or band saw and sand the edges smooth.

3. Cut the top to length from a 1-inch x 8-inch board.

4. Cut the back to length from a 1-inch x 8-inch board, making it 7 inches shorter than the top. Rip it 5-1/4 inches wide.

5. Locate the center points for the pot holes in the top board. To do this, draw a line the length of the board 1/8 inch off center (closer to the front). Then mark the center point for the middle pot by measuring half the length of the top board. (There's no need to find the center point of the

Hang the window box, fill your pots with a potting mix that drains well and plant your own "window-grown" herbs or flowers!

The Best of Birds & Blooms Bonus

20 Tips for Gardeners on the GO

Try these time-saving tips for making the most of your minutes in the garden.

By Ann Wilson, Geneva, Illinois

ILLUSTRATIONS BY KARA FELLOWS

There's no getting around it—cultivating a beautiful landscape is a lot of work. But you can labor more efficiently (and joyously) when you master a few shortcuts. During my 20 years of gardening, I've picked up my share of time-stretching strategies. To create this ultimate list, however, I turned to some of my expert gardening friends for help. It covers everything from tilling and tending to plant choices and pruning.

1. **Start with good soil.** Work in compost, manure or dried peat moss for nutrient-rich planting beds. Amended soil is lighter, drains well, makes for easy weeding and allows roots to establish themselves more quickly.

2. **Keep tools handy.** Stash a spare set of hand tools and garden twine in a waterproof container in your garden. When you spot weeds, broken rose canes or a stem that needs tying up, you won't have to run to the garage or potting shed for supplies.

3. **Mow less.** Limit grassy areas to reduce time spent on lawn chores. Combine trees, shrubs, boulders and decorative mulches to fashion eye-catching, maintenance-free island beds in your front and back yards.

4. **Play in the rain.** There's no better time to visit a garden center than during a cloudburst. Nurseries are less crowded, lines are shorter, and staff members are more available to answer your questions. Once the rain eases, go out and pull weeds—even clumps of crabgrass and deep-rooted dandelions pull easily out of wet soil.

5. **Don't wear yourself out planting in shaded sites with poor soil.** When you can't get anything to grow beneath trees or along fences, set up a multitiered container garden in the shady location. Plant shade-loving perennials and compact shrubs in appropriately sized containers; set the containers on metal stands in varying heights. Or use simple green pots that blend into the background, so as not to compete with the flowering show.

6. **Look around.** When walking or driving, take note of interesting plants and plant combinations. Write them down and take the list with you to the nursery—having an itemized list will speed up your shopping trips and reduce the urge to impulse-buy.

7. **Fertilize less often.** Nourish gardens and containers with time-release fertilizers that continue feeding for long periods of time.

8. **Avoid invaders.** Choose well-behaved perennials that don't send out runners—you'll have more time for enjoying your gardens if you don't have to keep your borders runner-free.

9. **Take preventative measures.** Add fresh mulch to your gardens every year. A 2- to 3-inch layer of mulch keeps weeds from sprouting and helps the soil retain water, so you'll be weeding and watering less often.

10. **Get an early start.** Divide and transplant hosta as soon as you see leaf tips breaking through the ground—since the stems and leaves have yet to unfurl, it'll be easy to cut the root-ball with a serrated knife. The planted divisions will leaf out beautifully in their new sites. You can divide and move fully leafed-out hosta, but you're likely to break off leaves and stems in the process, which results in ragged-looking plants.

11. **Consider color.** Don't waste a second searching for misplaced hand tools. Buy trowels, cultivators, forks and pruners with bright red or orange handles so you can quickly spot them amid the greenery.

12. **Place them in sight.** Plant vegetables and herbs in large containers placed near your back or front door. Since you'll see them often, you'll remember to keep them watered. And they'll be nearby when you need dinner fixings!

13. **Work smarter.** Make sure your tools are clean and sharp—they'll last longer and work harder in the garden. Use ergonomically designed tools, knee pads, or kneeling mats to lessen stress on your joints—pain-free bodies also work more efficiently in the garden.

14. **Take inventory.** Make a running list of newly added plants and their locations—this will help you remember what you planted where, which will prevent the inadvertent weeding (and replacing) of a "good plant." Save perennial-plant tags and store them near your favorite how-to gardening book—you'll have all your planting information in one spot.

15. **Go native.** Buy improved varieties of plants that are native to your region. They'll thrive with very little care and are likely to be the best-looking plants in your garden.

16. **Dig once; plant many.** When you've got a bag of tulip or lily bulbs to plant, or when using annuals to edge a border, dig a large, single planting hole instead of many smaller holes. Make sure it's large enough for all the bulbs or plants to prevent overcrowding.

17. **Be prepared.** At the beginning of the season, stock up on supplies like garden twine, twist ties, garden gloves, plant supports, plant markers and bags of compost to eliminate garden-center runs and the long lines on busy gardening days.

18. **Prune wisely.** Wait to prune evergreens, such as yews and boxwood, until they've produced most of their new growth. As a result, you won't have to prune them again until next year.

19. **Let them do their thing.** Choose plant varieties that readily self-seed, such as corydalis, larkspur and purple coneflower, or that quickly naturalize, such as daffodils and daylilies, to fill out borders inexpensively.

20. **Take a tour.** Walk around your gardens every day and check plants for pests and diseases—the sooner you spot a problem, the sooner you can take curative measures, which means less work later.

Author's Note: Thanks to gardeners Margie Archer, Cathy Byars, Christy Crafton, Denise Curtin, Pam Hamilton, Pat Kessler, Carol Mills, Shirley Remes and Brenda Spitzer, who all happily shared how they create glorious gardens by working smarter instead of harder.

Plant a Hummingbird Haven

W hat could be more exciting than seeing a hummingbird feast on the nectar of your backyard flowers? For *Birds & Blooms* reader Dottie Anderson of Rockwall, Texas, the encounter was so surprising it almost sent her head over heels.

"I was watching the butterflies in my garden when I spotted a tiny hummingbird flying from one bloom to another," Dottie explains. "When it landed just outside our patio door, I nearly fell out of my chair with joy. I simply couldn't believe my eyes! I'd never before seen one of

these beautiful birds up close.

"For almost an hour, I watched as it sampled the nectar from a variety of flowers. It was an amazing experience I'll never forget."

With the help of this handy garden plan packed with nectar-producing flowers, you, too, can become a hospitable host to some flying jewels.

And if you don't have the space or time to create an entire hummingbird garden, just add a sampling of the blooms profiled below to your existing flower beds.

Tad Stamm

Common Name: Phlox
Scientific Name: *Phlox species*
Type: Perennial
Hardiness Zones: Zones: 3 to 8
Height: 3 inches to 3 feet
Width: 1 to 2 feet
Light: Full sun
Soil: Well-draining
Bloom period: Spring or summer; varies by species

Common Name: Azalea
Scientific Name: *Rhododendron*
Type: Shrub
Hardiness Zones: 3 to 9
Height: 3 to 15 feet
(varies by variety and region)
Width: 3 to 12 feet
(varies by variety and region)
Light: Full sun to partial shade
Soil: Acidic, moist and well-draining
Bloom period: Spring

William H. Johnson

Common Name: Bleeding heart
Scientific Name: *Dicentra spectabilis*
Type: Perennial
Hardiness Zones: 3 to 9
Height: 2 to 3 feet
Width: 2 feet
Light: Partial to full shade
Soil: Fertile, moist and well-draining
Bloom period: Late spring

Alan & Linda Detrick

R. Todd Davis

Common Name: Hibiscus
Scientific Name: *Hibiscus moscheutos*
Type: Perennial
Hardiness Zones: 4 to 9
Height: 4 to 5 feet
Width: 1 to 3 feet
Light: Full sun
Soil: Fertile and well-draining
Bloom period: Spring to fall

Scott Zinck

Common Name: Geranium
Scientific Name: *Pelargonium x hortorum*
Type: Annual
Hardiness Zones: All
Height: 12 to 20 inches
Width: 12 to 20 inches
Light: Full sun
Soil: Moist and well-draining
Bloom period: Summer

Common Name: Delphinium
Scientific Name: *Delphinium species*
Type: Perennial
Hardiness Zones: 3 to 7
Height: 1 to 6 feet
Width: 1 to 2 feet
Light: Full sun to partial shade
Soil: Fertile, moist and well-draining
Bloom period: Summer

Mark Turner

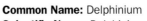

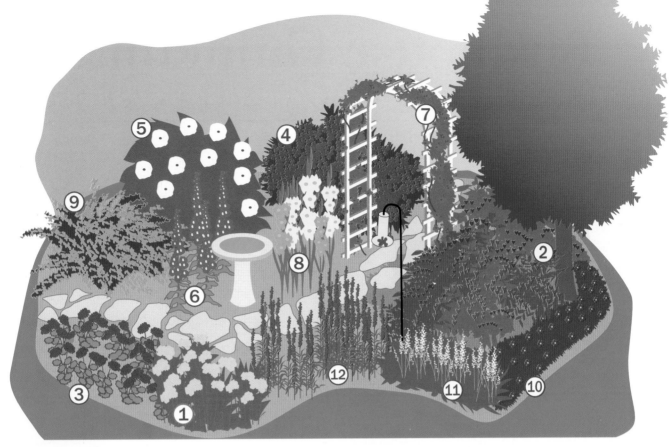

Common Name: Morning glory
Scientific Name: *Ipomoea*
Type: Annual vine
Hardiness Zones: All
Height: Climbs 15 to 20 feet
Light: Full sun
Soil: Well-draining
Bloom period: Summer to first frost

Scott Zinck

Common Name: Primrose
Scientific Name: *Primula*
Type: Perennial
Hardiness Zones: 3 to 8
Height: 6 to 12 inches
Width: 6 inches
Light: Partial sun
Soil: Cool, fertile and moist
Bloom period: Spring

Daniel Leach

Common Name: Gladiola
Scientific Name: *Gladiolus*
Type: Perennial (winter corms indoors in colder regions)
Hardiness Zones: 6 to 10
Height: 1 to 5 feet
Light: Full sun
Soil: Fertile, moist and well-draining
Bloom period: Early to late summer

Scott Zinck

Common Name: Coral bells
Scientific Name: *Heuchera sanguinea*
Type: Perennial
Hardiness Zones: 3 to 8
Height: 1 to 2 feet
Width: 1 to 1-1/2 feet
Light: Full sun to partial shade
Soil: Fertile and well-draining
Bloom period: Late spring and early summer; sporadic flowers

R.Todd Davis

Common Name: Weigela
Scientific Name: *Weigela florida*
Type: Perennial shrub
Hardiness Zones: 5 to 8
Height: 6 to 9 feet
Width: 9 to 12 feet
Light: Full sun
Soil: Well-draining
Bloom period: Late spring to early summer; sporadic flowers throughout summer

Larry Dech

Larry Dech

Common Name: Cardinal flower
Scientific Name: *Lobelia cardinalis*
Type: Perennial or annual
Hardiness: Zones: 3 to 9
Height: 3 to 4 feet
Width: 2 feet
Light: Full sun to partial shade
Soil: Fertile and moist
Bloom period: Summer

The Best of Birds & Blooms Bonus

Birdhouse Guidelines
Customize your designs for your favorite feathered friends.

Species	Dimensions	Hole	Placement	Color	Notes
Eastern bluebird	5" x 5" x 8"h.	1-1/2" centered 6" above floor	5-10' high in the open; sunny area	light earth tones	likes open areas, especially facing a field
Tree swallow	5" x 5" x 6"h.	1-1/2" centered 4" above floor	5-8' high in the open; 50-100% sun	light earth tones or gray	within 2 miles of pond or lake
Purple martin	multiple apts. 6" x 6" x 6" ea. (minimum)	2-1/8" hole 2-1/4" above floor	15-20' high in the open	white	open yard without tall trees; near water
Tufted titmouse	4" x 4" x 8"h.	1-1/4"	4-10' high	light earth tones	prefers to live in or near woods
Chickadee	4" x 4" x 8"h. or 5" x 5" base	1-1/8" centered 6" above floor	4-8' high	light earth tones	small tree thicket
Nuthatch	4" x 4" x 10"h.	1-1/4" centered 7-1/2" above floor	12-25' high on tree trunk	bark-covered or natural	prefers to live in or near woods
House wren	4" x 4" x 8"h. or 4" x 6" base	1" centered 6" above floor	5-10' high on post or hung in tree	light earth tones or white	prefers lower branches of backyard trees
Northern flicker	7" x 7" x 18"h.	2-1/2" centered 14" above floor	8-20' high	light earth tones	put 4" sawdust inside for nesting
Downy woodpecker	4" x 4" x 10"h.	1-1/4" centered 7-1/2" above floor	12-25' high on tree trunk	simulate natural cavity	prefers own excavation; provide sawdust
Red-headed woodpecker	6" x 6" x 15"h.	2" centered 6-8" above floor	8-20' high on post or tree trunk	simulate natural cavity	needs sawdust for nesting
Wood duck	10" x 10" x 24"h.	4" x 3" elliptical 20" above floor	2-5' high on post over water, or 12-40' high on tree facing water	light earth tones or natural	needs 3-4" of sawdust or shavings for nesting
American kestrel	10" x 10" x 24"h.	4" x 3" elliptical 20" above floor	12-40' high on post or tree trunk	light earth tones or natural	needs open approach on edge of woodlot or in isolated tree
Screech owl	10" x 10" x 24"h.	4" x 3" elliptical 20" above floor	12-40' high on tree	light earth tones or natural	prefers open woods or edge of woodlot
Nesting Shelves					
American robin	6" x 6" x 8"h.	none—needs roof for rain protection	on side of building or arbor or in tree	light earth tones or wood	use is irregular
Barn swallow	6" x 6" x 8"h.	none—does not need roof	under eaves of building	light earth tones or wood	prefers barns or outbuildings
Phoebe	6" x 6" x 8"h.	none—does not need roof	under eaves of building	light earth tones or wood	prefers water nearby

Note: With the exception of wrens and purple martins, birds do not tolerate swaying birdhouses. Birdhouses should be firmly anchored to a post, a tree or the side of a building.

Source: *Garden Birds of America* by George H. Harrison. Willow Creek Press, 1996.

What's Your Zone?
Plant Hardiness Zone Map

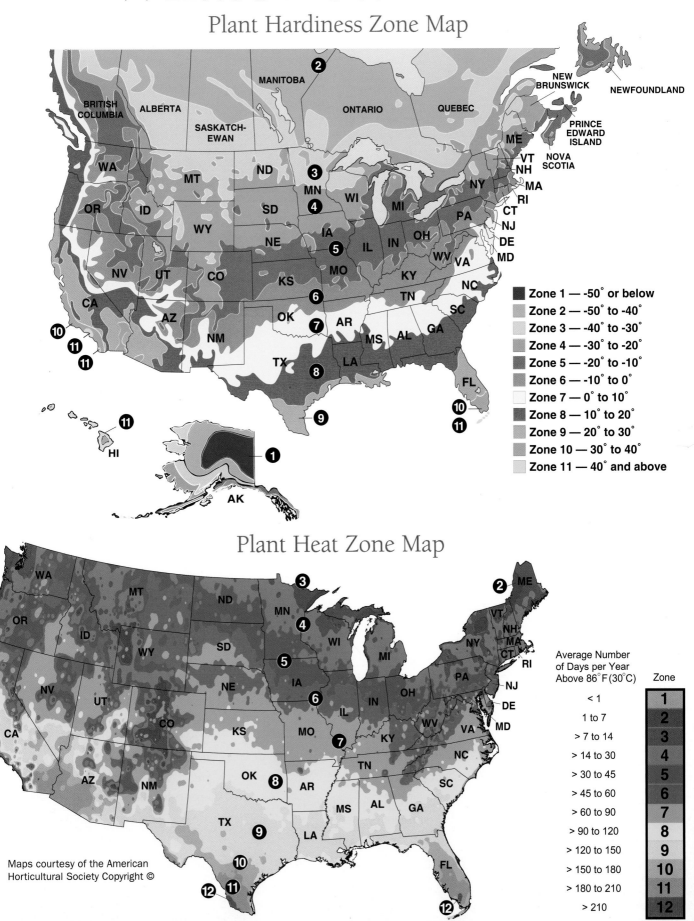

Zone 1 — -50° or below
Zone 2 — -50° to -40°
Zone 3 — -40° to -30°
Zone 4 — -30° to -20°
Zone 5 — -20° to -10°
Zone 6 — -10° to 0°
Zone 7 — 0° to 10°
Zone 8 — 10° to 20°
Zone 9 — 20° to 30°
Zone 10 — 30° to 40°
Zone 11 — 40° and above

Plant Heat Zone Map

Average Number of Days per Year Above 86°F (30°C)	Zone
< 1	1
1 to 7	2
> 7 to 14	3
> 14 to 30	4
> 30 to 45	5
> 45 to 60	6
> 60 to 90	7
> 90 to 120	8
> 120 to 150	9
> 150 to 180	10
> 180 to 210	11
> 210	12

Maps courtesy of the American Horticultural Society Copyright ©

*I*NDEX

A

Agastache, 105
Allen, Tom
  butterfly garden, 216-217
  "Glad You Asked," 220-221
  moths and butterflies, 210-211
Amaryllis, 168-169
Annuals, 236-237
Arborvitae, golden eastern, 99
Ash, mountain, 109
Ashes, 223
Aster, 150-151
Azalea, 248-249
Azure, spring, 122-123

B

Barberry, 109
Bears, 209
Bees
  attracting, 138-139, 150-151
  mining, 221
Bleeding heart, 248-249
Bluebird
  attracting, 215
  birdhouse for, 232-233, 250
  eastern, 7
  food for, 215
Bird feeders, 92-95, 107, 214-215, 243
  deterring bears from, 94, 209
  deterring cats from, 209
  deterring deer from, 209
  deterring raccoons from, 208-209
  deterring squirrels from, 93-94, 208
  hummingbird, 175, 182-187, 224
  mourning dove, 94
  oriole, 228-229
  sugar water, 175, 214-215
  suet, 94, 215

Bird feeding, 90-91, 92-95, 97-99,
  108-109, 214-215, 225, 243
  by hand, 175-175
  goldfinch, 93
  hummingbird, 91, 92, 174-175,
    177-178, 182-187, 214-215
  grosbeak, 51, 215
  northern cardinal, 41, 93
  oriole, 93, 214-215, 228-229
  white-breasted nuthatch, 44-45
  woodpecker, 48, 93-94
  yellow-rumped warbler, 20
Birdbaths, 215, 235, 240-241
Birdhouses, 100-103, 224, 232-233,
  250
  bluebird, 92, 232-233
  chickadee, 232-233
  deterring squirrels from, 92
  house wren, 36-37, 92, 232-233
  purple martin, 95, 103
Birds
  attracting, 90-91, 92-95, 97-99, 104-
    106, 108-109, 160-162, 214-215,
    234, 235, 240-241, 242-243
Bulbs, 56
Bunting, indigo, food for, 109
Butterfly, 210-211
  attracting, 113, 115, 117, 119, 121,
    123, 125, 129, 131, 133, 135, 138-
    139, 144-146, 150-151, 158-159,
    160-162, 216-217, 238
Butterfly bush, 217
Butterfly weed, 105

C

Canterbury bells, 223
Cardinal flower, 249
Cardinal, northern, 7, 38-41
  attracting, 95
  food for, 41, 95, 109

nesting of, 40-41
Caterpillars, 210-211
Cats, 209
Chickadee, birdhouse for, 232-233,
  250
Chickens, 225
Chokecherry, 109
Clay-tolerant plants, 213
Coffeeberry, 109
Coneflower, purple, 106
Conifers, 97-99
Containers, 239, 246
Coral bells, 140-143, 249
Coreopsis, 105
Crabapple, 109
Creeping juniper, 99
Crescent, pearl, 112-113
Crocus, 147-149
Cypress, sawara false, 99

D

Deer, 195, 209
Delphinium, 248-249
Doris longwing, 220
Dove, mourning
  food for, 94
Dragonfly, 220
Drought-tolerant plants, 213

E

Eggplant, white-fruited, 223
Egret
  great, 28-31
  nesting of, 30-31
  snowy, 10
Emperor, hackberry, 134-135

F

Fir, dwarf Korean, 99
Flicker, northern, birdhouses for, 250
Fritillary
    Aphrodite, 128-129
    host plant, 217
    meadow, 114-115

G

Gardens
    butterfly, 216-217
    container, 239
    herb, 244-245
    hummingbird, 248-249
Garden profiles,
    Arkansas, 70-72
    Connecticut, 54-57
    Maryland, 82-84
    Minnesota, 73-75, 196-198
    Mississippi, 64-66
    New York, 76-78
    Ohio, 58-60
    Ontario, 79-81, 85-87
    Pennsylvania, 67-69
    Tennessee, 61-63
    Wisconsin, 199-201
Geranium, 248-249
Germander, 105
Ginger, 222-223
"Glad You Asked," 220-225
Gladiolus, 155-157, 249
Goldenrod, 106
Goldfinch, American, 8
    food for, 91
Goose, Canada, 8
Grosbeak, evening, 49-51
    attracting, 51

    food for, 51
    nesting of, 50-51

H

Hardiness zones, 251
Heat zones, 251
Harrison, George
    attracting birds, 90-91, 108-109,
     214-215
    controlling critters, 208-209
    downy woodpecker, 46-48
    evening grosbeak, 49-51
    "Glad You Asked," 224-225
    great egret, 28-31
    house wren, 35-37
    hummingbirds, 172-173
    northern cardinal, 38-41
    rufous hummingbird, 176-178
    screech owl, 16-18
    tree swallow, 25-27
    tufted titmouse, 32-34
    white-breasted nuthatch, 42-45
    winter birds, 242-243
    yellow-rumped warbler, 16-18
Hawkmoth, 220
Hawthorn, Washington, 109
Hemlock, dwarf Canadian, 99
Herbs, 244-245
Heron, green, 224
Hibiscus, 248-249
Highbush cranberry, 109
Hornworm, 220
Host plants, butterfly, 216-217
    anise swallowtail, 119
    Aphrodite fritillary, 129
    black swallowtail, 217
    fritillaries, 217

    hackberry emperor, 135
    meadow fritillary, 115
    Milbert's tortoiseshell, 121
    monarch, 117, 216-217
    orange sulphur, 131
    pearl crescent, 113
    question mark, 125
    spicebush swallowtail, 133
    spring azure, 123
Hosta, 247
Hummingbird, 172-173, 179, 225
    attracting, 91, 158-159, 160-162,
     163-165, 175-175, 177-178, 179,
     182-187, 198, 214-215, 237-238,
     248-249
    banding of, 180-181
    feeders, 175, 182-187, 224
    food for, 91, 175, 177-178
    migration of, 172-173, 179
    nesting of, 177-178, 179, 187
    species
      Allen's, 172-173
      Anna's, 172-173, 181
      black-chinned, 172-173
      broad-billed, 172-173
      broad-tailed, 172-173
      buff-bellied, 13, 225
      calliope, 172-173
      Costa's, 172-173
      magnificent, 172-173
      ruby-throated, 172-173, 180
      rufous, 172-173, 176-178, 181

I

Impatiens, 236
Insects, 218-219

J

Jay
  blue, attracting, 91
  Steller's, 22-24
    food for, 23-24
    nesting of, 23-24

K

Kestrel, American, birdhouses for, 250

L

Lavender, 106, 138-139
Lettuce, 202
Lily, fawn, 7
Lupines, 10

M

Manzanita, 109
Martin, purple, birdhouses for, 250
Melampodium, 236-238
Migration
  monarch, 117
  hummingbird, 172-173, 179
  tree swallow, 26
  yellow-rumped warbler, 21
Milkweed, 216-217
Mockingbird, northern, 12
Monarch, 116-117, 216-217
  food for, 77-78
  host plant, 216-217
  migration of, 117
Morning glory, 249
Moth, 210-211
  attracting, 127
  cecropia, 10
  clymene, 220
  giant leopard, 221
  hummingbird clearwing, 126-127
  royal walnut, 221
Mulberry, 109
Mulch, 65, 212, 247
Myers, Melinda
  "Glad You Asked," 222-223

insects, 218-219
soil, 212-215

N

Nesting
  downy woodpecker, 47-48
  evening grosbeak, 50-51
  great egret, 30-31
  hummingbird, 177-178, 187
  house wren, 36-37
  northern cardinal, 40-41
  screech owl, 17-18
  Steller's jay, 23-24
  tree swallow, 26-27
  tufted titmouse, 33-34
  white-breasted nuthatch, 45
  yellow-rumped warbler, 20-21
Nuthatch, white-breasted, 42-45
  birdhouses for, 250
  food for, 44-45
  nesting of, 45

O

Oriole, Baltimore, 10
  attracting, 91, 93, 215
  food for, 93
Owl, screech, 16-18
  birdhouses for, 17-18, 250
  nesting of, 17-18

P

Pansy, 144-146
Pelican, 224
Penstemon, 106
Pentas, 158-159
Pesticides, 218-219
Petunia, 222-223
  wave, 237-238
Phlox, 248-249
Phoebe, birdhouses for, 250
Photos, 6-13
Pine, dwarf mugo, 99
Plant Hardiness Zone Map, 251

Plant Heat Zone Map, 251
Plants
  budget-friendly, 216-217
  clay-tolerant, 213
  cold-hardy, 144-146
  drought-tolerant, 104-106, 213, 238
  easy-care, 144-146, 150-151, 163-165, 236-237
  for arid climates, 160-162
  for attracting birds, 90-91, 97-99, 104-106, 160-162
  for attracting butterflies, 113, 115, 117, 119, 121, 123, 125, 127, 129, 131, 133, 138-139, 144-146, 150-151, 158-159, 160-162
  for fragrance, 138-139
  for attracting hummingbirds, 158-159, 160-162, 163-165, 177-178, 198
  for shade, 104-106, 140-143
  for sun, 140-143
  mutants, 190-193
Pond, 230-231
Poppies
  California, 10
  Oriental, 152-154
Primrose, 249
Projects
  birdbath, 235, 240-241
  birdhouse, 232-233
  oriole feeder, 228-229
  pond, 230-231
  windowsill garden, 244-245
  yardstick, 234
Pumpkins, 194

Q

Question mark, 124-125

R

Rabbits, 195
Raccoons, 208-209
Robin, American
  birdhouses for, 250
  food for, 109

Rose of Sharon, 223
Rudbeckia, 106

S

Salvia, 106
"Secrets to Grow on," 194-195
Sedum, 106
Seeds, starting plants from, 60
Serviceberry, 109
Snapdragon, 166-167
Soil, 212-213, 246
    improving, 57
Spicebuch, 109
Spruce, dwarf Colorado, 99
Squirrels, 12, 208
Star-of-Bethlehem, 222
Suet, 93-94, 215
    recipe for, 93, 95
Sulphur, orange, 130-131
Swallow
    barn, birdhouse for, 250
    tree, 25-27
        birdhouses for, 250
        migration, 26
        nesting of, 26-27
Swallowtail, 221
    anise, 118-119
    black, 217
        host plant, 217
    spicebush, 132-133
Sweet alyssum, 237-238
Sweetbay, 109

T

Titmouse, tufted, 13, 32-34
    birdhouses for, 250
    food for, 34
    nesting of, 33-34
Tobacco, flowering, 236-238
Topsoil, 213
Tortoiseshell, Milbert's, 120-121
Tulip, 8

V

Vinca, annual, 237-238
Virginia creeper, 109

W

Warbler
    black-and-white, 21
    yellow-rumped, 19-21
        food for, 20
        migration, 21
        nesting of, 20-21
Watering, 202
Wax begonia, 236
Waxmyrtle, southern, 109
Waxwing, cedar, 6
    food for, 109
Weigela, 249
Winterberry, 109
Wood duck, birdhouses for, 250
Woodpecker,
    downy, 46-48
        attracting, 48, 215
        birdhouses for, 250
        food for, 48, 93-94, 215
        nesting of, 47-48
    red-headed, birdhouses for, 250
Wren, house, 35-37
    birdhouses for, 36-37, 232-233, 250
    nesting of, 36-37

Y

Yarrow, 106
Yucca, 163-165

Z

Zinnia, 160-162